WHALE
warrior

WHALE warrior

PETE BETHUNE

Hodder Moa

National Library of New Zealand Cataloguing-in-Publication Data

Bethune, Pete.
Whale warrior / Pete Bethune.
ISBN 978-1-86971-223-5
1. Bethune, Pete. 2. Whales—Conservation—
South Pacific Ocean. 3. Whaling—South Pacific Ocean.
I. Title.
333.9595092—dc 22

A Hodder Moa Book
Published in 2010 by Hachette New Zealand Ltd
4 Whetu Place, Mairangi Bay
Auckland, New Zealand

© Text Pete Bethune 2010
The moral rights of the author have been asserted.
Design and format © Hachette New Zealand Ltd 2010

All rights reserved. No part of this publication may be reproduced or transmitted in any form or by any means, electronic or mechanical, including photocopying, recording, or any information storage and retrieval system, without permission in writing from the publisher.

Designed, produced and typeset by Hachette New Zealand Ltd

Printed by Griffin Press, Australia

Dedicated to my wonderful daughters, Danielle and Alycia, who love me despite my many flaws; and to Sharyn, the most extraordinary lady who will always have a piece of my heart.

Contents

Introduction   9

1	Fiordland Fury	11
2	Getting ready for Antarctica	18
3	Spies and Hobart hamsters	31
4	Playing cat and mouse	48
5	Rammed!	79
6	Lucky to be alive	96
7	Foul tactics	125
8	Battle stations	142
9	Boarding the enemy	171
10	Arrested, charged, incarcerated	196
11	Shocks to the system	236
12	The long wait continues	252
13	The most hated man in Japan	281
14	The day of reckoning	300

Epilogue   312
Acknowledgements   319

Introduction

For the last 23 years, Japanese have been illegally slaughtering whales in a whale sanctuary. This killing of whales is bad enough, but what really pisses me off is that it happens in my backyard. So, in 2009 when Paul Watson said he'd like me to take the *Ady Gil* — formerly *Earthrace* — a carbon fibre raceboat, down to Antarctica to try to stop the whaling, I jumped at the chance. Little did I know what a brutal and heart-breaking journey I was embarking on. The campaign itself had it all, a secret Sea Shepherd boat coming from Mauritius, brazen rammings in international waters, the destruction and sinking of a vessel, home-made weapons, a well-resourced enemy bristling with military hardware, and dangerous water-borne battles in the most inhospitable environment on earth.

Some of that was expected. What wasn't expected, though, is where I ended up. While the rest of Sea Shepherd partied in Hobart, I languished in a maximum-security prison in Tokyo preparing for the trial of my life. What was even more astounding was how I got there: arrested by the Japanese after boarding a whaler in the Southern Ocean. Looking back, I still can't quite believe how we pulled it off.

The year has gone down in history. It is the year that the world finally woke up to the barbaric practices that are happening each summer in Antarctica, and I was lucky enough to find myself in the thick of it.

This book follows the most extraordinary journey of my life — one that has seen me a hero in some people's eyes, villain in others, and the most hated man in Japan. Yet, looking back, all I did was stand up for something I believe in.

1
Fiordland Fury

'Dat wind be gettin up,' says Andy, in his thick Dublin accent. I look over at Andy, who is peering anxiously out the small starboard window of *Earthrace*. We are anchored up in a small fiord in southern New Zealand, waiting for a massive storm to hit. 'She's gotta be at least 50 knots already,' he adds. We've been swinging in a big star pattern around our anchor, and every change in wind direction places another dot on the star of our Simrad GPS.

'Diddly dee potato,' I respond nonchalantly. I'm not sure I've ever heard an Irishman say 'Diddly dee' actually . . . and I'm not sure they say 'potato' any more than we do, for that matter. But for some reason I keep saying it to any Irishman I come across.

Andy rolls his eyes, and goes back to his GPS. He's heard it a hundred times before and the funny side has long since worn off for him.

There's a long silence, as we both sit anxiously, hoping for a peaceful night, but realising the storm steaming in on us could be difficult.

'What're ya gona do afta *Earthrace*?' Andy finally breaks the silence. It's a good question really. In the previous year we'd set a new world record for a powerboat to circle the globe, and we'd done this using 100 per cent biodiesel made from waste cooking oils. Since then we'd been completing the promotional tours of Europe, Australia and now New Zealand, and in just a few weeks the programme would be complete. We'd visited 181 cities in 41 countries, and had over a quarter million people walk through the boat.

In a few weeks, though, it'd all come to an end, and the plan was to pull *Earthrace* out of the water until I managed to sort what we'd do with her. Which would make me a free agent. *Earthrace* had been my full-time life for four years now, but the thought of something new is appealing.

'You know I might go down south and hassle the Japanese whalers,' I finally reply.

A scowl crosses Andy's boyish face. 'What? In this boat?'

'Why not?'

Andy is about to respond when the boat suddenly lurches, and then starts to swing in a different direction. We both know something has changed, and we're hoping it is just another shift in wind.

'Pete, I think the anchor has pulled.' I look down at the GPS, and we've just started to inch outside the star pattern we'd been in for the last six hours. A massive gust of wind smacks into our starboard side, and within a few seconds we've moved some 50 metres towards the end of the fiord.

Amazingly, our large Fortress anchor has pulled despite the 30 metres of 10 mm chain and 150 metres of rope out. Another gust hits and our journey towards the rocks continues.

'Get on the bow, mate. I need you to throw the anchor line,' I command Andy, trying to sound calm. 'Everyone out of bed please and lifejackets on.' The crew scrambles up all looking a bit bewildered. I switch on the FLIR infrared camera and see Andy crouching down on the roof, and then inching his way down towards the forward cleat. The wind is whipping over the bow of *Earthrace*, and the arc of water is horizontal as it slices over us. Andy disappears into this mess, and in a minute is just a glow of blobs once he reaches the anchor line on the bow.

By now we are perilously close to the rocks, at least according to the GPS. My mind is grappling with two challenges we face in escaping this trap. Once the anchor rope is thrown, our speed towards the rock will increase and we'll have only a few seconds to get the boat turned. But we then need to avoid the rope which will now be dangling dangerously in the water, just waiting to tangle the props. If either prop is fouled, a smashed boat is inevitable. The only way out of here is to back away from the rope, and then rotate the stern into the wind, sneaking up a narrow passage between the anchor line and the rocks. To compound matters, it's pitch-black outside.

I look down at the radar to get our orientation. The GPS is only showing our drift towards the rocks, but not which way our bow is pointing. The radar has us side-on to the fiord which feels wrong. I struggle with it, rotating the image in my head. Trust your instruments, I say to myself.

Another huge gust has Andy flattened on the bow and clinging for his life. 'Throw the line,' I yell into my radio mike, unsure if any of it is getting through to poor Andy. 'Throw the bloody rope now.' Andy's infrared blobs move for a few seconds then there's a muffled sound over the radio, and Andy is flattened back down on the bow. There's no way to tell what Andy had said. Another 20 seconds and we're on the rocks anyway. I slam *Earthrace* into reverse and we lurch back, as 1080 horsepower of Cummins Mercruiser engines strain against the massive 36-inch propellers. The rudders are on full lock to swing us, but the wind is just too strong, and our stern passes into the green reef area on the GPS. I then slam my port throttle into forward to halt the reverse and start the rotation. Both throttles are pushed hard, and the propellers vibrate in an angry protest.

Slowly, the radar shows us inching around, then suddenly we're lined up directly in the fiord. I throw the port engine back into reverse and we start slamming into the waves, stern first, but thankfully inching our way out of danger. Andy is still lying on the bow. He lifts his head up and starts crawling his way back towards the hatch. I can now make out his face, a bright glow of white heat emerging from the infrared screen.

We pass the red X mark where our anchor was first dropped, and I turn towards the middle of the fiord, away from the rock faces and cliffs. There's a sudden gust of air through the helm as Andy emerges from the forward hatch. He's soaking wet, and shivering from the cold. 'That was easy,' he says laughing, and he raises his hand for a high five. He clambers up into the navigator's seat beside me, and shakes his head.

'You know mate. That is one of the gutsiest things I've ever seen,' I say to Andy seriously. Andy glances down at the GPS and back at me. 'Tanks Pete. Dat means a lot coming from you.' I don't give out compliments easily. I tend to be very selective in praising people these days, preferring to crew my boat with self-motivated people who make stuff happen, rather than people needing constant reassurance. But there is something very special about this gay leprechaun sitting beside me.

'So what do we do now?' Andy enquires.

'We drive up and down this fiord until the storm breaks. Then we'll come back and retrieve our anchor.'

'Which is how long'?

'Hmmm. Not sure really. Maybe 12 hours.' The winds have increased now, and great swirls of water are funnelling vertically upwards beside us.

'Well, it'll be a long night den. Would you like some company?' Andy scurries off to the galley and puts the jug on.

'Hey, Pete. Are you serious about going to Antarctica? I mean going round da globe is one ting. But the Southern Ocean is someting else.'

'Well, I'm thinking about it. And you know something. If I do go down, you'd be one of the first crew I'd pick.'

'Me?' There's genuine surprise in Andy's voice. 'You'd need warriors down there, not some little gay boy from Dublin.'

'Well, we'd always have someone to make us tea at least.'

Andy smiles.

This past week we'd been watching the second series of *Whale Wars*, a reality TV series about the Sea Shepherd Conservation Society who head down to Antarctica each year to try to stop Japanese whaling. While they have certainly made an impact, it strikes us that they are always short on speed to keep up with the harpooners. And so a boat like *Earthrace* might add a lot of value to things.

Also, it seems Sea Shepherd find the whaling fleet, but then are left a little shy on tactics. They focus all their energy on getting down to Antarctica and finding the whalers, but less on what they'll actually do to the whalers once they find them. So I reckon a fresh team with a new boat might be able to contribute.

We spend the night tossing around ideas on what we could do to disrupt the whalers. These ideas broadly split into three main categories. The first is to make it hard for them to get the whales. This could be through blocking their shot at the whale, or stealing the whale before it gets to the processing ship. The second set of tactics is to devalue the carcass in some way. This could be in say cutting or slashing the carcass so the meat is exposed to salt water. While it won't stuff the meat, any area exposed to the water will not be sold as prime sushi or sashimi. So the whaler's return is reduced a little. And the third idea is to disrupt their operations or make life difficult for them in some way. This is typically where Sea Shepherd's efforts have been focused in the past, deploying such things as prop-foulers, and throwing rotten butter onto the decks of the processing ships.

By morning we have a bunch of new tactics, some of them perhaps verging on crazy, some of them a bit limp, but a couple that might really stir things up. My favourite idea involves shooting the dead whales with a rifle and lacing the bullets with something toxic — like cyanide or arsenic perhaps, or maybe mercury. The good thing with this is you don't need to physically touch the whale. You just need to get within shooting distance. Also, assuming the whales are still processed, but with the affected areas removed, we can promote in media that poison-laced whales were processed, and this might play on consumers' minds in Japan.

If I was offered a piece of meat, for example, and I knew it had come from an animal that had possibly had poison injected into it in some way, I'd never eat the meat, regardless of how small the poison dosage. It'd just play on my mind. The whalers just couldn't resist processing a fat, juicy whale sitting on their deck either. Throwing away all that money just wouldn't gel with them. They'd cut out the areas around the bullets and throw it overboard, then hack the whale up into bits and package it up for the markets in Tokyo.

There's another idea, though, that we're tossing around, and that involves completely disabling the harpooning boats. I'd worked for a number of years in the oil industry as an exploration engineer, and I'd run a lot of explosives during different operations. Explosives are amazing, in that they allow a huge amount of energy to be released in a split second. There's no great mystery about them, and if handled correctly, they are perfectly safe. Now I'd never consider sinking a boat by placing explosives on it, but I would consider disabling it.

One of the weaknesses of propeller-driven vessels is their drive-train. It takes very little damage to render them useless or ineffective. Even a small charge on the tip of a prop blade and it becomes imbalanced. To then repair this would necessitate pulling the boat from the water, presumably back in Japan. So if we did manage to get a small charge onto a propeller and set it off, that vessel's campaign would be over. They'd be limping back to Japan or, better still, they'd be getting towed back, tying up two boats. Man, that'd hurt their bottom line.

We continue tossing around ideas and by lunchtime there's a couple more possibilities. The more I think about it, the more excited I get at the possibility of heading down to Antarctica. Gradually, however, the debate swings back to Sea Shepherd.

I'd wanted to go down with *Earthrace*, but I'm practically broke, and so how I'd fund an expedition to Antarctica I have no idea. If I can talk Sea Shepherd into it, perhaps they would fund the refit and fuel.

'You'd never last in Sea Shepherd,' says Andy. 'You'd never survive all the politics. It's Paul's way or the highway, and you'd just get pissed off and leave. And are you sure you want to be tied up with them? Look at that last episode of *Whale Wars*. What a bunch of clowns.'

'Yeah, but at least they're down there trying. No one else is. And I reckon I could fit in in a large organisation.'

Andy just smiles. 'Aye but day would never let ya use explosive either,' he says. 'Sea Shepherd are non-violent. And I doubt day would ever let ya use a firearm either. It just goes against their values.' Andy has a point. The use of explosives and firearms might be pushing things too far, regardless of how they are deployed.

Jason by now has risen from his scratcher, and is busy poking around in the galley looking for something to cook up. 'You could use an oxygen lance,' he says hopefully. 'They can cut through just about anything, even five-inch thick plate steel. And I know that some special forces use them under water for their missions.'

Jason goes on to explain the device. It has an oxygen tank, and the gas is directed out through a narrow array of magnesium tubes. Off the end is a flame at about 5000°C. Apparently, it's so hot it'll even melt through bricks. 'Two minutes with one of those on their propellers,' says Jason enthusiastically, 'and they'll be dead in the water.' I'd never actually heard of an oxygen lance before, so I add it to our growing list.

The storm gradually abates, and by late afternoon it's just a dark, brooding, overcast day, as we collect up our discarded anchor and head back out of the fiord. We plot a course for Milford, our next stop on the promotional tour, while I'm busy plotting how to get to Antarctica.

2
Getting ready for Antarctica

It's a month later that I fly to Friday Harbor, a small seaside town on San Juan Island in Washington State, USA. The plane rocks and jolts as we descend at the end of a short 50-minute sea plane flight. Waiting at the airport is Laurens de Groot, a tall Dutchman whom I recognise from the last series of *Whale Wars*. He stands out in his black Sea Shepherd T-shirt among all the middle and upper class Republicans who flock here for their summer vacations. A quick tour through town, and then we're back at the volunteers' house, tucked in among the woods.

It's early evening when Paul Watson finally arrives, back from his trip to the International Whaling Commission piss-up in Europe. Banned from the event, he and fellow Sea Shepherd people were limited to publicity stunts outside the main gathering.

He casually walks in and there's a certain humbleness about him that is quite surprising. I walk up and shake his hand, and he then greets all the other Sea Shepherd people dutifully waiting their turn. It's almost like he's the messiah, and certainly at times he has engendered an almost religious following among his supporters.

He's not as big as I'd expected, although he does look like he knows where the local pie shop would be. TV often makes people look bigger than they really are. I remember when I was young, there was this really popular politician called Winston Peters who was always on the telly, and he seemed so large and physical. One day I finally got to meet him in person, and he was anything but physical. Well, Paul Watson is by no means short, but he's certainly not the massive man he seems like on TV.

We sit down and chat about a few things, but he's a hard man to gauge. I was expecting someone loud and confident, but if anything Paul is quiet and reserved. But there's a certain hardness about the man. On many things he remains unconcerned or disinterested, and then something will pique his interest and he steps in with his thoughts. He doesn't speak in volumes, but rather just presents carefully thought out arguments. There's also a decisiveness about them, like he is the final word on things.

Something else that becomes apparent is his prodigious memory. I've known people who are perhaps cleverer than Paul, but his memory of historical events especially is quite astonishing. He slings out long since forgotten facts with unnerving ease. Not that any of us there have the knowledge to really question any of his claims. But I expect for the most part he's correct in what he says.

At times the conversation moves on and he becomes disinterested. The amazing thing with Paul, though, is he has been doing this for 30 years, and he still continues his campaign. I guess if I'd been doing his job for that long I'd be a bit distant at times as well. I'm just another one of his many disciples rummaging around for his attention.

Finally, I manage to steer the conversation to Sea Shepherd and *Earthrace*, and what role I might have. 'Look Pete, I want your boat in Antarctica, and I want you to captain it,' Paul says abruptly. 'I'll put you in touch with Rob, our financial guy, and you can sort out details with him.'

The surprising thing with this is there is no interview-like discussion. It's like he had made his mind up about the boat and my captaincy already, and the meeting here was just a formality. Or maybe he just wanted to make sure I wasn't a psycho before making his mind up. Whatever, I guess I've passed the first step in getting down to Antarctica and hopefully being part of a team that puts an end to whaling.

I end up walking away really impressed by Paul. From what little I'd seen of him on TV I didn't think I'd really like the guy, and yet I found him to be very likeable and extremely talented. He has been running Sea Shepherd for 30 years, and yet he remains totally driven by the same goals with which he founded the organisation. He takes virtually nothing. He has a humble house, and Sea Shepherd pays his expenses, but he has accumulated no visible wealth. To be honest, I don't think he gives a toss about money, except in terms of how it enables him to follow his vision for Sea Shepherd.

We went out to grab lunch the following day, and sitting at the table next to us was a family eating. Eventually, the mum leans over to Paul. 'Um, I know you're really busy, but my kids and I watch *Whale Wars* every week, and we love what you do, and we were wondering if we could have our photo taken with you?' Fifteen minutes later and the kids walk away with big smiles on their faces and the memory of someone famous who gave them his time.

Paul has the ability to connect with people and he is generous with this, despite everyone wanting a piece of him. He is constantly being asked to sign things, pose for photos, give his opinions, and yet he continues to oblige with a smile on his face, and the belief that he has a duty to share his knowledge.

His profile has also brought him his share of detractors. Cyberspace is packed with skinny little blokes with boring lives who snipe at others through their forums and chat rooms . . . and a chunk of them really hate Paul. It's not like their venom is well directed. They criticise him for so many things, most of them totally irrelevant. There was a long vitriolic chat about how Paul is too big to possibly be vegan. Another forum criticised him for being married to a stripper (his second wife was a Penthouse Playmate). Lucky bugger, I say, although apparently it never worked out. Maybe this is just jealousy on the part of the nerds on their computers. These people need to get a life. If they want to criticise him, at least do it constructively. It seems, though, that Paul doesn't care about all this. He just carries on doing his thing, and if people hate him he just brushes it aside . . . and if people support him, he is grateful for it.

I leave Friday Harbor a few days later with a new mission in life. *Earthrace* is to get a series of modifications, she'll be renamed the *Ady Gil* and, come December, she'll be on her way to Antarctica for the first time.

It's a dark, damp, windy day as I drive into the boatyard in Helensville several months later. The storm and unusually high tide sees murky brown water lapping up over the yard doors and onto the workshop floor. A couple of lads are busy sweeping the water out, but it seems like a pointless exercise as more water just leaks in around their brooms.

'Haven't you heard of climate change?' I say to Craig, the owner of the boatyard. 'Another 10 years and you'll be swimming in this shed.' It does seem odd that you'd build a brand-new boatyard so close to the high-tide mark. Craig gives me a dirty look.

'Climate change is a myth. It's been created so we can be taxed more.' Actually, I've heard this argument a bit lately. It allows people to kid themselves that our current levels of emissions are perfectly acceptable.

'Well, Craig, how about you are right and there is no such thing as climate change, and yet we are all forced to reduce our carbon footprint? You'd probably fly overseas a little less, consume a little less, and your SUV would have to go. Would that be such a bad thing anyway?'

'Yeah, but I like my SUV. It allows me to intimidate old ladies in little Toyotas.'

'Well, how about climate change is real, and yet we do nothing about it? What are future generations going to think of us?'

'Well, I'll be long dead anyway. And I reckon a few more degrees in temperature would be quite welcome.'

'Along with a boat shed that's under water?'

Craig just frowns, and goes back to the paint tin he's trying to pry open. 'What's this weird stuff?' he says.

'Well, it's got carbon flecks all through it that diffract radar signals. So it'll make *Earthrace* into a stealth boat.'

Craig has a dubious look on his face. He dips a wooden stick into the black oily mix and it emerges with a solid layer of jet-black gunk stuck on the end. 'This will block the paint guns,' he says in disgust, and he starts mixing the paint.

The paint in fact has been extremely difficult to source. The same product is used on Stealth bombers and certain military vehicles, but since September 11, such things have been extremely hard to come by. Anything with even a remote military application, especially if it originates from the US, has been banned from general export, so even something as benign as a special tin of paint has been very difficult to obtain.

I wander over to check out the progress on *Earthrace*. She was pulled from the water two months ago, and since then she's had a few modifications. I remember my meeting with Craig Loomes, the original designer, when I first got back. He was horrified at the thought of *Earthrace* heading down to Antarctica.

'She'll get smashed to bits on the ice,' he'd warned me. The biggest challenge we face is that carbon is amazingly strong, but also brittle. If you do have an impact, let's say from hitting a piece of ice, cracks will propagate and you'll end up with substantial damage. To compensate, you can add some Kevlar fibre, which adds a little in weight, but improves the impact properties. So it localises damage, rather than allowing small damaged areas to expand.

The designer had finally agreed to the adding of Kevlar over sections of the hull under the waterline. The number of layers was varied from four to eight, depending on the area. *Earthrace* when originally built was incredibly light. Her dry weight was only 16 tons, and these modifications will increase that by at least half a ton. This will reduce our speed fractionally, but we're not trying to set a record here; we're trying to stop Japanese whaling. Our maximum speed will come down a bit from the original 40 knots, but the whaling vessels only do 20 anyway. Speed is not an issue for us, but reliability is.

There was another problem with composite boats in freezing seas, however. Any water trapped inside the structure freezes, expands and causes the skin to blister, which in turn weakens the hull. So my plan is to cook the boat to 70°C for half a day to burn off any trapped water.

There is also an issue unique to multihulls heading into arctic conditions. They're extremely vulnerable to pack ice. The hulls get crushed, unlike a monohull, which if designed correctly, can ride up on the ice as it compacts — although I have no intention of going into pack ice. I'll just avoid it and stay clear. If I end up with a smashed boat from ice I will probably deserve it.

So in the end my cunning plan is to add heaps of Kevlar, cook the boat and then avoid pack ice. Simple, really.

As I wander down the hull, I run my hand lovingly along the yellow Kevlar seam. It's an impressive boat out of the water. Over the last four years I've become a little desensitised to how good looking she really is. Then I see her fresh or out of the water like this, and I'm reminded what an amazing-looking craft she really is.

A week later and *Earthrace* is gently lowered back into the water, and we head out across the bar of the Kaipara Harbour. While not a maiden voyage, all voyages after a refit make me nervous. You're always worried that something major has been forgotten or will fail. So it's with some trepidation that I line up the Kaipara bar. The Kaipara is the largest harbour in the southern hemisphere. Its massive volume funnels out through three narrow channels, and we're approaching the most northerly of these. 'Man that is a bad-looking stretch of water,' says Larry, my new engineer. The four-metre swell rolling in is standing up on end as it slows in the shallows, and where we are on the inside, it's a washing machine of confused waves jolting us around.

We idle out, and I'm carefully tweaking our course to match the GPS coordinates an old sea dog had given us the previous week. A minute later and we start hitting white water. Waves of froth come galloping in on us. There's a slight lull, and then big, breaking waves come racing over the top.

Earthrace is the most extreme wave-piercing boat ever built, and it doesn't take much to have water coming over the windscreen. Today with a full tank of fuel and tall standing waves, we're under the water almost as much as over it, and it is a bombardment of your senses. The 1080 horsepower of Cummins Mercruiser grunt roars behind you, the helm goes light and dark as each new wave covers us, the physical violence of tons of water crashing around you, and there's the stench of vomit, with two crew members chundering in the galley sink.

'We're about to lose the jet-ski,' Larry yells out, and the next thing I know he's scampering out the rear hatch to tie it back down.

'Leave it Larry. You'll get washed overboard,' I scream. Just then a wave comes over us, engulfing Larry on the back deck. He clings onto the hatch, and then clambers back inside, totally drenched and with a worried look on his face.

'We're going to lose the SeaDoo,' he pleads, but there's nothing I can do. The middle of the bar like this is the most dangerous place we can be. The SeaDoo can be replaced; people can't. Larry shakes his head, and goes back to the galley where he watches our prized 260-horsepower jet-ski getting smashed up on its rack on the back deck.

We're nearly through the bar, and I'm thinking the worst is over, when the steering starts to fade. It is taking more and more turns of the wheel to keep us aligned with the channel, and now at full lock it is not enough to turn us against the waves and wind. I throttle forward on the starboard engine and pull the port engine back to idle, and it is just enough to hold our course. What a time to have the steering fail.

One more massive wall of white water throttles us then we are through, with just big, lazy, four-metre swells ahead of us. We travel on a few more miles to get out of the dangerous bar area, and then we climb outside to survey the damage. The SeaDoo rack is a mess of twisted stainless tube, and the jet-ski itself lies on its side. 'Just a couple more waves and we'd have lost her for sure,' Larry says with relief.

'How long did it take you to build that?' I ask, pointing at his prized rack.

'Um. About three days. And it was all destroyed in three minutes,' he replies.

'Yeah. I think we need to come up with a better system, eh,' and I wander back inside to see what I can figure out with the steering.

It's the first mistake Larry has made. When he first approached me about going to Antarctica, I was pretty quick in saying I'd take him, which is unusual, as I normally make people crew for a considerable time before making any solid commitment. But there was a real toughness about Larry that I liked. He'd served in the South African army, had a solid engineering background, and enjoyed adventure. Most of all, though, there was anger in his eyes at the continued slaughter of whales. I remember thinking this guy will bleed his own blood for me.

Up until today, he hadn't let me down, but the SeaDoo rack was a disaster. Too light, not bolted down sufficiently, and poorly conceived. To be fair I had my reservations about the design, and I should have spoken up about it, so it's both our faults really. The good news is we still have the SeaDoo, albeit needing repair. We're also over the bar, so now we just have to make our way to Auckland, some 300 nautical miles away around the tip of the North Island, where we can effect repair.

The steering system gradually gets worse, and eventually we're only using the engines to steer. It's a constant job of tweaking the port or starboard speed to try to keep the bow pointed roughly in the right direction. Originally, I'd thought it was just some air in the hydraulic lines, but now I'm not so sure. Whatever the problem is it has rendered the steering virtually useless, making our voyage to Auckland a long trip of zigzags and a never-ending task of adjusting engine speeds.

Larry is just settling into his midnight shift when an engine alarm startles us. I've heard this noise many times before, and it always spells bad news. I jump up and check the control panel, and it is showing water in the fuel, which doesn't sound so bad, but on a common rail diesel engine, it's toxic. Just a litre or two sneaking through and it'll leave us dead in the water. 'There's water all through here,' says Larry. He's crouching in the engine room and viewing the watch glass in our Racor fuel system. Tiny bubbles of water are cascading down in the diesel, and there're several inches of water in the bottom.

We trace the water back to the galley floor. One of our water containers has burst, and water and sludge is sloshing around on top of the fuel tank lid. Larry looks at the mess in disgust. Six months of galley grime, from food and cooking oil, to dirt and now water, is mixed in a dingy sludge. Reluctantly he leans in under the spar and starts sponging it out. 'Anyone for tea,' he says with a grimace, as he squeezes the first lot into a bucket.

It's half an hour later, Larry's head still buried in the galley, when the GPS alarm starts beeping. The system is failing to get a GPS signal. I switch to the backup GPS and it, too, has failed. I've never had a single GPS fail, let alone two at the same time.

The GPS is our key navigational tool. It tells us where we are, and where we are going. So to lose it makes things very difficult, especially on a dark stormy night where we can't see any lighthouses or land.

I've got our last known GPS position, so I note that down, and get a compass heading sorted. We start on a course of 340 degrees magnetic, but with the steering problems, it's hard to tell if we're averaging the right line or not. I'm pondering this, when I realise we have a couple of additional GPS systems anyway. Both the iPhone and the Sony video camera have built in GPS receivers. We power them up and place them under the windscreen where they can view some satellites in the sky, and within a few minutes the camera has our location.

From there our voyage involves reading our GPS location every hour from the camera, updating this to get a new compass heading, and then steering to this as best we can. It's a long slow night into a building head sea, and it's with some relief that we cross above Cape Reinga early the following morning.

There's almost a sigh of relief as we commence our voyage south, the big head seas now following us. Lumpy waves smashing into our bow are replaced by a gentle push up our bum. Larry and I are having a last cup of tea before we head off to bed. It's been a long and exhausting night.

'Can you believe how many things failed?' asks Larry. 'The SeaDoo got smashed, our steering is gone, we had water in the fuel and both GPS systems went down. And all in one night.'

'Well, just be grateful we're not in Antarctica . . . and we are still in one piece.'

Larry peers back at the rugged stretch of water we've just come through. This is where the Tasman Sea and the Pacific Ocean meet, and it's one of the most amazing stretches of water anywhere in the world. Strong currents, massive tides and nutrient rich waters all make this a hugely rich marine ecosystem. It's also a very spiritual place for Maori.

'You know, legend has it that when Maori people die, their spirits exit this earth through that tree over there,' and I point to a rugged section of coast that has a lone pohutukawa tree jutting out over the water.

Larry nods his head. 'Do you believe any of that stuff?'

'What. You mean like spirits and life after death?'

'Yeah.'

'Well, who's to say that Maori religious beliefs are any more or less valid than, say, Christianity or Islam? Most cultures develop religion to help explain existence. Life after death can be quite appealing.'

Larry looks like he's deep in thought. 'Well, if we base it on numbers, then the odds are the Christians are right, but if they are, there'll be a lot of disappointed Muslims and Hindus cussing at the pearly gates each day.' A wry smile now crosses Larry's face. 'Hey, imagine you're a suicide bomber, you blow yourself up expecting to get in to Heaven and hang out with 72 hot virgins for the rest of your days, and you then find out someone else had the right religion and you were wrong all along. Not only did you blow yourself up for no reason, but now you're damned in hell for eternity.'

'Well, I'd be wondering if said 72 virgins had ever been consulted about this. How do they feel having to tend some bloke who's just blown himself up? Not the start of a long and lasting relationship I'd expect. Let alone competing with the other 71 virgins for the man's affections.'

'Well, I have a problem with this whole concept of heaven. It seems your ability to get in is determined by birth, your parents, where you live, your mates through school. It is so unfair if your place in the clouds is largely predetermined anyway.'

'Well, maybe the Maori are right,' I say. 'Maybe through some divine decision, Maori people go to heaven and the rest of us miss out. Heaven is covered in rugby fields, hangi pits, a brewery and dedicated areas for pig hunting and gathering kina. Ha ha.' I picture in my mind an idyllic East Coast community and all the bros hanging out at the marae (meeting area) after a day gathering kaimoana (seafood).

'Well, here's a thought for ya. When you go to heaven, do you take your same brain with you? Presumably so, otherwise we're not ourselves any more, but then we're taking all our intellectual flaws with us. The intellectual giants of this world destine simple people like us for eternal intimidation. Maybe we take our same physical flaws as well. So short ugly blokes like me are short and ugly forever.'

'I don't know bro,' I reply. It's all a bit early in the day for this discussion. Actually, I'm just knackered and wanting to get to bed now.

'I'm not sure I'd want to go to heaven anyway,' Larry continues. He's on a roll now, and I can tell he's thought this through long ago. 'Hell is nice and warm, and it's got parties, drugs, sex and alcohol. Heaven is cold, you're always worried about falling off the cloud, and the only instrument you can play up there is the harp.' Larry laughs at his joke, and he hands me his empty mug.

I take the cups to the galley then climb down to the sleeping quarters, where another crew member Jason Stewart is lying awake. 'You're up,' I say. 'Wake us when we're half an hour from the Poor Knights.' Jason jumps up, and I quickly slide into the already warm sleeping bag. It welcomes me in, and my body sighs with relief as the muscles all relax. A long night at sea like we've just had and all your muscles are worked, and mine are certainly looking forward to finally resting. A nice glow comes over me, and a few minutes later I'm asleep.

It's late afternoon when we cruise into the Poor Knights Islands. The group has two main islands and a few clusters of smaller ones scattered around. Originally, the marine reserve comprised just one of the islands, and it never really worked. Anglers could target fish on the boundary and, as a result, fish life never really flourished as it should in a reserve. A proposal was subsequently made to extend the reserve to both islands, and it divided the community down the middle. Eventually, and after bitter debate, the full reserve was approved and for a while nothing much changed. Then over a few short years, life in this area just went ballistic and, today, it rates as one of the best marine reserves anywhere in the world.

It is testament to what can be achieved when dedicated people band together to make something great happen. It took the vision of a few people, and then hard work and commitment from a bunch of others who bought into the vision. The fishing boats have long since changed to running dive charters and tourist trips, and Tutukaka, the local town on the Northland coast, is all the better for it.

Today, though, we're not here to check out the marine reserve. We have a different mission in mind. The Poor Knights are blessed with another asset — the world's largest open water cave. We idle into the dark, Rico Rico cavern, and I switch off the engines. The low growl of two Cummins Mercruisers is replaced by the gentle lap of water on cave wall.

We sit there for a while just soaking up the amazing atmosphere. Small fish erupt on the surface around us as larger fish chase them under our hulls. There's the occasional drip of water on our heads from the damp roof of the cave. A lone penguin circles around the stern, wondering if he can make our transom step his hangout. He eyes us up for a while, and in the end decides better of it and paddles away.

Eventually, we start getting too close to the walls, so I start the engines, and we idle out to get some film footage of the coolest boat in the world coming out of the largest open-water cave in the world. The footage and shots are stunning, and by dusk we are back underway for Auckland, where we'll do final repairs before heading to Australia.

3
Spies and Hobart hamsters

'How much did these dry suits cost?' asks *Ady Gil* crew member Jimmy, as he squeezes into one of our new black Mustang combat suits. He looks well impressed. He wriggles around for a few seconds, and then his head pops out the neck seal. He doesn't smile much young Jimmy. And with his skinhead haircut, he looks like he's about to rip someone's head off. It's a great bit of kit really. Underneath we have garments a bit like sleeping bags with arms and legs (a company in the UK called Weezle generously donated them to us), and on top the Mustang dry suit.

We finally get kitted up and wander outside. We're anchored up at a remote island out from Hobart, Tasmania, away from prying eyes. We arrived in here a week ago, and are on standby for the call from Paul on when he'd like us to leave.

Larry lowers our oxygen lance down to the seabed on a length of rope. We'd purchased this the day we left Auckland, and thus far the unit has never been tested. How good it'll be in cutting up the propellers of harpoon vessels remains a mystery to me. I still think it a really long shot. It is unlikely we'll ever sneak up on a stationary harpooner and deploy this beast, but the prospect of disabling a vessel and having it towed back to Japan I know would cost the whalers dearly.

The unit is pretty simple. A cylinder delivers oxygen through a special metal tube, and it burns white hot as it comes out the end. A trigger allows you to control the speed of burn. The metal, mostly magnesium, gradually burns away, a bit like an arc welder, and the flame itself is over 5000°C — hot enough to cut concrete and steel. This unit here is supposedly good for cutting plate steel up to four inches thick.

Simple as it is, though, we have one major challenge — how to light it in the first place. On land, a simple flame will suffice, but obviously that's not so easy to achieve under water. The guys involved in marine demolition work use electrical cables back to a battery bank on a boat to get the end lit, but in our case we need to be self-sufficient under water.

It was Larry who came up with the solution. Some types of flares will work when totally wet and in some cases even submerged. So today our tests are as much about getting the lance lit in the first place, hopefully using flares, as they are about seeing what sort of damage we can do with the lance once it gets going.

Larry squeezes half a dozen flares of varying size into a small bag. 'You ready?' he says to me, and there's a loud pssshhhht sound as he purges his regulator. We jump in the water and descend down to the bottom, about seven metres beneath us. I've figured this will be the approximate depth of the propellers of the *Nisshin Maru* (the largest ship of the Japanese whaling fleet), which is the deepest we'd be expected to go. The harpoon vessels will be a metre or two shallower than this most probably. So if we can make it work at this depth, we should be able to make it work on any vessel in the whaling fleet.

I struggle around on the bottom, finding the weight profile of the dry suits difficult to handle. I've still got excess air in my legs, and they keep floating up awkwardly. I crab around in circles, I roll over a few times, and I go upside down, until I finally get it sorted. Larry, meanwhile, in complete control of his buoyancy, is no doubt laughing at my ineptitude.

I hold the oxygen lance nozzle out, while Larry gets the first flare ready. On pulling the igniter, a small burst of liquid ash squirts out, but then nothing. The second flare does a similar thing. The third flare, however, bursts into life with a series of audible spluttering sounds. The flame, for want of a better word, dances around the tip of the flare, and the particles in the water all around us glow. I sling the lance nozzle into the flare and pull the trigger. There're a couple of loud bangs as it nearly gets to life, but then the flare dies, and all we're left with is a stream of bubbles and a liquid trail of dirty ash.

The next two flares go in a similar fashion. We're just not getting enough time for the lance to ignite, before the flare is extinguished.

Larry pulls out his last flare, and it's larger than all the others. A bit of variety is good, I'm thinking. Maybe a larger flare will last longer. But in the back of my mind I'm uneasy about something. I put the thought aside, and watch as Larry pulls the igniter. There's a loud bang, and a rocket comes shooting out the end of the flare. It zigzags around for a few seconds before settling down on the seabed. Larry, it would seem, has set off a bloody parachute flare, and the rocket, now hissing away angrily, would normally be zooming off up into the sky about now.

Thinking it might still ignite the lance I swim over and place the nozzle in the flame, then pull the trigger. The stream of oxygen, however, dislodges the flare from its hole, and it zooms off in the opposite direction, again settling on the seabed. We follow it, and again we dislodge it as soon as the trigger is pulled. Larry and I follow this flare and we zigzag around the seabed, then back towards the surface, and eventually we lose sight as it disappears off into the hazy blue distance.

A few hours later we are docked back in Hobart and discussing the training exercise. In fact 'training' seems a little generous. Larry is lying down on the dock and he can't stop laughing. 'How useless were you in that dry suit?' Larry chortles, 'I thought you were break-dancing on the seabed. Ha ha.'

'Yeah, I did struggle getting my balance right,' I concede. I don't like having Larry better me in something. A sly grin crosses his face.

'Well, you might not win a dive competition, but you'd sure be a candidate to win any dance off.'

'Yeah, well, I guess my diving is about as good as your flare selection. What were you thinking, a parachute flare under water?' We both have a cackle remembering the two of us, chasing a flare around under water, and me pulling the trigger each time we got the lance near it. Anyone watching us would be left wondering what on earth we were trying to achieve.

The training was in fact a valuable exercise, though, in eliminating flares as a suitable igniter for the oxygen lance. We sit there tossing around other possible options, but nothing leaps out at us as a likely solution, just long shots and impossibilities.

By mid-afternoon we've moved onto discussing our final purchases of tactical gear when a journalist turns up for an interview. I shake her hand, and motion for her to sit down on the dock beside me. She's from Japan, and has just arrived in the country today.

'Why do you hate the Japanese?' she asks me earnestly. She's got a slight American accent, like many young Japanese these days. This is the fourth journalist from Japan who's taken the time to visit us here in Hobart before we leave for Antarctica. Larry by now is back on *Ady Gil* and packing away our gear.

'Look, I don't hate the Japanese,' I reply. 'I just hate the whalers. And the people who eat whale meat. But if Japan continues to hunt whales, then it is possible that, in the end, most of the world will hate you.' She raises her eyebrows as though this is a very provocative statement.

'But if it is OK for you to eat kangaroo in Australia, why is it not OK for Japanese to eat whale meat?' I've heard this argument, or versions of it at least, from a number of Japanese reporters . . . and I roll off my usual answer.

'Well, I'm not Australian for a start. But even if I was there's a big difference between whale and kangaroo. Firstly, there are millions of kangaroos in Australia, whereas there are only a few hundred thousand minke whales left. The genetic diversity of kangaroos is assured by population size, whereas the gene pool for whales is very small. So every whale matters.'

'Secondly, the kangaroos are on Australian soil, and it is up to Australians to manage them as best they can. The whales, on the other hand are in international waters, or in some cases a whale sanctuary. Japan has no right to go stealing those whales.'

'Thirdly, when a kangaroo is killed, it doesn't have an explosive harpoon through its back and take 45 minutes to die. It is just wrong what your people are doing down there.'

I finish and there is a long pause while she sorts her next question. She's reading them off a list, like all the other Japanese journalists. And it's the same list; it's just that the order varies. I may as well just give them a press release with my answers, I think to myself.

'What about our culture?' she says slowly. 'Japan has a long, proud history of whaling, and it is part of who we are.'

I pause for a few seconds. 'Look, it was the Americans who encouraged you into ocean whaling after the Second World War. Until then it was only ever a couple of coastal towns hunting locally. So its not like you've been whaling the high seas for centuries . . . and culture doesn't make it right anyway. The Sudanese still practise circumcision of women, and they argue it is their culture, but it doesn't make it right. For a long time the Americans had slavery as part of their culture, but it doesn't make it right. And right here in Tasmania, for a long time, it was acceptable to shoot Aboriginal people on your land. It was part of their culture. But it doesn't make it right.' I've lowered my voice and there's an aggressive edge to it.

'Ummm, one last question. The whaling industry employs a lot of people. What do you say to those people who would lose their jobs if whaling was to stop.'

I'd like to say, 'They can get stuffed.' Instead I roll off my usual, 'Well, the Second World War employed a lot of people as well.'

She stands to leave, but there's a question that's been on my mind for a while. 'Can you tell me why the Japanese are so determined to keep whaling? I just don't understand why it is so important to you.'

She smiles at me, probably for the first time, and it's like she's happy I'm even interested in their perspective. She switches her microphone off and hands it to the cameraman, who hustles back to their van and starts packing up. She lowers her voice and goes on to explain that very few people in Japan really eat whale meat. It tends to be wealthy old men and, happily, demand is gradually waning. But part of the challenge is this demographic remains in power there. A scan of their parliament, and you'd be expecting a car park full of Zimmer frames and mobility scooters outside the lobby, and a prostate specialist on permanent stand-by. Young or female politicians are as common as fillet steaks on a vegan boat.

The problem extends further than this. Media in Japan is largely controlled by the state; that is, wealthy old men. Theoretically, there is free media, but it remains dominated by a state agency that promotes the government's agenda and, in the foreseeable future, this will include a continuation of whaling.

She then moves onto money, which I'd always seen as the main reason for the whaling industry's continued existence. The company that conducts the whaling, itself effectively a state-controlled entity, loses money — and lots of it. It only remains viable through generous government handouts and financial support. Taxpayers are propping up an industry that caters to old men, and while the company itself might be unprofitable, many individuals are making plenty of money along the way.

'So let's say we want to stop Japan from whaling,' I say, 'how do you suggest we do this?'

There's a long pause as she ponders this. Eventually, she says, 'I don't think you can.'

She stands and shakes my hand. 'Thanks for your time,' she says humbly, and starts wandering off down the dock. I'm not sure what she'll report. I doubt much of what I've said will make it into the papers. It's probably not what the old men of Japan want their public to hear. But the fact that we're heading down to oppose the cultural, economic and imperial rights of Japan most probably will.

She disappears past the gates, and I scan over the various tourists and locals peering down at us. Living on the *Ady Gil* is like living in a fishbowl, with people always looking in at your home. There's the usual array of locals there, and a few tourists off the cruise ship that arrived last night. But there's one guy who sticks out like a set of dog balls. While some of the people look like they'd cook on a wok instead of a frypan, something about this guy just doesn't look right.

Jimmy carries a dive bag aboard, and the man suddenly pulls up his camera and shoots a bunch of shots until Jimmy has disappeared through the hatch. He then turns back towards the fishing boat docked next to us, pretending to take interest in it instead. Larry then passes a box of equipment on, and again the man shoots a string of images, before reverting to his fishing boat.

'Hey Lochy,' I say quietly to the 14-year-old lad who's been helping us during his school holidays, 'I want you to go and get a photo of that guy up there,' and I motion towards the man pretending not to look at us. Lochy, alias 007, climbs up the dock and wanders nonchalantly towards him. Lochy lifts up the camera and the man suddenly jumps into a van and, with a little squeal of one tyre, reverses away, bumping over the gutter on the way. 007 grabs his pushbike and disappears after him.

It's a full hour later before 007 scampers back on the stern of *Ady Gil*. He's panting, and it takes him a few seconds to catch his breath. 'I lost him a couple miles away,' he starts, 'but then when I was coming back, I spotted the same guy parked up over there by the toilet block. He's got a massive set of binoculars, and he's now got a camera lens about this big,' and he holds his hands about half a metre apart.

I steal a glance over at the block and, sure enough, the van is parked there with just a small section of windscreen showing past the corner.

We go inside *Ady Gil* and throw around a few options of what to do.

'We could just go and beat the snot out of him,' says Larry.

'Yes, I'm sure that will gel well with Sea Shepherd's policy of non-violence,' I reply sarcastically. 'Much as I'd like to rough the bugger up a bit.'

Various ideas are thrown in, but in the end, we just decide to wedge a big potato up his exhaust — of the car, that is. This will stop the van from starting when he decides to move back to his hotel. It's not like he's a real threat to us; any secret squirrel stuff is well buried in *Ady Gil* already.

It's unsurprising I guess that spies would be sent over to keep an eye on us anyway. Our presence here is hardly a secret, and if I were the Japanese, I'd have us under surveillance as well. At the very least, it means it's costing them more money to run their operation this year. Although if boy 007 can outsmart them, I'm not sure it's money well spent on their part.

The following day we take a two-hour drive out to the Florentine, where there is a protest march happening. The Florentine is an old growth forest that is being logged, but incredibly, all the logs are being used for is paper. Today's march, though, is not so much to do with logging, but rather climate change. Labelled 'Walk Against Warming', it's a global march coordinated in many Western cities around the world.

An overcast and misty afternoon greets the six of us as we climb out of the small Toyota wagon and start the trek into the forest. It's a winding procession of hippies, students, academics and professionals. Hemp shirts, sacks, headscarves and ponchos mix with jeans, skirts and the occasional tie. In comparison we must look like a gang, our posse of six blokes all wearing black Sea Shepherd T-shirts.

'There's a lot of hamsters here,' says Larry, eyeing up a group of young girls wandering ahead of us. Their hair is in various stages of dreadlock development, there's a complete absence of makeup, and they walk along with a confidence that belies their tender age. Legend has it that the term 'hamster' was originally coined by one of the crew of the *Steve Irwin*. At the start of the voyage, he had decided that none of the ladies on board met his exacting standards. After a few months at sea, however, he changed his mind, and on the one boozy night aboard, he finally made a move on one of them, only to discover she smelt remarkably like a hamster. He decided to switch to a second lady, and she too had a rather feral smell about her. It is quite possible that everyone on board smelt a bit dodgy after such a long time at sea.

It's a great little community of eco-conscious people here in Tasmania, and as Larry points out, it includes a bunch of cool hamsters. Many of them are the same ones who visited us on the boat, some donating food and supplies to our campaign. As we walk off the road and up a logging track, an old Mitsubishi car lies buried across the middle. Inside is a lone hamster chained to the chassis. 'Go the Sea Shepherds,' she yells excitedly at us.

We climb inside and have a quick chat. She's been camped in the area for about a month now, and the car was brought in just over a week ago. She explains that the Florentine is such a large forest that they cannot protect it all. Gunns, the company logging here, just targets areas where the protesters aren't — it's a continuous game of cat and mouse but, unfortunately, every old-growth log removed is another loss for the eco warriors, and another blow for the planet. 'It just breaks my heart,' says the girl, almost in tears.

There's ferocity in her eyes, and you can sense the anger within her. It's one of the things I love about these young eco warriors. They care about the planet enough to come out here and camp in the bush, forgoing luxuries most of us take for granted. They give up a chunk of their life for something they believe in, but it's not just a passing fad. For many of them, this has become their life work.

It must normally be a lonely vigil for these passionate people, I think. And today must be a highlight for them, with all these new visitors wandering through. We say our goodbyes and move on through the camp, a mixture of old tents, canvas tarpaulins and cooking fires. There's a well-used feel about the camp, which apparently has been occupied continuously for many years now. A group of them come up and shake our hands, wishing us well in the upcoming campaign.

We wind our way along the track, which at times has bush and trees right to the edge and at others there are ugly scars where logging has occurred. Finally, we reach the protest area. Small groups of people are scattered around, waiting for things to begin. More of them come over to us for a quick chat and to wish us well. We clamber up on some tree trunks. I'm not sure if they are still to be removed, or whether they just weren't the right kind of logs for paper. It does seem a waste having cut all this timber down, though, to just leave it rotting. Regardless, the logs make a great seat for the team. We sit up there with Sea Shepherd emblazoned all over us, soaking up the atmosphere as more and more people arrive.

In recent times I've started to look at the conservation movement as tribalism. It gives people something bigger to belong to than just themselves. Humankind historically has been tribal but, recently, many societies have lost these familial connections. We've lost our natural tribes, being limited to small families instead, or in many cases not even that. So we look for other things to replace this. Following our local football team, national rugby team or some basketball franchise is one way we satisfy our tribal urge. The connections, though, are loose. We wouldn't bleed our own blood, or at least hopefully not, for the sake of a football team.

Conservation is uniting people in a similar way; however, the sense of belonging and contribution is much stronger. People are willing to sacrifice much more in support of their tribe. Further to this, their tribe is one of many subtribes making up the conservation movement in general. So Sea Shepherd, *Earthrace*, WWF and the Greens, we are all subtribes with converging values and ideals, and together we make up a very considerable tribe that is a growing and mobile force around the globe. The protest on this day is a demonstration of that.

Larry drags a bottle of Mudhouse Wine out of his bag. 'I bring you a fine wine,' he says with relish, and he passes it along to me. Mudhouse generously donated 25 dozen wine bottles for the launch function, and thankfully we never quite finished them. This bottle must be one of the last.

'And did you bring me a fine glass as well?' I enquire. Larry opens his hands towards me, as if it wasn't his job.

Scanning the crowd, I can't see anyone else drinking, and there're a few cops sniffing around as well. It's easier to ask forgiveness than permission I say to myself. In any case, this could be our last drink for the next three months, so we may as well make the most of it. I take a big, long, hearty swig. The wine is rich and luxurious and it fills my mouth with flavours. I wipe my mouth and pass the bottle on to Mike, who raises the bottle up, downing a few large gulps; not quite the way Mudhouse had intended their wines to be drunk I suspect, but I'm sure they'd be happy to see us enjoying it.

An hour later and the speeches have started, and there's an expectant mood among the crowd. Meanwhile a continual stream of small groups and individuals make their way up to us, wishing us well, or just wanting to shake our hands.

'Hey bro, I'm half cut,' says Mike suddenly. I look over at him and there's a silly grin on his face. He's clinging onto the bottle of wine like it's precious. In fact with his freshly shaven head and pale skin he looks a bit like Gollum on growth hormones and steroids.

Larry, who had given up on Mike's bottle ever making it back, now has his own personal bottle of wine going.

'Man, you got a vineyard in that bag of yours,' I say to him. 'How many bottles of wine ya got hidden in there?'

Larry smiles. 'Oh, enough. I came prepared at least.' He takes a swig from the freshly opened bottle, licking his lips. 'What a magic day,' he says, and we all toast each other.

The crowd starts chanting, and eventually Xavier Rudd, the main act of the day, takes the stage. Amazingly, he's wearing a Sea Shepherd sweatshirt. He talks for a short time about climate change, about the need to preserve old-growth forests, and then he points to a small platform about 40 metres up a tree that overlooks us. A Kiwi bloke has been living up there for the last month, moving from tree to tree on an elaborate spider web of cables, as the police tried to bring him down. 'Much respect to you,' Xavier says, and he raises his fist to salute him.

He then looks up at our small posse . . . 'And much respect to the Sea Shepherds,' and he raises his fist to salute us. 'Going down to save the whales. We're there with you in spirit. Be safe and be courageous.' He sits there looking at us for several seconds as the crowd turn towards us cheering.

It's a moment I'll never forget. We came up here to show our support for the climate change and Florentine forest activists, not to be recognised ourselves, but there's respect, admiration and belonging among all the groups here, and to be recognised by them is something special indeed.

Mikey is almost overcome, and he leaps to his feet yelling and screaming, exactly what I'm not sure. Laurens jumps up as well, but starts to lose balance and sits back down. Larry sits there with a big grin on his face, and he then raises his bottle to the crowd. I just sit there, soaking up the atmosphere. We are privileged indeed to be here and to experience this.

Xavier then starts his first song, a haunting melody that comes soaring out of the massive banks of speakers stacked against logs, filling the valley up with his emotions. A lone hamster makes her way through the crowd and starts gyrating to the music. An ample breast oozes out from beneath her orange top, and she stands there with one leg raised up in the air, before lowering it down and gyrating back the other way. 'That's the mother hamster,' says Larry, and he laughs. A few younger hamsters jump up and start gyrating as well, as the song slowly builds. Man, there must be a hamster burrow in that hill somewhere, I think to myself.

Xavier gets to his last song. Music can be a powerful medium. At times it's just sounds we like to hear. A given beat or sequence connects with us and we enjoy it, but it is simply sounds. Sometimes, though, it's more than that; it's when a musician and a crowd join. Some musicians spend their entire career trying to reach this nirvana and never achieve it, while others somehow manage to reproduce it in many performances.

'With Mine own Eyes' is a personal song Xavier wrote about some of the injustices he'd seen in the last few years. It's a powerful song filled with emotion and passion. His voice resonates and it lifts the crowd up, carrying us along on an amazing journey. It connects us all in this shared belief in looking after the planet. This tribe that wants to save the whales, that wants to stop climate change, that wants to stop the destruction of old-growth forest; a tribe that is tired of seeing the planet trashed, and that is now prepared to make a stand.

Xavier finishes the song, and we drift back down. He doesn't say anything — he doesn't need to. His song has said it all. He just stands, bows and wanders off the stage.

We sit there for a while until the wine is all finished. The crowd has mostly wandered off, and there are just a few still hanging around, starting the long clean-up. Larry and I finally get up, and we stand on opposite ends of the log, rocking it backwards and forwards. We can't quite dislodge it from its perch, despite our efforts, and we're about to give up when Larry loses his footing. He stumbles backwards, collapsing in a heap among the brush and dead logs. There's a confused look on his face, and he gives a muffled moan.

'Aha ya loser,' I yell at him, and I jump off the log and down onto the logging track.

Several minutes later Larry extricates himself, and he climbs gingerly down to join us. He moves slowly and deliberately, and sits down in a heap and groans. His face is grey and pale, and he closes his eyes. 'I think I broke my ribs,' he finally says.

'Yeah whatever,' I reply. I grab his camera, and Laurens, Mikey and I pose for a photo with Larry looking bewildered.

'Seriously guys. I'm a bloody trained Army medic, and I know my ribs are broken. I heard three cracks when I landed.'

Laurens becomes concerned and decides to get him to a hospital, while Mikey and I wander off down the track, convinced that Larry is just pretending. Our razor-sharp minds have decided we should meet with

Xavier and get him onto the *Ady Gil* for a few quiet ones later in the evening.

Xavier does in fact make an appearance. Late in the night he and a few mates turn up, and we sit in the sleeping quarters thrashing around ideas, and solving the world's problems. He's certainly passionate about many things — marine conservation, climate change, deforestation and the Aboriginal people of Australia. He's well versed in the arguments and has had these discussions many times it would seem. He's agreed to let us use his music in any video we might care to make.

The following morning and Larry is still not back from the hospital. In all the mayhem the previous evening we'd forgotten about him, but on sobering up today, we're all suddenly worried. I track him down to a small room in the pneumothoracic ward of Hobart Hospital, and he's lying there with a solemn look on his face.

'Zer is no vay he can go vis you to Antarctica,' the young doctor says, with a strong German accent. There is firmness in his voice, suggesting there is no discussion to be had. He's a good-looking bloke. He'd have no problem picking up nurses and local ladies looking for an eligible young man.

'It's just a couple of broken ribs bro,' I reply. 'There's nothing he can do anyway aside from rest, and he can do this on the boat.'

The doctor gives me an unfriendly scowl. 'No, it is vay vorse. Larry also as a punctured lung.' There's a long pause, and then he adds, 'Zis is a very serious condition.'

It is easy to stereotype people, and I do it a lot. Not because I like to lump people with negative traits, but more because of their positive ones. Germans as a rule can be pedantic, and at times awkwardly so. Not all of them, of course, but many of them. Now if you want someone to design you a car, for example, a German would probably turn out something that's pretty good, although it won't be cheap.

The same might go for your doctor. I watch the German, as he explains the condition Larry is in, the way he methodically steps through the various X-rays, and what he is proposing for Larry. He is totally lacking in compassion, which can be a German trait as well, but there is a thoroughness about him that is compelling. He completes the discussion and I just nod. It would be foolish to take Larry with us, despite the key role he was to play on *Ady Gil*.

I thank the doctor for his efforts, and he just replies, 'But of course,' as most Germans would, and he wanders off to his next patient, who is hopefully not about to head to Antarctica.

Larry, I know, is gutted. He lies there with a permanent scowl on his face. He'd already made his mind up about not coming. He knew he'd be a liability for us anyway. And it took the doctor to convince me. Larry has been volunteering now for months, though, and of anyone to lose on my team, he's by far the hardest to replace. But the decision is made and I just need to move on.

'I reckon you just need to harden up,' I say to Larry. He starts to laugh, then winces in pain and stops.

'You'll be fine without me Pete.' His voice is a whisper.

'You gonna head back and see your whanau [family] as soon as ya get outta here?' I say to Larry.

He twists a bit to adjust his pillow then winces.

'Oh Christ,' he says, flopping back onto the bed. 'Nah, mate. I'm coming down to Antarctica.'

'And how exactly do you intend getting down there?' Larry reaches over to the bed control and presses an arrow button. The top half of the bed starts rising up.

'The *Steve Irwin* will be back here to refuel soon enough. They can't do a full campaign on one tank.' He lets the control panel go and it hangs down limply beside him.

'That'll be ages away. Why don't you go back to NZ and see Madlaina and ya daughter in the meantime?' Larry turns his head slowly towards me.

'Look, Pete, I'm like a bull elephant.' His tone of voice suggests that I should know what he's talking about, but I just look puzzled.

'Actually bro, I'm not really sure what bull elephants do. Perhaps you could enlighten me on the linkages between an elephant rutting on the savannahs of Africa, and you lying here with broken ribs in a hospital bed?'

'Well, bull elephants don't spend much time with family. They just roam around, sometimes alone and sometimes with a few other males. They wreak a bit of havoc, scare the locals, rob a few maize paddocks . . . maybe a boozy night or two . . .' his voice trails off.

'And do they have any wives or kids while this is taking place?'

'Nah, piss off. Occasionally, they might get lucky and pick up a bit of fluff in one of the reserves. They'll go berserk for a short time, and then they'll bugger off back to the bush. So, you see, I'm just like a bull elephant.'

'Well, ya look more like a wounded badger that has been run over by a car and is on its last legs.'

'Yeah, well, when ya're robbing farmers and trampling their fences, ya gotta expect a few injuries along the way. I'll just chill out here and get better and as soon as the *Steve Irwin* returns, I'll jump aboard and join all the boys down in Antarctica — and wreak a bit of havoc I hope.'

There is a long pause between us.

'In many respects Pete I'm just like you. You're a bull elephant as well. How much time you spent with your family over the past four years while you've been skippering *Earthrace*?'

I sigh and look out of the window. The first droplets of a rainstorm are coming down. There's a semblance of truth in what Larry says. My times at home with my family have been few and far between for quite some time now. Sharyn and I have split up, mostly because of it, and I've seen little of my girls in ages.

I wander out, maybe not as upset as Larry, but certainly aware of the big hole in the team that won't be easy to fill, and thoughts of my family languishing in New Zealand without me.

I start to imagine all the discussion this will bring about within Sea Shepherd. I've deliberately recruited a group of risk takers, confident and physically capable people who climb trees, wakeboard, river swim, sky dive, play rugby; people who regularly put their bodies on the line and back themselves to come out the other side. When you have these people, they'll push the boundaries in many ways. They'll jump on a whale being towed, clamber up a security fence, or take a wave on a SeaDoo at 40 knots.

People like these also tend to be survivors. When things turn pear-shaped, instinct and reaction will see them turn the right way, jump at the right time, or make good their escape. Or that is the hope at least. Certainly, I believe these lads with me will survive this voyage intact, despite the considerable risks we face.

Of course, the downside of a team full of physically active risk takers is a few bumps and bruises along the way — or, in Larry's case, unfortunately, broken ribs and a punctured lung.

Consider the alternative, though. If I had a group of conservative, risk-averse characters with me yesterday, well, we wouldn't have been trying to topple off the log. In fact we wouldn't have been up there in the first place; we'd have been seated down on the track. We wouldn't be drinking a bottle of wine each either. That same group, though, would struggle crewing the *Ady Gil*. The constant risks, the physical exertions, the lack of structure and the deprivation of amenities would drive them nuts . . . and they'd baulk when asked to clamber up a moving vessel or to jump on a dead whale being towed by a harpooner.

I start my laptop, and I start scrolling through past crew to see if there are any who might be available. It's a big call, however. While many people might want to go to join us in Antarctica, few would be able to leave at just a day's notice, and fewer still that are engineers. I come up with just two possibilities, and hurried emails are beamed off to New Zealand.

4
Playing cat and mouse

Pam, one of the local volunteers, comes bouncing into the helm. She is beaming from ear to ear. 'His Holiness, the Dalai Lama, has given you his blessing,' she says with relish. Actually, I wasn't sure the blessing would happen at all. The Dalai Lama is currently in Hobart, and he was asked to bless the *Ady Gil* and her crew, and keep us safe in Antarctica. I was worried that he might not want to bless us, given our tactics might be considered dangerous. Or perhaps slightly illegal, depending on what law book you're reading from. So it's welcome news to know he has given us his blessing.

'He read your names out after his lecture,' Pam says, 'and he has asked that you and your crew all return safely.'

Laurens comes up and plants a big kiss on Pam's cheek and hugs her. 'Thank you so much for sorting that,' he says. Pam blushes.

Paul Watson told me a story about how a small Buddha statue turned up on the *Steve Irwin* a few years back, and the crew nearly threw it out. In the end they placed it away on the vessel and forgot about it. A year later, the Dalai Lama finally met up with Paul, and he asked if his Buddha had gotten delivered OK. If the Dalai Lama blesses a Buddha for you, regardless of your religious persuasion, you don't throw it out.

Now it seems that Sea Shepherd has two vessels with the personal blessing of His Holiness.

An hour later and we're ready to leave. Jimmy, Laurens and I have one last look through our lists to make sure we're not forgetting anything. Jason Stewart, our replacement engineer, meanwhile is stacking away the last of the galley food.

It's a stiff breeze rollicking up the Port of Hobart as we say our final goodbyes to people on the dock. 'You be careful down there,' says Pam, 'and make sure you all come back in one piece.' It's a sentiment expressed by many. There are certainly risks in the campaign. We are taking a small boat into the most treacherous waters on earth. There're the roaring forties, furious fifties and screaming sixties to deal with. And that's before we deal with any ice.

This boat has never been in ice before, but it's certainly well proven in big seas. What worries me more are the whalers. Or scientists, should I say. Actually, I've decided I'll call them scientists from now on — which is a total farce, of course. The only science going on down there is how many steaks they can eke out of each carcass. But what the 'scientists' will do to us remains an unanswered question. If the initial skirmishes between the *Steve Irwin* and the *Shonan Maru #2* are anything to go on, the scientists are ready for a fight this year . . . and they remain well funded from state support in terms of subsidies, as well as access to restricted military hardware.

The scientists are just well-paid employees doing a job. It does involve the killing and butchering of whales, but it is still just a job. The *Ady Gil* crew, in comparison, are volunteers giving up a piece of their lives to work on something they believe in. We're all extremely lucky to have this opportunity, and we will tolerate a lot of hardship in hopefully putting an end to the professors, doctors and lab technicians, with their harpoons, knives and butcher's hooks.

A few minutes later and we ease away from the dock and, shortly after, Hobart is fading in the background. The crew is busy outside and I'm alone in the helm pondering the voyage. I'm not elated to be leaving. Maybe relieved a little. It's been a long wait here, and I wish we'd been down a week ago to support the *Steve Irwin*. If anything, I'm nervous.

I'm worried we'll be a failure down there, and we'll come back with the Japanese scientists laughing at us. All we can do is our best, though. And hopefully it's good enough to make a difference.

The lads all come clambering back into the helm. 'We're sorted on the back deck,' says Jimmy. 'Anything else you need us to do?'

'A cup of tea'd be good bro,' I reply.

'Man, it is so good to be under way,' says Laurens. He raises his hand and we all high five each other, happy to be on our way at last.

Despite my anxiety, there's a good feeling among this crew. Certainly, it's a talented team — a range of ex-military people, although that wasn't really intentional; it just happened that way. People displaying the qualities I was looking for tended to be ex-servicemen. Aside from losing Larry, the team is as good as I could hope for.

The scientists (whalers) often portray Sea Shepherd as a bunch of unemployed extreme activists with tattoos and nose studs. While in the past there were examples of this, Sea Shepherd in reality comprises a range of people . . . and the *Ady Gil* crew certainly can't be labelled as extreme activists. Most have spent their working lives upholding laws.

We sit there dissecting the crazy last few days. In the back of my mind something is nagging me. It takes me a while to figure out what it is. There's a slight diesel smell wafting through the helm. The smell has been there for some time, just gradually sneaking into my consciousness.

For the last three years, we'd run *Earthrace* almost exclusively on biodiesel, and so the smell of diesel in here is relatively new. Eventually, I convince myself the smell tonight is from more than just when we refuelled a few days back. I wander into the galley and lift the hatch and, to my horror, there're several centimetres of diesel sloshing around on top of the tank.

I trace the problem to the back fuel tank lid, which is an aluminium disc about the size of a Frisbee. It isn't sitting right on the top of the tank, and diesel is sloshing through a narrow gap. Our tanks are so full, though, that if I take the lid right off to repair it, I'll have a mountain of fuel suddenly sloshing around. In the end I tighten things up as best I can, and then sponge up the remaining diesel. It's not perfect, and the galley will stink of diesel for some time yet, but at least the flow will be stemmed. In a few days when we've burned a bit more fuel, I'll get the lads to do a proper repair, I say to myself.

I wander back into the helm, where Jason is tweaking the autopilot. 'Man, I feel crap,' he says slowly.

'Yeah me too,' I reply in disgust. Diesel is all over my arms, and my clothes reek of the stuff. The fruit and vegetables in the galley will all stink of the fumes now as well. Here we are heading out for what we hope is a few months, with no shower on board, and on the first night at sea I'm already covered in crap. Not a good start.

I clean myself up as best I can, and head off to my scratcher. We were up the entire previous night on final preparations, so all the crew are knackered. Various emotions are racing through my mind: anxiety, elation and relief. There's this nagging doubt about having forgotten something vital . . . and disappointment at not having Larry with me. My body, though, is exhausted, and it's not long before my mind starts to wander and I sink off to sleep.

'Hey, Pete. There's something wrong with the steering.' Jason is trying to whisper, but he's not so good at it. His husky voice is either on or off. His words echo a few times around my head before I register where I am. I stumble out of bed to look at the clock on the engine controls: 9pm. So I've had a few hours sleep at least. My body tugs at me, saying it needs more.

Jumping into the driver's seat, I see the autopilot has the error 'rudder angle not adjusting', which means the system is trying to turn the rudder, but seeing no change in the rudder angle. I've seen this error before, and several different things can cause it. Cancelling the error, I turn the steering wheel manually, and *Ady Gil* starts a slow turn to port, and back towards Antarctica.

'What's wrong?' says Jason with concern.

'Well, I reckon the hydraulics are all OK, so it's probably a problem with the electronics. We'll just steer her manually overnight, and hopefully fix things in the morning.'

Steering this big boat manually is a challenge, however. The waves picking us up skew the stern to starboard, and then back to port as we fall off the back. The trick is to anticipate the waves and adjust before you're too far off course. Jason slowly gets the hang of it, now running off the compass for his bearing, and I head back to my little scratcher. I scored a bottom bunk tonight, which is always nice.

My scratcher welcomes me back in like a generous lover. It wraps me up and engulfs me, and a smile crosses my face. If there's one thing you appreciate after spending time at sea it's a good sleep. And right now I'm really looking forward to it.

It's mid-morning the following day before I rustle up the energy to troubleshoot the system. The electronics and pumps all seem OK, so it suggests the problem lies in one of the outriggers, where the rudders are located. Getting there to do an inspection, however, is not so easy.

The water looks cold and uninviting. Three-metre waves roll in on us, and the outrigger slaps in and out of the water as each new wave comes charging through. I'd tossed up sending Jimmy or Laurens out to do the job, although if the problem does lie there, I'd probably have to go out to follow up anyway. In the end I decide to just do it myself, saving the rest of the crew for another task.

In the months ahead I'll be asking the crew to do some unpleasant and at times dangerous jobs. It is good to have them aware that their captain will only send them on jobs he'd be prepared to do himself. I've always believed your crew should respect you, and that respect is earned by actions, rather than being bestowed on you by title.

Despite all this, it's with some trepidation that I climb gingerly along the outrigger and down to the rudder access hatch. My bum is pointing up in the air as I poke my head and torso through the round hole. The problem is immediately apparent — the hydraulic ram has actually come away from the rudder. So the other rudder is steering normally, and this one is just floating in the breeze — or, in this case, current.

I'm picking up the various washers and bolt that are lying beneath the tiller arm when a wave comes shooting over me, soaking my bum and legs, and sending a cold shiver up my spine. I can hear Jimmy and Laurens laughing from the spar, and it leaves me wishing I'd sent one of them anyway.

The nut it seems has gradually unscrewed until it finally fell right off, but it is nowhere to be found. It must've been washed out the drain hole.

'Grab us an M24 nut will ya.' I yell at Jason. He scarpers off to do some digging in our collection of nuts and bolts. It's half an hour later and the rudder is back together. The repair is a quick and dirty job, though. The nut is not a Nylok, nor is it stainless. So it'll corrode quickly in the harsh salt environment. But it does keep us on our way to Antarctica, and we'll do a proper repair at a later date.

We make our way south and the rudder holds up in one piece. 'This is not the furious fifties,' I say to Laurens a few days later, 'its the fluffy fifties. Laurens is busy scoffing his breakfast; he finishes his mouthful and looks around the horizon. It's a crystal blue sky, and the wind is a gentle 15 to 20 knots on our stern, giving a nice rolling three-metre swell up our bum. And the barometer is firmly planted at 1000 hectopascals. About as good as you can expect here really.

When we left Hobart our latitude was around 42 degrees, then as we headed south we passed through what are commonly referred to as the roaring forties, and now the furious fifties. By tomorrow, we'll be into the screaming sixties. That's not to say they are always roaring, furious and screaming, but they often are — although not today by the looks of things.

'You wanna be careful what you say,' Laurens finally answers me. 'This ocean can be treacherous.' How the Dutchman learnt a word like 'treacherous' is beyond me. Let alone the other five languages the Dutch all seem to know.

He's been an interesting crewman, young Laurens. I wasn't so keen on taking him initially. He arrived on the boat a few days before we were to leave, and I hate big voyages with people I haven't had on the boat before. But he's turned out to be awesome. The best thing about him is he is always so damned happy. I've never seen him without a smile on his face. Not that you want everyone on your boat running around with Valium grins. You need a mix of people really. But having someone who's always happy certainly lifts the team when things are not going well. And, for sure, we'll have a few tough days ahead.

By late afternoon the barometer suddenly starts sinking. There was a depression showing on the forecast, although I'd thought we were going to clear most of it. 'Down to 970 now,' says Laurens, who has suddenly taken an interest in the barometer. I look out the starboard window, and the gentle three-metre rolling swell has morphed into angry four-metre waves on the beam. Winds increase over the next hour to at least 40 knots, and soon the waves are towering above us.

'Oh, check this wave out,' I say to Laurens, who is perched in the navigator's seat beside me. There are white wind trails up the face of it, and on top there's about three metres of foam thrashing around. Rather than being like a wall, it's more like a mountain, with a peak only 30 or so metres long. It passes ahead of us with a whoosh. Five minutes later and one of these monsters lines us up. I turn the boat to port, hoping to take a little of the wave on the stern. There's a sudden smack as the wave engulfs us. It flicks us round and lifts up the starboard outrigger, then unceremoniously dumps it back down. We slide off the back face, and the wave races away.

'Do you still get scared at sea?' Laurens asks shortly afterwards. The smile has gone.

'Yeah, I do. I'm nervous now,' I reply slowly. 'No two waves are ever the same. They all differ in some way. We're only ever one wave away from being flipped upside down. And while I've been in seas much bigger than this, the oceans are unforgiving. If you don't treat them with respect, they will bite you.'

'That was a big wave back there though, eh?'

I look over at Laurens, who remains serious. 'Yeah, that was a good wave alright.' It was a bit like we were irrelevant though. It just came crashing through and we had almost no impact on it at all. It just smashed right past us. We sit in silence for a few minutes. 'But you wanna know the best thing? We are the only people who will ever get to see that wave.'

Laurens nods his head slowly and his smile returns. 'Unless some surfer gets to ride it in New Zealand,' he says hopefully.

We continue heading south and towards the *Steve Irwin*, which for the last week has been tailed by a Japanese security vessel. As we approach their position, two blips show up on our radar. We were instructed to come down the 145 longitude line, but I've swung a couple of miles to port to give them some practice at detecting vessels. I know there will be a number of people in the helm, and they'll be scanning the horizon and poring over the radar screens trying to find us.

The satphone rings again. 'Paul Watson wants an update on our position,' Laurens says hurriedly.

'Tell him we're four miles ahead of them, that we have them on radar and a visual, and we will be alongside in 15 minutes,' I reply.

At 2am we slide silently up beside the *Steve Irwin* — all black, and with those distinctive lines I've seen in so many books, newspapers and on TV. It is great to finally see her in the flesh.

'Man, she's a good-looking boat,' says Laurens. He's the only one of us who has set foot on her before, and he talks as if she's an old friend of his.

I grab a set of Generation 4 night vision goggles and watch the *Steve Irwin* crew battle to get the *Delta*, their rigid inflatable, launched. A guy donated the goggles to us, and they'd be one of the coolest bits of kit I've ever come across. I've been using them on my night watch on the voyage down to get used to them. The image clarity on a pitch-black night is quite astonishing. They're illegal in fact in most countries, but thankfully, in Arkansas, you can buy just about anything.

Once on board the *Steve Irwin*, we're quickly ushered up to the helm where Paul Watson and his officers are waiting. Red lights and electronic screens glow in the large space, and it has the feeling of a battle control room. There's a welcoming disposition about the officers; they all seem genuinely happy to see us.

'Would any of your crew like a shower?' Paul enquires.

'No thanks, Paul. But a hot chocolate would be nice.' One of the crew scurries off to get it, while Paul starts giving us his thoughts.

'We've had this damned *Shonan Maru* following us for over a week now,' he explains, 'and as long as they are on our tail, it's impossible for us to find the fleet. They just keep relaying our position to the fleet, which can then skirt around us. I need you to get them off our tail.'

I look around the group and I can see them all looking expectantly at me, and I'm thinking this is where I'm supposed to go 'Sure — no problem', but the trouble is I have no idea how I can get this tail off them. If the *Shonan Maru* is determined to keep following the *Steve Irwin*, there is little I can do to stop them, aside from perhaps fouling their propellers.

'Do you have any special tactics in mind?' I finally reply.

Paul pulls out a small metal tube and hands it over. 'This,' he says proudly, is a blah blah blah laser.' I don't remember any specifics about the laser, other than that it is green. 'Point it at the crew of the *Shonan Maru* and this will blind them temporarily.'

I take the laser, trying not to reveal my disappointment. How is a pissy little laser going to do anything helpful for us I wonder to myself?

'We also have a new prop-fouler for you,' says Paul. 'The *Delta* crew will drop it off to you once we're finished here.' Just as well, because my crew has done no work on prop fouling. Sea Shepherd has been working on these for the last three seasons, so I figured they'd have it well sorted already.

'One more thing,' says Paul, as I'm about to leave. 'The crew on the *Shonan Maru* are not whalers; they are trained military people and they are extremely aggressive. You be careful.'

'Yeah, no worries.' We shake hands, and with that, Laurens and I are shuttled back onto *Ady Gil* to an anxious crew. The prop-fouler is loaded, and we idle a mile away from the *Steve Irwin*. We lie there in wait for the *Shonan Maru*.

It is just getting light as her sleek form gradually emerges from the darkness. There's a certain sinister air about these vessels, in part I guess because of how much I hate their activities. She is sliding past, maybe just 200 metres away, and my crew is silent.

Suddenly, she stops. She sits there almost stationary for a short time then she turns to starboard, looking straight at us. She's like a hunting dog that has just found new prey, and is evaluating us, looking for a weakness or deciding when to pounce. Then there's a puff of ugly smoke and she comes racing in on us. For several minutes she circles then she comes steaming right in on our stern. As we increase speed, the *Shonan Maru* matches us all the way up to 20 knots, before we finally pull away. The gap increases to over 100 metres, and she eventually veers away. There's an indignant air about her as she turns back towards the *Steve Irwin*, maybe preferring a quarry she can catch.

Jimmy, Mike and Laurens are stationed on the back preparing things. We've done no training with the prop-fouler, and I'm worried about how to deploy it effectively. Our weapons, namely the spud gun and the laser, will just serve to harass the scientists and make us feel good, but only the prop-fouler can disable them.

The lads are finally ready, so I slam *Ady Gil* into gear and we're off after the *Shonan Maru*. For the last week the engines haven't gone over 1500 rpm, and they don't like it. They gradually carbon up and get clogged. As they accelerate now over 2000 rpm, the turbochargers start to whistle, and there's almost an audible sigh from the engines. A nice raspy tone comes rumbling through our thin carbon hull. These engines like me.

We're up around 25 knots and travelling into three-metre swells, and each wave comes lurching over the top of us and smothering the back deck in an icy-cold blanket. I look at the camera screen and I can see

Mikey and Jimmy cowering behind the horns. It looks like a miserable place to be right now.

In a short time we catch the *Shonan Maru*, and I slow down beside them to get a good look at this vessel. Hardened security men ('lab technicians') glare down at us from behind their flak jackets, long-range acoustic devices (LRADs) and water cannons. There's an arrogant air about them. They don't smile, nor do they give us any signals; they just glare down from their stations.

We circle a few times, noting where the different stations are. On the bow and stern are water cannons. They don't look very grunty. Up close they'd do some damage I reckon, but over 20 metres away it'd be spray only. It means to get really close to the vessel the safest place would be around the middle of the ship, where you're a reasonable distance from both water cannons. You'd probably just get a misty spray from the one on the bow.

Both cannons, I note, are also controlled remotely. The bow cannon started off pointing directly ahead, but it was then gradually shifted to be pointing down the port side. No one has been near it, however, so they must be controlling it remotely, perhaps from the helm. If you were to zip in and out around either cannon, it'd be difficult for them to keep it directed on you.

As we slide closer, a female voice suddenly comes booming in on us. 'This is the captain of the *Shonan Maru* speaking. Stop your agglessive action or we will be forced to blah blah you off.' I listen to it a few times, trying to make out the last bit of the sentence.

'What's she saying at the end there Jason? Is it "*fend* you off"?'

'Well, it could be "suck",' he replies with a chortle.

The female voice is then replaced with the LRAD's wah wah wah wah noise. A US company developed the LRADs as a non-lethal form of crowd control. They are a military product that has seen them deployed through Iraq, and more recently by local law enforcement agencies. They have thousands of piezoelectric crystals all aligned in the same way. They have various noise types pre-programmed in, such as the standard crowd dispersion noise they are playing at the moment. They can also run as a standard loudspeaker system, which, presumably, is how they gave us the 'This is the captain' message a few minutes earlier. The LRADs are positioned in the middle of the ship, one on the port side and one on the starboard.

There are also a couple of random blokes stationed around the *Shonan Maru*. They are at specific locations with a role each I figure, as they are not moving, but what their roles might be I'm not sure.

As we get closer still, the net becomes apparent. Virtually the entire vessel is shrouded in it, a giant spider web, extending almost right to the bow, and then back and around the stern. All up, the *Shonan Maru* has been transformed from a harpoon vessel into a formidable fortress.

We normally use hand-held radios to communicate among the crew. The scientists, however, have used jamming devices in the past, which would render them useless. I'd hate to be using them, and then miss a crucial instruction if the scientists were selective in when they turned their jammer on. Also, the scientists are bound to have scanners that could intercept our radio transmissions anyway. So I've decided I'll just use Jason as a gopher. 'Tell the lads they can deploy the laser and the spud gun as they like,' I yell over the din of the LRAD. Jason nods and disappears out of the stern.

Mikey crouches behind the horn and starts pointing the laser. Through the misty gloom, an intense line of green light shoots over onto the bridge area of the *Shonan Maru*. I'm actually quite impressed with how bright it is. Mikey methodically targets anyone who looks at us; from the LRAD operators, the random blokes whose roles we don't know, the bridge team, the people filming and photographing us; anyone attracting Mike's attention basically.

Jimmy meanwhile is rigging up the spud gun. It is linked to a compressor in the engine room, and the first few shots fall well short. In due course the compressor gets up to full pressure, and there's a solid thumpssshhhh each time Jimmy pulls the trigger.

He starts off with apples, and then moves onto some sweet potatoes, which are slightly denser, and provide a virtually airtight seal. It takes a few shots to get his eye in, and from there, he's able to pretty much hit targets at will. We're not trying to hit anyone, but certainly we'd like to make life difficult for the scientists. He then loads one of the bottles of foul-smelling butyric acid (an organic acid found in rancid butter). Tape has been wrapped around the bottle so it's a snug fit. It is pushed right to the bottom, and the *Shonan Maru* is then targeted in the red dot sight.

Jimmy pulls the trigger, the pressurised air is suddenly released, and the beer bottle of butyric acid goes shooting out the 70 mm barrel. It sails up at about 45 degrees to the *Shonan Maru*, some 80 metres away, smashing onto the bridge. 'Wahoo. Bull's-eye,' yells Jimmy. By now the *Shonan Maru* is basically cleared of scientists. Only three remain visible; one holds a handicam filming us, but he's hidden behind a wall. One is hidden behind the port-side LRAD. And one whose job we haven't figured out yet sits peeking at us from behind the superstructure. The rest have decided their life expectancy is better off if they're below decks. Or perhaps they were ordered off? Either way, the lads now have scant targets to intimidate. Mikey by now has shifted onto harassing the officers in the bridge. They're well hidden behind the glass, but we know they'll be in there.

The laser has been quite a revelation actually. I'd figured it was hardly worth the effort, but on seeing it, the scientists all seem scared of it. The spud gun has also been a huge success. On last year's campaign, not a single projectile was landed on any of the whaling vessels, while we've hit them with over 50 in the last few hours.

The trouble, though, is the *Shonan Maru* just continues its relentless pursuit of the *Steve Irwin*, despite all our efforts. So while we might be successful in pissing the scientists off, we're hardly fulfilling Paul's objectives.

'Tell Mikey to rig up the prop-fouler,' I yell at Jason, who's sitting in the rear hatch watching them. It's a terrifying feeling putting your boat on the line in front of a 70-metre harpooner. What makes it more difficult is the astonishing speed and manoeuvrability of our quarry. It means you need to get incredibly close and cross directly in front of them to have any chance of snaring their props — which is terrifying indeed.

As we line them up, Jason calls distances. 'Throttle hard bro,' Jason yells urgently, as we start to cross their bow. I've got our FLIR infrared camera looking astern and the giant vessel engulfs the image. The screen then suddenly goes blank as their water cannon hits us from above. I can hear yelling from the stern, but over the LRADs and water it's impossible to tell what's happening.

'It's going to be real close,' Jason says for the second time. 'Oooohhhhhh.' A slight hint of relief in his voice. 'Shit, was that close.'

Mike and Jimmy drag themselves inside. 'We threw the fouler bro,' says Jimmy, panting, 'but it ended up in a big ball and missed them. I reckon we'd be better off towing it,' he says.

We retrieve the fouler, while Mike and Jimmy get a new rigging set up. The fouler is suspended between the two horns and towed, and a small rope linked to a release mechanism. We catch back up with the *Shonan Maru* and I make another pass across their bow.

'It's right up our arse Pete,' Jason yells. There's genuine fear in his voice for the first time. 'Throttle hard now, bro.' His voice trails off, and he watches the giant whaling vessel loom over our stern. Water smashes in on us from the remotely controlled cannon mounted on their bow and, for a moment, it drowns out even the LRADs.

'They never deployed it,' Jason says slowly. 'The release mechanism jammed.'

We make a second pass, and again the mechanism jams.

On the third attempt, we tie the fouler off with a small rope. Jimmy sits up on the horn, and as we slide in front of the *Shonan Maru* he cuts the line and it slides away from us.

The buoy on the end sits idle in the water, as the captain of the *Shonan Maru* turns his vessel hard to starboard to avoid it. It's too late, however, and he slides over our prop-fouler. As the stern passes our buoy, it is suddenly sucked under water. The *Shonan Maru* continues on her way, and 100 metres further on, the buoy and rope suddenly pop back on the surface. The rope now has two big gouges in it, but otherwise it looks OK.

The *Shonan Maru* unfortunately is also OK, and she changes her heading back to tailing the *Steve Irwin* again.

We're rigging the fouler up for another attempt when the satphone rings.

'You are to disengage from the *Shonan Maru*. Take a heading of 90 degrees true and await further instructions.' Paul sounds disappointed. It was always going to be a long shot — an 18-ton vessel trying to stop an 800-ton vessel from following its course. The laser and spud gun were only ever an annoyance for the scientists, and perhaps enjoyment for us. Our only hope lay in the prop-fouler and it failed.

I call the lads inside and give them the news. Mikey and Jimmy are both exhausted. In fact we all are. We're into our second day with no sleep, and now that the pressure is off, we're suddenly stuffed.

I get Jason on watch, while the rest of the lads head off to bed. I sit there pondering the day's action. Certainly, the spud gun and laser were valuable tools. They'd be great in hassling a harpooner who's lining up to shoot a whale, for example. Perhaps they'll come into play once we catch up with the whaling fleet.

The prop-fouler was disappointing. It definitely got around the propeller but failed to stop the vessel. The rope is pretty massive too. Thinking about it, some wire in there would be helpful. One of the Sea Shepherd vessels fouled a harpooner last season, but the scientists managed to just cut the rope away from on deck. Some decent wire rope, like half or three-quarter-inch, would really make it difficult to extract. It'd almost certainly need a diver to go down, and that would hold them up for ages. What a crap job that'd be as well!

We're heading east now at a leisurely 16 knots, the *Steve Irwin* and *Shonan Maru* back on their dance heading north. I head into the galley and take a look at things. There's one container of pancake mix left in the back. An hour later and there's a hot plate of pancakes ready for the lads. None of us have eaten anything today, and we are all so exhausted. I hand a plate to Mikey who nearly rips my hands off getting it. He gulps the lot down in about two minutes, burps, skulls his glass of orange, and rolls over. 'Thanks bro. That was awesome,' he mutters before drifting back to sleep. Jimmy and Laurens are equally as grateful, albeit without the burp.

They've been a good team today, I reflect. It was freezing cold, with a chilling wind, and all the team were hosed down by icy water on many occasions. They had waves come over them and they got blasted by LRADs. They did everything I asked of them and no one complained. They just got stuck in and did it. And I'm actually quite proud of them. In many respects they complement each other. They have varying skills and strengths, and they all have a great attitude in common. A formidable group. Right now, though, they are shattered, and a good long sleep on a full belly of pancakes will do them good. A few minutes later and I crawl into bed as well.

'Hey there's an iceberg up ahead.' Mike is on the early morning shift, and his eager voice wakes me from a deep sleep. Aside from a shift on watch, we've all basically slept for the last 12 hours. I clamber out of bed and climb into the navigator's seat beside Mike.

'It's over there,' he says, pointing at a berg a few miles ahead of us. It's probably a few hundred metres long and, as we get closer, lots of smaller bergs show up in the water. I've told the crew 20 times to be super-careful when on watch. If we hit a single berg, even a small one, our campaign is probably over. I can't help myself saying it again, though.

We slide silently towards the big iceberg. Birds circle around it, diving and weaving to pluck little scraps of food from the frigid waters. Icebergs like this act as fish aggregation devices — a bit like a reef. Only here the reef gradually decays away. Small fish, bigger fish, birds and the occasional unlucky penguin all share this shrinking ecosystem.

'You know, a lot of people talk about the amazing colours down here,' says Mike thoughtfully. 'But I can't see it.'

I look over at the iceberg, with big waves crashing up on its northern edge. It's just white, and the water is green. 'You know, I reckon the real beauty down here is in the barrenness of it all. We've been at sea for nearly a week, and the only thing we've seen above the water are a couple of shrinking icebergs. Romantic, Photoshopped pictures of blue skies and icebergs are used to lure tourists down here to make money — in some respects just like the Japanese come here to make money. But the reality is there is bugger all here, above the water at least. It is nature's way of telling us we shouldn't be here. It has made this the most inhospitable place on earth.'

We sit there in silence for a while, a couple of simple blokes trying to think deeply. Mike's brow is furrowed. 'Yeah, but under water is a different story, though, eh?'

Indeed it is almost the complete opposite under water. These waters are among the richest on earth. Over summer, huge amounts of plankton are harvested by the krill, which in turn base-load a massive ecosystem. The whales come down here and pig out over the summer months, fattening themselves up in a three-month feeding frenzy. Kind of like what UK chavs do over summer.

'Do you think the Japanese will ever stop whaling down here?' Mike changes the subject.

'I hope so. I wouldn't be down here if I didn't think we had a chance of stopping them. And I hope that this year is their last. We don't belong here, mate. The Japanese don't belong here. No one belongs here. We should just leave this as the one place on earth that man hasn't stuffed up.

As we get closer, the lads all hear us chatting and decide to get up. I jump into the driver's seat, and the rest all get on the roof to check out the iceberg.

It'd be the most amazing iceberg I've ever seen. Not that I've seen many icebergs to compare this one with. But this one sure looks wicked. For a while it looked like several icebergs, but as we got closer it turned out to be a single chunk that has eroded into three massive towers, water gradually eating away the base.

'Oh ders a leopard seal,' yells Laurens excitedly. The seal eyes us up suspiciously for a minute or so, then goes back to playing on the surface. We circle the berg several times, coming back each time to the lone seal. It's not a leopard seal, but what species of seal we're not sure. A big one was about all we conclude in the end.

He seems quite oblivious to his situation. And in fact many penguins and seals end up perishing in the same way. They live on an iceberg that drifts north, eventually taking them so far from Antarctica that they can no longer get back. They continue to exist on these bergs, but as the ice melts, so does their existence. In the end, the berg is all gone and they perish, simply becoming another part of the food chain in this harsh environment.

At the moment, though, this lonely seal has tons of food. As do the many other inhabitants of this ecosystem, I suspect. Hundreds of birds flit across the surface. One cheekily lands two feet from the Animal Planet cameraman, Simeon, who is perched on the forward hatch. He turns his camera around and films his new friend, who seems content to just cheep at him. There are few predators of the birds here, and so they can become very tame — or unafraid at least. The bird finally becomes bored with the cameraman and flies off to join his friends.

There's suddenly a loud crack, and an enormous chunk of ice breaks away from the second tower, crashing into the clear blue water, and sending spray everywhere. Seconds later and a second chunk breaks away. We sit there marvelling at the spectacle, but also all too aware of what we are seeing. This iceberg has been part of Antarctica for 10,000 years. And what we are witnessing is the blunt end of climate change. Slight rises in temperature sees increasing numbers of these bergs drifting north and melting.

'What do you reckon that is?' asks Jimmy, pointing at a dark line running through the berg. In fact the line runs through all three towers, and I've seen the same line on a couple of other icebergs as well.

'It could be from the Aussie bush fires,' says Jason hopefully.

'Nah. The roaring forties and fluffy fifties would never let the dust down this far bro. It's gotta be something way bigger.'

'Well, how about Mount Pinatubo?' he suggests.

'Oh come on bro. That iceberg would be 10,000 years old. So whatever did that was thousands of years ago. And it would have to be massive.'

'Mmmmm. How about the Taupo eruption? Or Krakatoa?'

'Yeah, now ya talking.'

We drift past the lone seal one last time. Nature can be brutal, I muse, feeling suddenly quite sorry for the poor guy.

As we idle away, I get the lads to rig up the jet-ski and get it in the water. Mike and Laurens come idling after us on the SeaDoo, lining up the jet-ski ramp. There's a solid thump as it lands into the ramp. I'm busy attaching the line to it when a wave picks up the stern of the jet-ski and it slides off the side. Laurens is leaning one way, Mikey the other, and as they skew sideways, the pair topple off. The SeaDoo is on its side, then flips back upright indignantly.

This is actually our fourth attempt, and it's the second time the jet-ski has rolled.

'It's just too hard to land with two people,' comes Mikey's crackled voice over the radio. He and Laurens by now are back on the SeaDoo and licking their wounds.

The trouble is I also need three people to pull the jet-ski in. Two just isn't enough. I need one to pull the bowline, a second to latch the line and a third to winch the jet-ski in.

'Mikey, can you drop Laurens off and then come in by yourself please?' Mikey nods, and a minute later there are three of us ready to land the jet-ski.

Five minutes later and we finally get the jet-ski secured down in its cradle, but it's been a salutary lesson for us. We'd trained on this in Auckland and Hobart, but here in the Southern Ocean swells, it's much more difficult. The jet-ski was only going to be a fine weather piece of equipment, and that has certainly been reinforced here today.

'How was the water?' I finally ask Laurens, as we dissect the last few hours of training.

His eyes light up. 'These suits are amazing. I'm not cold at all. In fact, going in the water was refreshing.' We're all wearing black SAS combat dry suits, and they are probably the best bit of kit we managed to secure. They seal around your neck and arms, and the feet are fully enclosed. They also have Kevlar patches on all the normal wear points, which make them extremely abrasion resistant.

The thing with training is you learn a lot, but hopefully you undertake it in a situation where if things turn to custard, it doesn't really matter. Today we figured out that it takes three to land the jet-ski; we should only have one on the jet-ski for the landing; we need a better clip and U-bolt to latch the jet-ski with; and falling in the water is no big deal.

We'd also spent some time on deploying the prop-fouler. The lads are convinced that towing the rope allows for the most accurate placement of it into the path of the whaling vessels. As the harpooners come into the danger zone, they will often turn away, be it to port or starboard. As they start to turn, however, the boat will lean right over, giving you an early indicator of which way they are going to turn. By watching them, then, you can take a good guess at the line they'll be on when they pass the fouler.

Given we are going to tow the fouler, we need a reliable way to release it. The stainless release mechanism we bought in Auckland specifically for this purpose has been found wanting. It works at low speed, but as soon as there is any real tension on the line, like when you are deploying the fouler at speed, it jams — which sucks really, since it is specifically designed as a release mechanism. Eventually, we just tie some smaller rope onto the end of the prop-fouler and have this wrapped twice around the winch bar. Mikey can just sit on the stern holding this line, and when he's ready to release, he just lets it go. Simple, really. During this morning's training we released the fouler successfully five out of five times.

We pack up our things and head inside. There's a new email with instructions from Paul. He's given us a series of coordinates that he would like us to check out over the next few days. They seem to correspond to interesting structures near the ice shelf. I plot the first one on the GPS and we change our heading slightly, now heading directly for the ice shelf. We'll reach the first of them tomorrow morning, which is Christmas Day.

It's a stiff 25 knots, snow and three-metre waves that greet us the following morning. 'Merry Christmas,' says Jimmy, as he wanders past me in the galley. I'm busy packing heaps of vegetables into tinfoil for Christmas dinner. There are potatoes, pumpkins, sweet potatoes, onions and a vegan turkey roast.

'You still going for a swim?' I ask him.

'Yeah, I'll do it,' he replies with a glint in his eye. 'No worries.'

But Jason is adamant straight away. 'No way, man. I'm not swimming in that.'

'Oh, you're such a wuss man. You need to harden up.'

We're all tossing up the merits of a quick dip in the minus 1°C water. Finally, Mike, Jimmy and I accept the challenge, with Laurens abstaining, as he did it last year, and with Jason wussing out.

I tuck the vegetables, now neatly packed in tinfoil, around the exhaust manifold and turbochargers of both engines. The heat will gradually cook them through the day — at least I think it will.

Then it's down to my knickers and I scurry out the rear hatch, where the others are already waiting. The conditions are miserable. Waves come crashing in on our stern, and little flurries of snow are whipped around us in gusts of wind. We're freezing already and we haven't even jumped in yet.

A few seconds doubting the merits of this crazy idea and I plunge into the dark water, still clinging onto the rope so I don't get dragged away in one of the waves. The cold is instant. There's this shock to your body, and every instinct tells you to get out immediately, which is exactly what I do. Jimmy is already out of the water as well, and there's a pained look on his face. 'Whose stupid idea was that?' he yells over the wind, and he disappears through the hatch into the relative warmth inside.

Mike by now has all his kit off and is climbing over the SeaDoo jet-ski for his jump. 'Oh you'll make us look bad going naked ya bloody horse,' I yell at him, and he disappears into the water, white arse and all. A few seconds later he's back on deck, covering his ample dangly bits with his hands, while Simeon films his quick escape.

A minute later and we're all in the sleeping quarters putting our kit back on and warming up. Funnily enough, it wasn't as bad as I'd thought. I'd heard horror stories of how cold it was, but in the end it was bearable. And, in fact, we all feel quite invigorated by it. I'm thinking I might make it a weekly event. Given we're not having showers, a swim each week, albeit for only 10 seconds, might do us all good.

'How long would you survive in that water if you fell in?' I ask Jimmy. He's warming up with a cup of chai, and has a big smile on his face. The smile disappears. 'I reckon half-an-hour,' he finally replies optimistically.

'You know, I don't reckon I'd last five minutes in that.'

'Best you don't fall in then, eh!'

It's late evening when I climb back down into the engine room to check on our roast. The smell of cooking vegetables welcomes me. It seems so out of place. Engine rooms smell of oil and fuel, not food. I poke one of the potatoes, and I can feel the flesh squashing easily under my finger. Cooked to perfection, it seems, and I collect them all up and throw them in our salad bowl.

Laurens meanwhile has whipped up some gravy. Mushroom gravy to be precise, which is quite a mission, given we have no mushrooms. The galley is starting to look bare now, so I'm not sure what's gone into it. But it looks and smells OK at least.

Half-an-hour later and we're all sitting down in the sleeping quarters. The top bunks have been folded away, the red lights switched on, the stereo is pumping, and we're all ready for a feast.

'Oh I nearly forgot the tea,' says Laurens, and he disappears one last time, returning with a cup of hot tea for each of us. 'This is Antarctic tea,' he announces proudly, 'made from snow that I've been collecting all day.'

So we sit down to our first, and hopefully our last, Christmas dinner in Antarctica. The sleeping quarters make for a cosy little den. The six of us squeeze in and tell stories, while dining on roast veggies, vegan turkey, mushroom gravy with no mushrooms and Antarctic tea.

There's a good spirit among this team. The *Steve Irwin* is now almost back in Australia to refuel, and the *Bob Barker* is still over a week away. At the moment we're the only Sea Shepherd vessel down here, and yet no one has complained. The crew just accepted it and continued with our job, which is to find the fleet.

'I wonder what's happening on the *Bob Barker* right now?' says Jimmy.

'They'd be getting pissed I expect,' replies Laurens. Sea Shepherd vessels normally carry a small amount of alcohol, and on days like today they'd have an open bar, which can be done on a big vessel where you have plenty of crew and are relatively safe. A small vessel like ours, on the other hand, is only ever one piece of ice away from sinking, and to have some of the crew drunk just isn't worth the risk. We tell ourselves we'll make up for it when we get back on land. The truth is we'd love a drink right now and yet, somehow, Christmas in Antarctica without alcohol is quite OK.

We sit there shooting the breeze and solving the world's problems for a few more hours, and then the beds are made back up, and we head off to sleep. Jason is on the helm, and we have a new set of coordinates to head for.

It's early in the morning a few days later, and the smell of fresh bread wafts in and wakes me from my slumber. Grabbing the rail, I slide back out of the top bunk and poke my head up in the helm. The winds have died down from last night, and all that remains is a lazy two-metre rolling swell. Mikey is driving, and he has a bored look on his face.

'How are ya my homie?' I ask enthusiastically.

He takes his eyes away from the endless ocean and looks over at me solemnly. 'You know bro, this is hopeless. We're just driving around

Antarctica and we have no clue where the whalers are. It's like finding a needle in a haystack.'

In some respects, Mikey is right. Generally, the whalers operate in a narrow band of water, say 300 miles deep, but it extends for over 3000 nautical miles in length. They could be beneath New Zealand, beneath Australia, or all the way over near South Africa. It's like we don't even know which haystack to start looking in.

In finding the scientists, though, we have a little help. This is mostly in the form of tip-offs. You'd think there is no one down here, but in fact there are lots of people coming and going from these waters every day. New Zealand, Australia, France, Poland, Russia and Canada all have bases in Antarctica, and there is a procession of boats and planes coming and going. Then there are the various research vessels, fishing vessels, as well as an increasing number of tourist ships. And, finally, there are surveillance flights from New Zealand and Australia.

Now, out of all these visitors, you'd be hard pressed to find a single individual, excluding the Japanese, of course, who would support the whalers. Many in fact are openly angry about what is happening just a short distance from their research centres. I wonder what sort of response the whalers would get if they visited the genuine scientists at the French base of Dumont d'Urville Station.

There's a certain bond between the many researchers in Antarctica. A short time here and they realise what a precious and yet fragile place this is. And the taking of whales is viewed as nothing short of raping the place. The whalers have bent Antarctica over and are taking her from behind while slapping her arse, and the rest of us watch on helplessly.

Over the last few years, the West has become increasingly united in opposing the Japanese whalers, although ineffectively it would seem, at a political level at least. Politicians speak in volumes of their opposition to whaling, but the rhetoric is seldom matched by action. There are economic reasons for this, of course. We all want Japanese cars, Japanese electronics and Japanese tourists, which is why in many instances the tip-offs are anonymous. People working on Australian or New Zealand research projects, for example, don't want to inform us at an official level, lest they lose their funding. But, anonymously, they may be quite willing to provide us with information.

The point is that tip-offs tell us which haystack to look in, and sometimes which part of the haystack as well. After that, we also have a few tricks up our sleeve. It might be past knowledge of where the whalers have operated or been successful, likely looking structures under the surface that would encourage krill, and hence attract whales, and closeness to the ice shelf. Whalers are simply hunters. If we find the whales, we also have a chance of finding the whalers.

I explain this to Mikey, who remains unimpressed. 'Yeah but we've had no info in ages bro. We don't know which bloody haystack they are in.' He goes back to looking at the ocean. He's tired of driving around, running grid patterns in the hope of finding the whalers. We all are. It's just that Mikey is the best at expressing his frustration. But we have a job to do here. Right now our job is to try to find the whalers. And while we are here we still have a chance. If we were back in Hobart, we'd have zero chance of finding them.

I wander into the galley. The loaf of bread is wrapped lovingly inside a tea towel, and just one slice of crust has gone. I cut off a couple of thick slices, and get some jam and peanut butter ready. I'm pondering this haystack analogy. If I really was looking for a needle in a haystack, I'd burn the haystack down, then use a metal detector in what remains to find the needle. I'm just not sure how to do the equivalent in an ocean. Which means we'll just continue to run grid patterns in the hope of finding the whalers, or until we get any new leads.

'To be perfectly honest Pete,' says Mikey, 'I'm really worried about our water situation.' I look over at Mikey, who has a serious look on his face. Whenever he says 'to be perfectly honest', I know something is eating at him. He's been bemoaning our lack of water and support for some days now. Our stocks of water have started to make even me nervous. We started with some 200 litres a couple of weeks ago, and we're now down to 15 . . . and given we have six thirsty lads on board, that is only enough for a couple of days. This was going to be OK, except this morning we found out that the *Steve Irwin* is currently in a storm, and it'll be at least six days before we see any sign of them, and the *Bob Barker* is in fog and making slow progress.

'We could go to the French base and get some water there,' says Laurens hopefully.

The trouble with going there is we don't actually know if we can even make it. When the *Steve Irwin* visited it a few weeks back, they could only get to within a few miles because of the ice, and they are way more ice-proof than our little carbon boat.

'What about one of those icebergs?' It's Jimmy's turn. He's wanted to clamber on one of the icebergs for some time now. He's pointing at a big berg on the horizon. The trouble is we don't actually know if the iceberg is salt or fresh water. My guess is probably fresh, as it is large enough to be from the old ice shelf that is gradually breaking apart.

An hour later and Jimmy and I are kitted up in our dry suits and climbing into the frigid cold waters. There's a rolling 1.5-metre swell, and we slowly swim in to line up on our entrance onto the berg. What lies before us is a narrow rising gut cut away in the ice. Our equipment is a couple of meat hooks, some rope, and two 20-litre containers. I line up on a wave and go shooting up the gut, but only make it halfway, before the wave tumbles me back down. The second wave then picks me up and dumps me unceremoniously on a slippery little saddle. I'm trying to bury my meat hook in the hard ice, when suddenly there's a tug on the rope around my arm, the other end of which is still back with Jimmy, and I'm dragged back down the slope. I'm going down, Jimmy is coming up, and we collide in the middle, then both of us get shunted all the way back up on the slippery saddle. We get our meat hooks into the ice, and sit there marvelling at our precarious little nest.

We are perched on a small ledge part way up the iceberg. But the way up to the top doesn't look easy. A slippery 45-degree slope worn smooth by months of saltwater erosion suggests you'd need crampons and proper ice picks to have any chance of getting up. Undeterred, Jimmy grabs his meat hook and starts dragging himself up. It's a short journey before he realises the hopelessness of his situation, and he slides back down to where I'm sprawled out.

I chip away a little sliver of ice and throw it in my mouth. The initial saltwater burst is replaced by sweet fresh water as the chip melts. So it is fresh water at least. But the ice is so hard that it'd take us days to fill the containers. Another wave, bigger than the previous ones, suddenly washes up around us, nearly dragging us back down our slide.

'This is hopeless,' I finally say to Jimmy. 'Let's go back down bro.' I wait for the next big wave, jump on the tail, and race down the narrow slide. I'm monstered by the next incoming wave. It smashes into me, flips me over a few times then, thankfully, spits me out into open water. Seconds later and Jimmy comes racing down beside me, dragging the rope and 20-litre containers with him.

We swim back to the *Ady Gil* and clamber on board. Jimmy has a massive smile on his face. 'Man, that was amazing,' he says excitedly. 'That's the most wicked slide ever.'

We relive the slides a few more times, still buzzing at the experience. 'Yeah, having fun is all well and good, but it hasn't solved our water crisis.' Mikey brings us back to reality with a thump.

'Well, I can confirm the iceberg is fresh water,' I say hopefully, 'but getting it into containers isn't so easy.'

'Why don't we just grab some of the little bergs around it,' says Laurens, pointing to a patch of little growlers some 50 metres away.

Jimmy and I scramble back into the water, and drag a few back. We're a bit ambitious with the first, and we soon give up on a slippery 100-kilo monster. But the smaller chunks are easy pickings, and in just a few minutes we have a collection of mini icebergs clumped up on the deck.

Mikey has one of the meat hooks and is chipping away at the largest chunk. Small chips break away and he passes them around. I place one in my mouth. There's that initial hit of salt, but then this washes away to a nice sweet taste of fresh water.

The lads are all smiles, as we sit there, devouring chunk after chunk. 'This tastes amazing,' says Laurens, 'Antarctic water.' He tilts his head back and drops a piece into his expectant mouth. 'And to think this water has been part of the Antarctic ice shelf for thousands of years, and now, finally, I get to drink it.'

'Yeah, and tomorrow you get to piss it as well,' I reply.

'Actually, the average piece of water that enters our body remains in us for nine days,' say Jason. 'And water that becomes ice in Antarctica remains that way for typically ten thousand years. Just a useless bit of information I thought I'd share with you.'

'Well, thanks for that Jason,' I reply. 'My apologies, Laurens. That means you'll be pissing that out in nine days. Not one.'

'Hey, here's a thought.' Jason isn't finished. 'Water is actually the ultimate recycled product. The total amount is fixed on earth, and it's remained the same for millions of years; it's just the percentage tied up in animals, the atmosphere, as ice, and in oceans and lakes that varies. And so this water we're drinking now, well it's been ice for say ten thousand years, and at some time before that, it was dinosaur piss, and before that it was in a lake somewhere, and before that . . . it is endless. If only this little piece of ice that I'm about to gobble up could tell us its story. It'd probably be amazing.'

'Yeah, like the time it was squirted out the pizzle of a tyrannosaurus rex.'

'Well, here's a useless fact for ya. Ice is unique, in that it is the only element that expands when it freezes, which is why ice floats. All other elements compress as they freeze.' The lads look less impressed with my fact. Dinosaur piss is clearly the more interesting concept.

We pose on the back deck with our chunks of ice. It's been a good blowout for the lads, and Mikey, for the time being at least, has his smile back. We finally head back inside, heading for our next set of coordinates.

It's early the following morning when we start to notice the first possible signs of the whalers. We're right in close to the ice shelf, and Channel 68 has started to give the occasional clicking sound, like electrical noise. Channel 73 also has some noise. We look on the charts but there're no buildings or bases anywhere near us, so it suggests there are some vessels in the vicinity.

We gradually idle in among the ice, and the signal gets stronger and stronger. I'm just getting excited, when a humpback whale breaks the surface in front of us. We come to a stop and wait for it to reappear. A minute later and three humpbacks appear briefly. As we sit there, they gradually make their way towards us.

Over the next 30 minutes, we have the most amazing whale encounter I've ever seen. The three whales circle us, they go under us, and they poke their head out of the water and check us out. One slides past our stern on its back in an amazing display of pectoral dexterity.

Eventually, they tire of our inactivity, and they turn and head further into the ice, one of them rolling on his side and waving a fin at us as it leaves.

'Oh that is the coolest whale encounter ever,' says Laurens, who is grinning from ear to ear. 'Did you get that on film?' he asks Simeon.

'I think so,' he replies. He heads off inside to check his footage, while the rest of us sit there reliving the experience. 'That is a once in a lifetime,' says Laurens. 'This is my third campaign in Antarctica, and that is by far the best encounter I've ever seen.'

Slowly, we head back inside to work out our next move. The radio signals remain active. We cannot head further into the ice, so our choice is to go east or west. The French base is to the west, so we decide the whalers would most probably head away from them, so east is the decision.

We gradually pick our way out of the ice, before making a slow turn to the east, zigzagging our way around patches of ice and growlers. Jason meanwhile heads into the galley to sort lunch. 'Gee, there's not much food left,' he finally says in disgust. He's fossicking through the food bins, but they're mostly empty. The shelves are all almost empty. And the trays under the floor are empty. What remains is a barren pantry, devoid of any meaningful food.

Mikey watches on anxiously. It'd be fair to say he takes a bit of feeding this lad. He's 197 centimetres tall and weighs 110 kilos — and maintaining that body requires a lot of grub, which right now is not so easy to achieve.

'There's plenty of these left,' Jason says proudly, holding up another box of biscuits. These crackers were donated for the launch function, and what was left over has been hidden away for the last two months. They still taste OK, and they've become our latest staple. But after a few days of them, the gloss starts to wear off. Mikey is unimpressed.

There remain plenty of spices as well. So you can spice up your crackers with exotic tastes from all over the globe. But there's a limit to how much sustenance can be gained from curry powders and peppers.

And then there're the pastas and canned foods, hidden away in various nooks and crannies around the boat. These are OK as well, and have become the mainstay of our diet over the last few days.

But it seems like we lack any really meaningful food, like fruit and vegetables, for example. I glance into the veggie bin, and what lies there is a solitary garlic bulb, and two sweet potatoes. They'll be gobbled up in tonight's dinner no doubt.

'Hey, what about this?' asks Jason, and he holds up a rock melon. In fact this lone melon was donated to us three weeks ago, and it has sat at the back of the fruit bin ever since, albeit gradually moving to the front, as all the other fruit were consumed. Now it sits in the middle, the only remaining piece of fruit anywhere on the *Ady Gil*.

Each time I wander through the galley I'd see the melon sitting there, and it'd mock me. It laughed at us losers because we were so dumb not to eat him in the first week when he was ripe, and now he's old and rotten we won't get to eat him anyway.

'You can cut it up,' I say to Jason, 'but don't get ya hopes up bro. I reckon it'll be rotten.' In fact I know it'll be rotten.

A few minutes later and Jason walks out with half a dozen slices of rich orange rock melon, neatly placed on a plate. 'Would you like to taste my melons,' he says proudly. I look at the pieces suspiciously. They all look OK — in fact when all you've been eating for the last week is tinned foods, pasta and rice, the slices look fantastic. I pick up a slice and nibble a corner. Amazingly, the flesh is still firm, and my mouth fills with the sweet, rich taste of a perfect melon. 'Wow, that is fantastic,' I say. 'Who'd have guessed that wee gem was still sitting in there?'

Jason passes the plate to Mikey, who turns his nose up. 'Nah, I don't do fruit,' he says. I grab the one remaining piece and gobble it up before anyone else gets his dibs on it.

'Hey Pete, any word on the *Bob Barker* yet?' asks Mikey, changing the subject a little, although he is well aware any new food we get from here on will be from the *Bob Barker*.

'Still three days away, bro.'

Mike looks disappointed. A frown crosses his brow and he heads back down to the sleeping quarters. I am starting to get concerned about Mikey, in part because he worries so much about things. It can actually be a good thing to have a worrier on the team. They will sometimes make you aware of things that might otherwise slip your mind. But there is a danger that they can affect other members of the crew. Thus far everyone else has remained positive, but I can sense a definite downward slide in Mikey.

5
Rammed!

We continue heading east. With no fresh intelligence coming in, the radio is all we have to go on, but the signals are difficult to interpret and inconsistent.

We're now over 65 degrees south and right against the Antarctica ice shelf, working our way eastwards. There is no night now to speak of. The sun dips beneath the horizon, revealing a twilight period, and then the sun comes up again. Darkness just never arrives.

It's 10pm and a cold blast of polar air greets me as I poke my nose out the rear hatch. The sky is dark grey with ominous clouds on the horizon, and the wind looks like it's the forerunner to the big storm that has been looming up on us these last few days. Already the water has chopped up to three metres, and it's a precarious position I take up on the roof.

I do a quick scan of the horizon, looking for any telltale signs of the whalers. I then use the binoculars, gradually working my way around in a full circle. I follow this same procedure each time, taking about four minutes to complete the scan. There's nothing showing, as per usual, so I scamper back down into the relative warmth of the helm.

There's a decidedly whiffy odour about the place now. I'd first noticed it a few days ago, and each time I go outside, I notice it when I come back in. Only now it seems to be more pungent than ever.

'Man, this place travels,' I say to no one in particular. I screw my nose up and look at Simeon. He's sitting in the navigator's seat completing his daily report. It's probably him, I reckon. He's got budding dreads going already. And he just looks like a smelly bastard anyway.

'Oh it's not me bro,' he says indignantly. 'It's Jimmy, man. He reeks.'

I look over at Jimmy, who is busy reading a book. He's too preoccupied to hear the accusation.

To be fair, I reckon we're all starting to smell a bit. We've been down here for three weeks now, and no showers in that time starts to take its toll. We have, of course, had a few swims in the frigid waters, albeit 10-second dips. But we're still living in the same set of clothes, day in, day out, and after a while the entire boat starts to pong. And the odd smelly person tops it off.

There're also bits of food buried behind things, the sweaty undergarments that go beneath the dry suits, and damp socks, underwear and singlets. All up it's a male dormitory from hell . . . and that's exactly what it smells like.

I clamber up into the driver's seat, with another two hours of my shift to go. It's freezing, though, and eventually I drag my sleeping bag out. A warm glow comes over me as I slide into it. I like my sleeping bag. It's like an old friend who is always there when you need them. I pull the hood part up over my head, and it's just my nose and eyes poking out the top. I must look like a possum. The others all meander off to bed, although it's an angry sea outside, so I doubt anyone will be sleeping well tonight.

It's been an ordinary day, really. Like so many other days down here lately. Just driving around Antarctica running grid patterns, trying to find the whaling fleet. The weather, though, has been especially crap today, a cold south-easterly biting at us all day, and lumpy seas rolling in and tossing us around. On top of this the heater stopped working a few days back, so inside our little haven has become cold and damp, which sounds really bad. The good thing, however, is we have six bodies squashed in here, and apparently each body puts out about 300 watts of heat. Mikey more like 500, I expect. So we have the equivalent of a two-kilowatt heater burning in here. While it is cold and damp, it could be a whole lot worse.

I look down at Laurens, his face just visible in the twilight. His eyes are open but there's a blank look on his face. He's been to Antarctica enough to know that crap weather like this is generally followed by good weather. He just has to see it out — although the good weather will then be followed by crap weather again. It's a cycle that just repeats itself with monotonous regularity. Like a three-day menstrual cycle maybe, only you're menstruating for half the time.

A wave suddenly slams us, closing the lid on our laptop. I reach over and open it again, lapping a little piece of duct tape onto the top to hold it in place. I then quickly drag my arms back into my sleeping bag to stop the loss of that snugly warm air. The laptop is another one of my friends down here. It's our conduit to the outside world, bringing us little snippets of information from all over the place.

On the screen is the final page of Danielle's email that I'd received earlier in the day. I've read it about 20 times, and it makes sobering reading. Things haven't been easy between us of late — mostly my own doing to be fair. But she, Alycia and Sharyn are just getting on with things — like they always have while I'm off elsewhere doing my thing.

What am I doing here? I think to myself, as I look out at the angry sea thrashing us. I could be on the beach lighting illegal fires, sleeping in a bed that doesn't toss you out, eating snapper and crayfish, and teaching the girls drinking games, which, despite popular opinion, will stand them in good stead once they go to university.

What am I doing here indeed? As if to answer me, a dark shape slides up alongside us, followed by another and then another. A small pod of minke whales is battling along in the waves and checking us out, despite the weather. They remain the most curious of all whales, so it's little wonder the Japanese whalers have targeted them. The whales stay with us for several hundred metres, and then veer off, no doubt waiting, like us, for the weather to clear. If they could speak to me, I wonder what they'd say? 'Thanks for ya help' perhaps? Or 'The whalers went that a way.'

I glance down at the clock: just 15 minutes until the end of my shift.

Not that I'll be sleeping much tonight. But I will at least be snugly and warm tucked up inside my sleeping bag . . . and tomorrow is another day.

I'm just about to head off to bed, when I decide to do one last check of my emails. There's the usual array of media requests, but there's one that looks interesting. It's from a lady on the *Orion*, a tourist vessel that takes paying passengers on voyages to Antarctica. We'd met her in Hobart, and she'd promised to email us any information on the whaling fleet if they came across them.

I open up the email and my heart starts to beat a little bit quicker as I read. 'Dear Pete. Today we came across the Japanese whaling fleet. It looked like they were in the process of refuelling. There was one tanker, one very large vessel, which we presume was the processing ship, and four smaller vessels, presumably the harpooners. Following are their GPS coordinates as of 20:15 today.'

I sit there reading the email for a second time, when the satphone suddenly rings. My emails have been forwarding automatically onto Amy, the Sea Shepherd Media Manager, and she has forwarded the information onto Paul. And he's now on the phone to me with new instructions.

'How much fuel do you have left?' he asks.

'Um. About one day's worth.'

'Well, I want you to refuel from the *Bob Barker*, and I then want you to engage the whaling fleet,' he says with finality.

New coordinates are entered onto the GPS, and we're suddenly off with renewed vigour. The coordinates are only a few hundred miles away, and as we get closer overnight, Channel 73 slowly starts to chatter again. Not the voices of Japanese, but rather continuous noise, like a frequency on or near 73 is being used for data transfer of some kind.

It's late evening, and nearing the end of my shift, when Laurens suddenly spots something on the horizon. 'What is that you reckon?' he says slowly. I study the dark shape, and like many times before, it's hard to tell. Probably just an iceberg. Laurens wanders outside with the binoculars, while I study it from inside. For a second or so, I think I can see a faint light.

Laurens comes running back inside. 'It's definitely a boat,' he says excitedly.

Picking them up on the radar, we idle closer to take a look, while a hurried phone call is made to Paul. We can tell from the shape it is not a harpoon vessel, nor is it the main processing ship. Which means it's a security vessel, a spotter vessel or a fishing vessel. We study it for a while. It is not moving, making us even more suspicious. Fishing vessels down here run 24 hours, moving from long-line to long-line. This one is dead stationary.

'I'm sure it's a security vessel,' I say to the crew a second time. A big boat in Antarctica, no long line equipment on the deck, stationary just 60 nautical miles from where the whaling fleet was spotted earlier in the day. It's here protecting the fleet.

We slide past the vessel, silhouetting it in front of a setting sun. Paul is back on the satphone, instructing us to avoid the security vessel, and to continue on towards the fleet. We relay the coordinates of the suspect vessel to the *Bob Barker*, suggesting they keep well south of it.

By now all the crew are up. No one was able to sleep anyway with the rough conditions, and now we're all amped and raring to go.

Two hours later and the satphone rings again. This time it's Peter Hammarstedt, First Officer on the *Bob Barker*. 'How's the Hammer?' I ask him jovially. I've never met the Hammer. I've only seen him on TV and exchanged a few emails. But I think I'll end up liking the guy.

He has an excited edge to his voice. 'I have great news. We are just two miles astern of the *Nisshin Maru*,' and he then provides us with his GPS coordinates and bearing. 'We are launching our Zodiacs now,' he says. Laurens quickly plots the location on the GPS. I look down at the blobs blinking on the screen. The *Bob Barker* is just 40 miles south of us!

The challenge for us now is that we are extremely low on fuel. We're so close to the *Bob Barker*, but with it engaging the *Nisshin Maru*, there is no way they'll want to stop and refuel us.

'What do you reckon they'll do now?' asks Jimmy.

'Well, the whalers will be expecting this, given they were spotted by the *Orion* yesterday. They know that everyone down here hates their guts, and their position will have been blown. So they will have a plan already. The *Nisshin Maru*, given its role, will take priority. You can bet it was refuelled first, so it now has a full tank of gas. The whalers have been hunting this area since the start of the season. So they have probably cleaned up here already. I reckon they will just run. They will pack up their gear and head west.'

'Or they could go east again,' says Laurens.

'They've already come from the east. And the Ross Sea is not open yet. I reckon they're just going to head westwards to see how long it is until we run out of fuel. As soon as we turn around to refuel, they'll resume whaling again.'

Laurens nods his head slowly, and a smile crosses his face. 'Well, if they're hoping they can outrun the *Bob Barker*, they're in for a surprise.' The *Bob Barker* is an amazing vessel. Firstly, for a big boat, she's fast. Her top speed is around 17 knots, a couple faster than the *Nisshin Maru*.

Secondly, the *Bob Barker* doubles her weight in fuel, and can travel for many months on one tank. She's come all the way from Africa, and yet she still has three-quarters of her fuel left. If the Japanese whalers think they can outrun the *Bob Barker*, they're mistaken. She'll now be with them until the end of their season.

I decide to sit there and wait for the *Nisshin Maru* to reach us. We're low enough on fuel as it is. Our job now will be to just sit and watch the fleet pass us, and to wait for the *Steve Irwin* to arrive and refuel us. Paul was right in demanding we refuel before engaging the fleet. The refuel location, though, was set ambitiously close to the whalers, and in now stumbling over the fleet our refuelling opportunity has been lost.

'Hey, did you say the *Bob Barker* was launching the Zodiacs?' Laurens asks.

'Yep. Why?'

We both take a look outside. There are solid 2.5-metre waves and 20 knots of wind blowing from the south, which would be hard work in a Zodiac — although you could hardly blame the crew for getting stuck in. They've been at sea for almost a month already, and this is their first encounter with the whalers, so you can bet everyone there is excited as hell and raring to go. Just like we are.

An hour later and the phone rings again, with yet another update from the Hammer. 'Pete, we're now six miles astern of the *Nisshin Maru*. We need you to engage it and slow it down please.' We get an updated position and heading from Peter.

'They must have lost ground launching the Zodiacs,' says Laurens hopefully.

We plot in new coordinates, and take a heading to intercept the *Nisshin Maru*.

An hour later, and her dark shape emerges from the gloom. She's a big boat — 170 metres in length, with over 150 people working in her bowels. For the last 10 years, she's processed about five thousand whales, more than half of all whales taken globally over this period.

'That's the bloody Death Star,' says Laurens angrily, as he looks at her through the binoculars.

We move slightly westwards so that our approach will be masked among the ominous clouds.

A plate of cereal lies untouched before me. The human body has many ways it deals with situations. When we are very excited or anxious, adrenalin is pumped into our veins, giving us greater strength, and in some people, increased cognitive powers. It also inhibits digestion. There is no point, for example, in expending energy in processing food when our survival may depend on our ability to escape from an angry lion. It's a defence mechanism honed through many thousands of years of evolution.

The cereal sits there looking at me. We might be engaged with this fleet for some time, however, and once the skirmishes start, getting a feed will become all but impossible. I eventually force the food down my unappreciative mouth, as we angle closer to the *Nisshin Maru*.

Mike and Jimmy are on the back deck preparing the prop-fouler. After our training the previous week, I'm pretty sure we'll get it well positioned in front of the oncoming monster, but whether the fouler is big enough to stop the boat I'm not so sure. It's a solid mooring line of about three inches diameter, so it's certainly possible.

Jason again becomes my gopher, and he relays a constant stream of instructions backwards and forwards between the deck crew and me. Our plan is to first deploy a couple of fenders in front of the vessel, simulating a prop-fouler. We'll see how they react to it. The captain will tend to use the same technique each time to avoid the prop-fouler, so I'm keen to see what he'll do. We only have the one fouler as well, so once the fouler is gone, so is our opportunity to stop the whalers.

I line up the vessel and come sliding up past her port side. She's an imposing sight. I've seen her many times on TV, in videos and photographs, and yet it doesn't prepare you for the sheer size of this vessel. She is simply massive.

Her huge water cannons are turned on and, as we edge closer, a stream of water comes blasting in on us. 'Man, those cannons are grunty,' says Jason. Even at 50 metres away, they are strong and relentless. Once again I'm glad to be inside, rather than on the back deck, which I know right now will be a miserably cold place.

'This is the captain of the *Nisshin Maru* speaking,' comes booming in on us. It's the same female voice and the same basic recording that we got from the *Shonan Maru*. Then a loud horn sounds, as we cross in front of the bow. We're a reasonable distance in front of her — maybe as much as 75 metres — and Mikey throws out the buoys. I can see them disappear into the water cannon spray, but the vessel remains on course.

We make a second pass with two more buoys, and again the *Nisshin Maru* continues, with no alteration in heading or speed.

Mikey then gets the prop-fouler rigged up. As we tow it in, I'm determined to get as close as I can. We want the middle of the *Nisshin*

Maru to go over the middle of the rope. I take a similar line to the past two passes, running past the port side, but it's a steeper angle we run in crossing their bow. The enormous structure looms over us, and Jason has an edge to his voice as he relays distances. 'Go, go, go,' he yells urgently, suggesting we're about to be run down. I push the throttles forward and the engines roar in protest. The water cannon suddenly blasts us, and it's not a spray but a full-on impact that pummels along our deck, over the windscreen and then onto the back deck.

'You can stop now,' says Jason, with relief in his voice. We drift away from the hulk, watching the bright orange buoy tied to our prop-fouler. Mikey has released it perfectly, and the *Nisshin Maru* drives directly over the fouler, a buoy neatly placed on either side of its hull. As the stern passes the buoy, it jerks once, and then is suddenly sucked under, disappearing from view.

'Suck on that one,' yells Jimmy from the back deck.

The engines are thrown back in gear on the *Ady Gil*, and we race in astern of the *Nisshin Maru*, praying that she will be stopped. The prop-fouler doesn't emerge, though, but nor does the vessel alter course or speed. She just continues her relentless passage northwards, with the *Bob Barker* in pursuit.

I get our radar locked onto the *Nisshin Maru* and the *Bob Barker*. Amazingly, the *Nisshin Maru*, at 15 knots, is a good knot quicker than the *Bob Barker*, and so far from having superior speed, Big Bob might actually be slower. Or in these conditions, at least, which is immensely disappointing. Laurens and I are digesting this information. We call the *Bob Barker*, and Chuck, the captain, confirms they are close to full power, and continuing to lose ground. He also reaffirms that they will not refuel us, and we must await the *Steve Irwin*'s arrival down here in two days' time.

Chuck then suggests they will make up a new prop-fouler for us and we should deploy this with the last of our fuel.

'Let's take a break,' I yell at the lads, and they all come wandering in off the back deck. Jason puts the kettle on, while the rest of us discuss options.

'We could just go and nail them with butyric acid and potatoes,' suggests Jimmy. 'We've come all this way, and it'd be a shame not to get stuck into them now.'

Mikey also raises the issue of food. Our boat is long since devoid of anything remotely nutritious, and we need to get some decent food transferred from the *Bob Barker* while we have the chance. So instructions are given to the *Bob Barker* crew to attach some food parcels onto the end of the prop-fouler.

Half an hour later and we're back beside the *Nisshin Maru*. I drive up and down both sides, at a distance of about 70 metres, which is an ideal range for both the spud gun and the laser. Jimmy now starts a relentless barrage of both butyric acid and apples, showering the vessel with projectiles. Several hours later, and with their deck crew now all but gone, I make the mistake of passing astern of the giant vessel, and the stench of rotten butter is nauseating.

'If it is unpleasant for us, imagine what it must be like for the whalers,' Jason says with a wee laugh.

In time, the new prop-fouler is ready, and we drop back to the *Bob Barker*, now some 11 miles astern of the *Nisshin Maru*. We pull astern of them, watching their deck crew prepare the package. After about 10 minutes, they dump what looks like a couple of bodies overboard, and a long skinny rope with buoys on either end.

It takes us a full quarter hour to pull the lot in. The food has been packaged up in Mustang suits, which are now not only packed full of food but also water. Each one, weighing over 100 kilograms, is dragged onto our stern. The prop-fouler is tied off, and a few minutes later we're back off after the *Nisshin Maru*, now a good 15 miles ahead of us.

Jimmy comes in scowling. 'Um, Pete. I think you need to take a look at this prop-fouler.'

I wander outside, and take a look at the fouler, neatly tied off and ready to go. The rope is just 18 mm in diameter, with a little 3 mm wire trace wound around it. If 75 mm rope cannot stop the *Nisshin Maru*, this little toy has no hope at all.

'What were they bloody thinking?' asks Jimmy in disgust. 'This is just pathetic. We may as well deploy tampon strings.'

'It might get into the seals,' says Laurens hopefully.

'Nah, that's just a myth mate,' I reply. 'Their driveshaft seals will be way up inside their stern tubes. There is no way this prop-fouler will make any difference to them at all.'

Laurens has a determined look on his face. 'Yeah, well, we've been tasked to deploy this, and that's what we should do. The people on the *Bob Barker* are doing their best. It might not be the prop-fouler we were hoping for but our job is to still give it a try.'

Jimmy shrugs his shoulders and wanders back outside, with Mike following him.

An hour later and we sight the *Nisshin Maru* ahead of us. Jason by now is checking the fuel every 15 minutes, and it is getting extremely low. We have just a few hours left before we'll be pulling back and leaving the *Bob Barker* with the task of keeping up with the fleet.

One thing about the new prop-fouler is it certainly is long. So long in fact that we manage to double it over, and it is still easily long enough to launch effectively. We tie a few big buoys and a couple of short fat ropes around it to make it look more intimidating.

As we pass the *Nisshin Maru*, I am again reminded of its bulk. It must be immensely expensive to bring this behemoth, complete with crew, harpoon vessels, security vessels and tankers down here each year.

Pulling in front, we tow the fouler behind us, and the *Nisshin Maru* gradually turns to starboard, before finally making a hard turn to port to pull away from the line of the fouler. We continue this for at least an hour, the *Bob Barker* gradually making up ground with every slight turn that the whalers are forced to take.

Jason comes forward from the galley. 'Hey Pete, we're down to just 250 litres.'

'Ok then mate, let's deploy the prop-fouler. We'll give Jimmy one last blast on his spud gun and then we'll call it a day.'

I pull ahead of the *Nisshin Maru*, and turn sharply to starboard, cutting in front of its bow. I ease off on the throttle and Mikey releases the fouler. Again the vessel runs directly over the middle, and again the buoy is sucked under.

The *Nisshin Maru* suddenly slows right down to five knots, turns slightly to port, then gradually increases back up to 13 knots. At this speed the *Bob Barker* may actually start to make up some ground. Jimmy lets loose with one last flurry of apples, and we call it a day. With no one on the deck now, he has free rein to aim at radar domes, LRADs, satellite dishes, with varied levels of success.

Finally, our fuel hits 200 litres, a dangerously low level, so we stop, and await the *Bob Barker* to pass us.

We sit there and as each harpoon vessel passes, Jimmy lets off a few apples. Two of the vessels follow us in a slow circle. One thing about these vessels is their impressive speed and manoeuvrability. They can make a full turn in little more than a few boat lengths. As Larry once said, they are an engineering marvel.

The *Bob Barker* is now looming up on our starboard side, so I jump up and get Jason to drive. 'Just pull alongside her for a half mile mate,' and I jump up on the roof with the rest of the crew to wave them goodbye and wish them luck.

The five of us sit on the roof and wave to the crew, most of whom are now standing on their port deck. It's a great-looking boat, the *Bob Barker* — perhaps slightly smaller than the *Steve Irwin*. It makes a good pirate ship I reckon, all decked out in black. When the boat was in Mauritius the crew painted only part of her black, leaving the deck and superstructure until after they had left port. That the *Bob Barker* exists at all has been a well kept secret, and I bet there are lots of hurried phone calls between the whaling fleet and Tokyo now as they try to work out where this vessel has come from.

She sits very low in the water. She's still three-quarters full of fuel, so that'll be part of it. She's also looks slightly bow down, which might reduce her boat-speed a tad. But this may easily change once they burn a little more fuel.

The *Bob Barker* slides on by, and I pass word down to Jason to put the *Ady Gil* in idle. It's been a massive day all up. The crew never got any sleep through the night, and we've just had a constant 12 hours of engagement. There's a few high fives as we settle back on the roof and watch our fellow Sea Shepherd vessel head off in pursuit of the Death Star.

One last vessel starts pulling up astern of us. Their profile suggests it is our old friend the *Shonan Maru*. I bet they were mad as snakes after we smothered them in butyric acid the other day. No doubt they've been made aware of today's activities as well.

'Just be staunch, guys. They'll hose us down, but I don't want you to do anything. Just stand here and take it. That'll piss them off even more.'

Jimmy wants one last blast on his spud gun, but I convince him to just sit on the roof with the rest of us.

As they come in, the LRAD gets louder and louder, and then the water cannon suddenly gets us. A small trickle of icy cold water sneaks down the back of my dry suit, and I curse myself for not tightening up the neck seal. The cold blast on my face is short and sharp, and then gone.

We sit there with arms folded, glaring up at the security personnel, busy manning their various devices. A small face pokes out from the bridge, and I glare at him, before he disappears behind a wall of fine spray.

At this stage it looks like they'll pass us by about 20 metres, but then the *Shonan Maru* suddenly turns to starboard. In the space of two seconds, we go from being quite contented little activists, to fearing for our lives. There is a little blip on the throttle as Jason tries to turn the *Ady Gil* to starboard, but it is way too late. We are an 18-ton sitting duck, with an 800-ton monster bearing down on us.

The five of us on the rear deck all have the same thought. We jump over the horn and tumble down onto the rear deck, away from the exharpooner now metres from us. There's a sickening crash as their bow lands on the *Ady Gil*. The impact is massive and violent. The boat turns as we get pushed almost right under water, and a wave comes racing over the top of us. In a split second, the boat is ripped in two. A three-metre section of bow has been sheared right off, and the forward sleeping quarters are completely demolished.

I start to stand and get hit by something on my back. Looking around I can't see what it was. My mind is racing, and I'm not quite sure what has happened. I check my arms and legs to make sure they're all intact. The other lads are a tangle of limbs and are now getting to their feet as well.

'Mike, give us a hand with the life raft mate.' The two of us run inside. I'm not sure what sections are intact and what are damaged, but there is the definite possibility we'll sink quickly. Looking up in the bow, there is water sloshing all through the sleeping quarters, and there is a gaping hole where the bow used to be.

'Put out a mayday call,' I bark at Jason. 'Channel 16 and Channel 77.' Jason starts the mayday calls, while Mikey and I struggle with the life raft. Laurens comes clambering inside. 'Grab the Epirb, the flares and the emergency bag,' I yell at him, as Mikey and I struggle out the rear hatch, the life raft hardly fitting through the door.

The life raft is placed right on the stern and ready to go. In fact the rest of us with our dry suits would all be OK if we took a swim, but Jason's dry suit was in the forward sleeping quarters and is probably long gone, so if the boat is going to sink, we need to get him into it before he gets wet. Laurens emerges clinging onto the safety equipment.

I sneak a quick look back inside. It doesn't look like we have sunk any further. So I scurry back in and grab some paperwork. Our passports, log book, port clearance papers and charts are all stuffed into a bag and handed to Laurens.

Again I check the water level, and again it hasn't changed. I start going through and checking for structural damage. It looks like the sleeping quarters and everything forward of this is gone, but astern of that the structures seem relatively intact. The wave of water has made it into various places, including the helm, galley and engine room, but the water level doesn't seem to be increasing at all. The engine room and storage section alone are sufficient to keep the *Ady Gil* afloat, so for now at least the vessel is safe from sinking.

Whether she will ever be a boat again is another matter. The damage is huge. Her campaign is clearly over. The best we can do from here is rescue whatever we can in case she sinks. The engines are still going, so I shut them down, and I turn off all the electrical circuit breakers.

I wander back outside and the first of the rigid inflatable boats (RIBs) off the *Bob Barker* has arrived. Simeon has been struggling the most. His eyes are sunken and he's struggling for breath. He clambers onto the RIB and collapses on one of the seats. We pass a little bit of gear on as well, and it zips off back to the *Bob Barker*.

The *Shonan Maru* sits just a few hundred metres away, a couple of crew watching us through powerful binoculars. They idle there, surveying their handiwork. Mikey lifts up a fist and shakes it at them. 'You assholes,' he yells out angrily. He's an intimidating figure indeed. Man, it'd be great to just dump him on the *Shonan Maru* right now and see what sort of damage he'd do to those little bastards, I think to myself. He'd wreak some havoc indeed.

The forward sleeping quarters have been practically demolished. Unfortunately, this was also where most of our personal gear was stored. Clambering up on the horn, I can see our clothes, books, shoes, bags and various items sloshing around in the waves. Some are sinking, while others look like they'll float for ages. The second RIB arrives, and it is instructed to go and pick up as much of this gear as they can before it disappears.

Gradually, this amazing boat that was lovingly packed over our last week in Hobart is emptied out. The crew methodically work through, an occasional joke failing to lighten our mood.

Finally, I decide we've removed enough, and we climb into the RIB and idle over to the *Bob Barker*. I climb slowly up the stepladder, and into an orgy of Animal Planet cameras and crew.

I look around my hand-picked team, all in various stages of shock. Jason has climbed into a red Mustang suit, and is busy sorting our gear, but his face is long and drawn. Laurens is being hugged by one of the female crew off the *Bob Barker*. Mikey is leaning against the rail with a blank look on his face, while an Animal Planet cameraman focuses in on him. Jimmy comes walking slowly over to me. 'What do you want me to do bro?' he says.

'Maybe sort ya personal gear for now, bro,' I reply. Jimmy just nods, and heads over to our mountain of gear piled up on the deck. I guess it doesn't really matter what Jimmy does. Or what any of us do for that matter. Our boat is stuffed and our campaign is over. This amazing team of tough men have been emotionally raped and right now they are lost.

I throw my gloves into the wall and wander over to the rail where I can see what remains of the *Ady Gil*. The incredible boat that has been my life for four years lies like a dead animal behind us. Its bow is ripped right off, entrails of hoses and wires protruding out the gaping hole. Her carcass bobs lifelessly in the water, while several sheets of carbon flap away on the sides.

A tear slides down my cheek, and my throat starts to swell up. Up until now I'd had things to do: ensure my crew was safe, get the rescue equipment sorted and secure the vessel. Now, suddenly, I have nothing to do, and my world collapses around me. I think about Sharyn and my girls back in New Zealand. My family had all expressed their concerns about us coming to Antarctica. Perhaps they've been vindicated; maybe coming down here was a crazy idea.

One of the *Bob Barker* hamsters comes and puts her arm around me, and I just burst into tears. The *Shonan Maru* sits a mile away, her crew no doubt elated at the demise of this thorn in their side, but perhaps also now wondering at what the ramifications will be. 'Those arseholes,' I blurt out between sobs.

I wander over to Laurens, who is still being consoled. 'Hey, can you go sort a satphone for us, mate? We need to make some calls.' Laurens nods and wanders off.

I can see the Animal Planet producer fossicking through all the videotapes, ensuring they get them all secured. They're suddenly very valuable, I guess.

I wander over to him. 'Did you guys film the ramming?' I enquire. My eyes are bloodshot but at least the tears have stopped.

He nods. 'Yes, I think so. I haven't seen the footage, though.'

'I'd like to see the footage please.'

'Um. I can't do that just yet. We're still sorting other things out.'

'Look bro. My boat has just been rammed and sunk. And you guys probably have it all on tape somewhere. I want you to get that tape and play it for me.'

He looks at me carefully, and decides he doesn't want to mess with me in the mood I'm in. He sighs, and wanders over to one of his helpers, and I'm ushered downstairs. A tape is loaded into a player, and the *Ady Gil* comes up on screen. I can hear Peter Hammarstedt talking away about what a good looking boat she is. Or *was*, I think to myself.

As the *Shonan Maru* comes into view, she's moving well to port of the *Ady Gil*, and then there's a sudden turn to starboard as she lines us up. A few seconds later and she comes crashing down on top of us. The footage is so crisp and clear . . . and there is little doubt — we were deliberately rammed.

6
Lucky to be alive

'Here's to being alive,' I say to the lads, as we toast each other. The six of us are alone in the mess, still trying to come to terms with things. We have no permission to drink any alcohol, but no one is prepared to confront us. 'Asking forgiveness is easier than permission,' I'd said as I opened the first bottle.

The smile is back on Laurens. 'You know, we are like cockroaches. You can squash us, but you can't kill us.' We all laugh at his joke. But it's a nervous laugh. We sit there trying to discuss other things, but we just keep coming back to the ramming. It's like a dark cloud hanging over us, and each time we try to get away, it moves back over us. Mike and Jason say very little.

'You get a diagnosis?' I ask Simeon. He still looks like crap, although he has at least had a hot shower.

'Yeah, bro, broken ribs.' He's got a thick Kiwi accent, and the bro bit rolls off his tongue. He lifts his shirt and one side of his rib cage is dark and bruised.

'Oh, you're just soft,' says Jimmy. 'That's not even a flesh wound.' There's another nervous laugh from a few of us.

By now we've all seen the footage several times, and exactly who falls where remains a mystery. We just know we all collapse in a heap. Although I'm pretty sure what hit me after the collision was the water cannon.

We drink a few bottles each and, surprisingly, it does help. We gradually relax a little and head off to bed. None of us has slept in 36 hours, and our bodies and minds are exhausted.

Two hours later and I still can't sleep. My mind keeps racing back to the collision. What if we'd refuelled first like Paul wanted? What if I'd been driving? What if Jason had hit reverse?

I hear a sigh from Mikey. 'You awake bro?' I ask. There're various murmurs and groans from the entire team. We're all lying there awake, and despite our exhaustion, our minds won't let us sleep — or not yet at least.

Eventually, I give up, wandering up to the helm. Malcolm Holland (Mal) is there. 'You OK Pete?' he asks sincerely.

I look over at Mal. He's sitting in the navigator's chair, and has a cup of hot something in his hand. He's not as tall as I thought he'd be, and his face is unshaven.

'Yeah, I'm all good. Just struggling to sleep, bro.'

'Oh, not surprising. You guys have been through a lot today. Let me know if there is anything you or your team need, OK.'

We sit there and just shoot the breeze for a while. He's a nice guy Mal. Of all the people I've met in Sea Shepherd, he's right at the top. He is so positive and professional in everything he does. But there's also something very human about him. He genuinely cares for everyone on his vessel. Not because it's his job, but because that's the kind of guy he is. In some respects he's quiet and humble, but he has immense respect from all the crew.

The satphone rings in the communications room, just off to the side. It's a guy from ABC in Australia who we'd spoken to just before leaving Australia. 'Hey Pete, it's media, are you OK taking their call?' I nod and take the receiver from Mal.

'The Japanese have accused you of deliberately stopping in front of their vessel,' the ABC guy says, in a crisp radio-like voice. 'What do you have to say?'

I'm suddenly really angry. 'Look, they deliberately rammed my vessel today, and we are lucky no one was killed. They were on our port side, meaning we have right of way. They were the overtaking vessel, meaning we have right of way. We were virtually stationary. We were just a sitting duck, and they came in and rammed us.'

I put the receiver down and it immediately rings again. This time it's Radio New Zealand. Word is definitely out. And for the next 24 hours, I am virtually continuously on the phone to media. From New Zealand, Australia and Japan, to the USA, UK, Canada, Portugal and Spain, everyone wants the story. At the same time, Paul Watson on the *Steve Irwin* and Jeff Hansen in Australia are also both fielding calls continuously.

For much of the day I'm just angry. I've subsequently listened to some of the interviews I gave that day, and I have no recollection of saying those things. There is real venom in my voice, and I was probably the angriest I've been in my life.

By lunchtime the Japanese story has switched from we deliberately stopped in front of them, to we deliberately turned in front of them. By now, however, footage shot from the *Bob Barker* is doing the rounds on YouTube, and the media starts to swing in behind us.

This changes the Japanese story yet again. They start to say that at the time of the collision they were under attack from us and they were defending themselves. We then release the footage shot from the *Ady Gil*, and it shows my crew just chilling on the back deck, taking the LRAD and water cannons on the chin, and then being rammed. Their story changes yet again.

At lunchtime there's a call from Ady Gil, the generous millionaire in the US who purchased the boat from me and donated it to Sea Shepherd. 'Look, I'm so sorry about your boat,' I say to Ady, a tear rolling down my cheek once again. You'd think I'd be out of tears by now, but little things still seem to trigger me off.

Ady is upbeat. 'You know Pete. I wasn't famous before, but I am super famous now. My name is on the front page of the *LA Times* and every other paper.' He laughs for a long time on the other end of the phone.

'We can fix the boat,' he says optimistically. 'And if we can't fix her, we can build another one. We can do that, can't we?'

Finally, we finish the phone call. I'd actually been dreading speaking with Ady. I feel like I've let him down. I was skippering his boat when it was rammed, and I'm responsible. And yet Ady was so cool about it all. He remains one of the most generous and positive blokes I've ever met.

By mid-morning a call comes through from Paul Watson. He wants the *Ady Gil* towed to the French base, and at the end of the summer it'll be transported back to Hobart. From there it will be either rebuilt and placed in a museum, or perhaps placed in a museum as she is.

We pull the *Ady Gil* alongside the *Bob Barker* and empty her of fuel, water, food, electronics, batteries, spare parts and anything else we can lay our hands on. I clamber on and take a look at the structures. There is water lapping into the main fuel tank, which is a worry. The line linking the main and day tanks is broken, so water will be sneaking in through there. Of more concern is the engine room. There is a leak down the main girder, and water is seeping around this and into the bilge.

I sit there doing the numbers. I have the rear storage area and one outrigger intact. These two alone, however, are not sufficient to keep her afloat. We also need the engine room or the main fuel tank as well, but both of these are compromised.

'Will she last all the way to the French base?' Mal asks when I get back on the *Bob Barker*.

'I don't know, mate. There's a lot of damage. I think we need to empty all the water from the engine room and then get her to the French base as quickly as we can.'

Mal sends instructions down to the deck crew, and I head back down to rig up the towline.

Late in the evening we start towing. It's a sad sight, but the thought of having the *Ady Gil* as a permanent exhibit in a museum may be a fitting end for such an amazing vessel. I still have my doubts on us getting her all the way to the French base, however. It is over 120 nautical miles, and our speed is limited. I head off to bed, instructing Mal that if the *Ady Gil* sinks, to not bother waking me.

I clamber into the bed. It's not a bed really — just a mattress on the floor, along with all the other crew spaced out around me. For the first time in 60 hours, I sleep.

It's 6am the following day and I climb slowly up into the helm. Mal is there. Does this guy not sleep? He sees me and his smile disappears. I can tell straight away what has happened.

'I'm really sorry Pete. She just took on too much water. Our towline snapped this morning, and we ended up having to abandon her. Again, Pete we're all really sorry for your loss. I know that boat meant so much to you and your team.'

'Nah, that's OK, Mal. It's just a boat after all. And I got six guys happy to be alive.'

The satphone rings. My media duties start over again.

'Ady Gil is talking about an *Ady Gil 2*, would you support that?' It's a lady from a San Francisco newspaper. Apparently, Ady has already committed a million bucks, and wants to get started on a new boat as soon as possible.

'Well if Ady raises the money, and Sea Shepherd wants a new vessel, then I'd love to see that happen.'

'How do you feel at the loss of the *Ady Gil*?' This has become a common question over the last 24 hours. Obviously, I'm pissed off. And the previous day, I'd said words to that effect. But, today, things seem a little different. For the first time, I start to realise that good things will come from this.

By midday I head down to the galley for a feed and a break from the phones. I pile up a big plate of beans, salad and bread. The food here is certainly amazing compared to the fare we'd had over the last few weeks on the *Ady Gil*.

My lads are all seated on the end table. 'How are ya my homies?' I say, sitting down on the end of the bench. There are muted grunts and moans from them. Laurens has about 2 kilos of food piled high on his plate, and he's tucking in like it's his last meal. Jimmy has already finished, and I can see him looking expectantly at the queue, wondering about getting up for some seconds.

'Any news?' Laurens asks hopefully.

'Not really. Oh Ady Gil is talking about a new ship. And the media coverage on this is humungous.'

'You know Pete, I was thinking this morning about all the positive karma that boat had. Maori in New Zealand and also Aboriginals in Australia blessed it. We even had the Dalai Lama bless us just before we left Hobart, and yet it still didn't help us.'

I ponder this for a few moments, while Laurens goes back to his plate of food. 'Well, in many ways the Dalai Lama would approve of what has happened. We had skirmishes with all the whaling vessels during the day, and I'm not so sure he'd approve of those tactics. The exception was the *Shonan Maru*. It was the only boat we never messed with. As it came past we just sat there and looked at them. We took their water cannons, their LRADs and their intimidation, and we did nothing. We just stood there and glared at them, and I reckon it really pissed them off. It tipped them over the edge and they lost it, ramming us in the process.'

'Yeah, but that's my point. All that blessing and then doing nothing never helped us at all, did it?' A piece of food dangles on his lip, wiggling as he speaks.

'Look, like I said last night, we got six blokes happy to be alive. All we had was a couple of broken ribs to Simeon. And he just needs to harden up anyway. It is a small miracle no one was badly injured or killed. I reckon someone was looking over us. And on the other side . . . the fallout for the Japanese I believe will be huge.'

'How do you see that?' asks Jimmy. He's back with his second helping. 'With the *Ady Gil* gone, the whalers will hunt whales all season and the *Steve Irwin* and the *Bob Barker* won't be quick enough to catch them.'

'Well, the impact long term will be what hurts them. The whalers have been shown up for what they really are. The media spotlight is on them like never before. And the Japanese public and politicians will be looking at them like never before. Trust me guys, what has happened will achieve way more in stopping the whalers long term than anything else we could have done with the *Ady Gil* in one piece. Our five minutes of peaceful protest, which then precipitated the ramming, will contribute enormously. As for the two vessels left, time will tell if they really are too slow. Maybe the *Bob Barker* was slow today, but this campaign has a long way to go. I think they'll still deliver.'

Laurens nods his head slowly. The bit of food still hangs there on his chin.

'Trust me guys, good has, and will, continue to come from this, and for years to come. You guys have been part of a team that will be instrumental in bringing an end to whaling. We came down here with bows and arrows, oxygen lances, butyric acid, spud guns, prop-foulers, cyanide, slingshots and many other things, and yet the ramming two days ago will achieve way more than all of those combined ever could have. You guys have achieved something special; it's just not in the way we expected.'

'Yeah, but it is such a shame. We could have achieved so much more if the *Ady Gil* was still rocking in Antarctica.'

'Look, I wouldn't worry about it,' I reply.

Mikey hasn't said a word yet. He's normally quiet, but I can tell something is eating at him. 'You OK, bro?' He looks up at me and doesn't smile. His meal is largely untouched.

'Look, Pete, I know I'm lucky to be alive right now. And I know you lost a lot more than anyone else with the sinking. But all I can think about now is getting home, and I'm worried it's not going to happen. Chuck has done absolutely nothing.'

Mikey was to head back home before the end of the season. The plan was to slip him on the *Bob Barker* or the *Steve Irwin* if either headed back to Australia and, failing that, I'd take him back on the *Ady Gil*. With the sinking of our boat, however, he has one less option.

'I've spoken with Chuck and he said he will get you off OK. The plan was to get you into the French base, but with the *Ady Gil* sinking we're not going there now, which is a shame, as they have several flights a week from there. That leaves the *Orion*, which I think is still in the area, or perhaps some other option.'

'What's the *Orion*?'

'That's the boat that gave us the coordinates of the whaling fleet a couple of days ago. They are really supportive of Sea Shepherd, and I'm pretty sure they'll sneak you on board there somewhere.'

Mikey just nods and looks away. I am worried about him. He's hardly said a word in the last few days. He has always been the most easily affected of my crew. Lack of water, lack of food, lack of support all festered inside his head, but when it was just my small team we could manage it OK. On the *Bob Barker* it's a different story, because I have little control over what happens. We're just an add-on to a boat of 40 people, and they have many priorities to juggle, including getting Mikey back to land before he goes mental.

When at sea, it can be a very slippery slope. A few things going wrong in a row for certain people and they can suddenly find themselves suffering depression and psychosis — what may seem like a small issue for us can become a festering sore, and ultimately affect all the crew.

In looking at Mikey, the signs are there. He has been the most affected by the ramming, and now is totally obsessed with getting home. He has idle time and dwells on it all day. He's got a problem with his neck, which is affecting his sleep. He's also hardly eating at all. Finally, I tell Mikey I'll have a word to Chuck.

In the end I phone up the *Orion* directly, but unfortunately they'd left the area the previous night. Amazingly, they were only 40 miles from us at one stage, and could have easily taken Mikey aboard if they'd known about it. By now, though, they are some 300 miles north and unable to meet us.

I grab Mikey and we head into Chuck's cabin. 'Look Chuck, Mikey here is worried about getting home. Can you give us an update on what's happening please?' I look over at Mikey and his emotions are just simmering under the surface. He sits there trying to control himself.

'Well,' says Chuck, 'we're talking with the *Orion*, and with several of the bases down here, and we're confident we'll sort something for you.' He has that American confidence about him, and the words roll off easily.

Mikey starts shaking with rage. 'You haven't even spoken to the bloody *Orion*,' he says in a low growl. 'We just spoke to them now and they left this area last night. And the worst part is they could have easily taken me.' There's a long pause and Chuck says nothing. 'Look, mate, you'd better sort this out or I'm going to rip ya bloody head off.' There's a slight gulp from Chuck as Mikey's massive frame towers over him. Mikey then storms out of the office, snarling, 'You'd better show me some honesty from now on as well,' as he exits.

I stay behind and Chuck looks shocked. He makes a weak joke but I can tell he's been shaken up, which might be a good thing, I consider. Mikey has certainly moved up the in-tray a little now.

'Look Chuck, you just need to sort this out. The best chance we had for getting Mikey off was the *Orion*. That option is now gone, and it's a shame advantage of it wasn't taken. There will be other options, though, and I need you to sort them out. Mikey right now is a festering sore. The way to get rid of the sore is to get him off here.'

Chuck nods his head. He's in a difficult situation. This is not like getting someone back from Perth. This is a remote part of the planet with very few transport options. I walk out of the office.

I've always seen managing people as the hardest job in the world. People have different motivations, different objectives and different perspectives. It's like we all look at the world through glasses, and the tint on these glasses varies. With some people the tint is blue, with some it's red, and with some it might be almost black. Two people look at the same thing and they see it completely differently. It makes managing people so difficult, and Mikey and Chuck are examples.

I remember this guy Tino who was my engineer in the successful record attempt in 2008. He just looked at the world differently to everyone else, and it pissed many of the team off. He could be such a hard bugger to deal with. But that he saw things differently was also an advantage. He would see opportunities where the rest of us saw nothing, and he ended up being one of the most talented blokes I've ever worked with. There was this amazing energy about the guy and he really made things happen. But managing him sure wasn't easy. I remember thinking about him that the tint on his glasses was actually infrared; he saw things so differently to the rest of us.

In many respects, a good manager realises people all see the world differently, and what motivates people differs. We are then better able to get the best out of our team, which is after all just a collection of individuals. Crap managers just treat everyone the same.

I think back to Mikey, who by now is probably in his bed. He'll be simmering, I reckon, although he'll feel better having had his rant at Chuck. On the *Ady Gil* he was such an amazing asset. He always did exactly as asked, he was enormously strong, and he brought coolness under pressure, perhaps from his experience as a fireman. On here, though, he has become a liability, and if he is not kept in the loop, or gets lied to again, he'll be a real handful.

I head up to the media room, where Laurens is busy at work. 'Hey Pete, it says here you're asking for the arrest of the captain of the *Shonan Maru*. There's a fat chance of that just quietly.' Laurens hands me the news article he's reading from. Actually, I never asked for his arrest. That was Paul. But I do agree with him. If it was Paul or me who'd sunk a Japanese whaling vessel, we'd be under arrest already and facing a period in prison. No one will be coming down here to arrest the *Shonan Maru* captain, though. He'll head back to Japan a hero.

'Maybe I should arrest him,' I say jokingly.

'Well, if we were in the Netherlands, you could arrest him. You could do a citizen's arrest.' Laurens, being an ex-cop, would know of course.

Actually, I could probably do this in New Zealand and many other countries as well. I'm pondering this, and it seems there might be a possibility of attempting it at least. Given the ramming occurred on a New Zealand vessel, if the captain was in New Zealand, or on another New Zealand vessel, I could in fact arrest him. He'll probably never set foot in New Zealand, however, and the *Ady Gil* rests in two kilometres of water, so there's no way I can get him on there.

Once I step onto a Japanese vessel, say the *Shonan Maru*, I could ask for the captain's arrest, but he's under no obligation to comply — Japanese law, rather than New Zealand law, would apply. Legally, though, given he's sunk my vessel, he'd be hard pressed to bring a charge of piracy against me for boarding him.

I give Paul a call on the *Steve Irwin* to discuss it. 'If you did get aboard,' he says, 'they'd just arrest you and take you back to Japan,' he says dejectedly. 'Which would be good in stirring up debate in Japan, but you might end up facing some serious charges as well.'

'Yeah, but maybe that's a good thing. I've got no role on the *Bob Barker*. This boat is fully crewed anyway. They don't need me here. If anything I'm a burden. If I can get on the *Shonan Maru*, I'd become their burden at least. It'd force them to take me back to Japan, and maybe that could be used in a positive way.'

There's silence for a while, before Paul answers slowly. 'Well, if you're happy to go back to Japan, I'll support you boarding the *Shonan Maru* and attempting an arrest.' He fails to mention again the bit about being charged and spending some time in prison.

I hang up the phone. That was what I like about Paul. He thinks about things then makes his mind up, and you can go for it. My job just became to board the *Shonan Maru*, attempt a citizen's arrest, and when that fails, which of course it will, have a free ride to Japan. The tricky part of course is getting onto the *Shonan Maru* in the first place. And perhaps the bit about what happens once I get on there. The easy bit will be finding the *Shonan Maru*, because ever since we left the final resting place of the *Ady*

Gil, she's been on our tail, and relaying our position back to the whaling fleet, allowing them to avoid us.

The following day, both RIBs are prepared for an 'engagement' with the *Shonan Maru* — although I prefer to call it a 'skirmish'. Epirbs, flares, laser and radios are all loaded into the small inflatable boats.

The *Bob Barker* slows down and we lower them into the water. We head over to an iceberg for cover, as the *Bob Barker* steams away, and the *Shonan Maru* comes heading towards us. She's still a few miles off when she suddenly turns away from us. We emerge from behind the iceberg and Matt eases the throttle forward but we get bashed around in the one-metre waves.

I look down at the GPS and we're barely doing 15 knots, so catching the *Shonan Maru* will be a tall order indeed. The inflatable we're in is flat bottomed. The bow has very little V in it, so instead of punching into a wave, it just gets airborne over the top, which is fine in really small waves, but even in relatively benign seas like this, their performance is extremely limited. The driver Matt Kimura, and navigator Marcus Graham, decide it's not going to happen, and we head back to the *Bob Barker* with our tails between our legs.

'How'd it go?' asks the Hammer, as we clamber over the rail onto the deck.

'Well, we never got within striking distance of them. The waves were just too big for those boats to get any speed going.' I look over at the first inflatable as it is hauled in. It's more suited to taking tourists and divers around harbours and holiday spots than battling seas in the Southern Ocean, I reckon. Fine in flat water but limited in big seas. 'The good news, though, is you get my dubious company for a few more days.'

Peter smiles. 'Hey, you're welcome back any time,' and he pats my back. 'Hey do you think it's still possible to get you on board the *Shonan Maru*?'

I think about this for a few moments. 'Their crew knew we were up to something. I reckon they saw us slow down on the *Bob Barker* and figured something was up. Maybe they saw the launching. They skirted right around the iceberg we were hidden behind. I'm not sure they saw us — probably not as we were well hidden. But they were suspicious as hell.'

Peter nods his head.

'I think they're a really good crew on there. These aren't fishermen. They don't need to worry about whales, and harpoons and stuff. They are trained security people and their job right now is to just keep our tail and to keep out of trouble. You watch the way they follow us. They don't follow our path. They're always a few miles off on our starboard side. That means if we drop something in the water, be it an RIB, jet-ski, propfouler, diver, whatever, they won't just drive blindly over it. To get to them we must therefore move over open water, exposing us to their radar and sight. It also means they can watch us launch any RIBs on the starboard side. These guys are extremely professional in what they do. For me to get on board, we'll need to be really clever. But I reckon it can be done.'

Peter nods his head again. 'Well, there is a long way to go in this campaign,' and he heads back to the bridge.

The weather chops up for a couple more days, and we continue heading westwards, following the fleet but not within striking distance. As Paul explains so well, when the whalers are running like this, it means they are not whaling. So while it may not be grabbing headlines, it will be reducing their kill.

The weather finally abates, and with the *Shonan Maru* still tailing us, another attempt is made at boarding it. We enter an area of icebergs of varying sizes. It's also on dusk, with the sun hanging low in the sky.

We lower a single RIB into the water, this time on the port side, so the whalers won't see its launching. We then sneak along beside the *Bob Barker*, out of view of the security vessel. As we pass the first decent-sized iceberg, we slip in behind it, and then iceberg hop our way over to line up with the track of the *Shonan Maru*, now just four miles away. It's a fine line, waiting for the *Shonan Maru* to be behind a berg, then blasting to our next concealed position before we get picked up on radar. We end up about a mile from the line of the *Shonan Maru*. This is as far as we can get with any cover, so we lie here in wait for our target, its sinister form growing as it closes the gap.

A group of penguins perched on a smaller iceberg look at us curiously. Their pad is drifting past us slowly. Orcas and leopard seals will chase them around, and they'll often jump onto a berg like this to escape. Some orcas, however, have figured out they can climb onto the smaller bergs, tipping their next meal back into the water.

A thought runs through my head. Predators seem to be the most intelligent animals. I don't know if this is a fact, but the thought lingers. Predators rely on being clever, whereas prey seem to rely more on instinct. Orcas have figured out how to drown young blue whales. They separate them from their mother then climb on top, drowning them under a few metres of water. Once dead, just the tongue is eaten, and the carcass is then left to sink. It's a brutal end for such a magnificent creature. That's nature, though . . . and the carcass will form a small and vibrant ecosystem on the seabed for a year or more.

One of the penguins comes cruising past, poking his head out of the water to take a look at us. He circles around, eyeing us up suspiciously. For such ungainly creatures on land, they are incredibly adept in the water. His little wings propel him along in an effortless display of hydro dexterity. The penguins here are fat little guys. There's plenty of food around at this time of the year, I guess. He eventually skips back towards his iceberg, lines up his landing, and then shoots up out of the water, sliding along on his belly as he lands. Not for the first time, I count my blessings at being able to visit this amazing wilderness.

Our bow pokes around the corner of the iceberg and I sneak a look at the *Shonan Maru*. Nearly time to go. The sun is sinking on the horizon behind us, and it'll provide good visual cover. The plan is to drive towards the *Shonan Maru* with the sun exactly behind us. Their visibility either side of the sun will be excellent, with everything in silhouette, but they'll be unable to look directly into the sun.

'Go, go, go,' I whisper to Matt, and our engines are put in gear. We go shooting out from behind our lair, leaving behind our bewildered friend on his iceberg. I give Matt continuous instructions on his heading, gradually having him shift to port, ensuring the sun remains directly behind us. We cover perhaps the first mile and no sign of any changes in our prey. We're just 400 metres away when there's a puff of dirty black smoke and the *Shonan Maru* turns sharply to starboard.

'They must have picked us up on radar,' I say to the lads. It's a small boat we're in, but with dead flat water like this, decent military radar would still perhaps pick us up. Certainly, the line of our approach has been spot on, so I'm doubtful they'd have seen us by eye.

As we pull alongside there are already four men on deck and they are busy turning on the water cannons and LRADs. 'Warning, warning, this is the captain of the *Shonan Maru* speaking, stop your agglessive actions,' comes blaring out at us again. I've heard this recording a few times by now, and I know the words by heart. I give a little smirk, imagining the debate the Japanese PR people would have had over the recordings, and especially the use of a female voice.

As we circle, looking for a point to board, one guy dressed in black follows us around. He glares down at us from behind their net. Boarding will be a tricky exercise, and I can tell straight away it'd be a real challenge to do it now when the crew are expecting us. It'd take 30 seconds or so to cut the net away while you're clinging to the side — plenty of time for them to push you off or dislodge your fingers, tumbling you back into the frigid waters.

'Isn't that a gun?' yells Marcus. I follow the line of his hand, and spot a guy with some kind of gun pointed ominously at us. Not a firearm by the looks, but clearly some form of weapon. We back away a little and watch him closely. He seems content to just follow us around, keeping a watchful eye back at us.

With the decision made that the boarding will never happen today, instructions come through to attempt a prop fouling.

I open up the bin and reluctantly pull out the little white buoy on the end of a little 5 mm cable. I'm embarrassed to deploy this. Three-foot mooring lines never stopped the *Shonan Maru* before, so this tiny little toy has no hope at all.

'You sure it's worth it?' I say to Matt.

'It's good practice at prop fouling,' Matt says, 'and it might just work its way into the seals.' I know this will never happen, but I bite my tongue and say nothing. To be fair, my team never spent any time on developing prop-foulers anyway, so perhaps we've only got ourselves to blame. I make up my mind to spend some time back on the *Bob* building new prop-foulers.

We hassle the *Shonan Maru* for several hours, but we have no real impact on them. In due course Matt decides it's time to leave, and we head back to the *Bob Barker*. The Hammer is again waiting expectantly for us. 'Welcome back, Pete. Remember you can stay as long as you like,' he says jovially, and he pats me on the back again.

The following morning, Jimmy and I climb down into the rope locker. It's a plethora of handy bits and pieces. 'What about this rope?' asks Jimmy, dragging a two-and-a-half-inch mooring line out from under some fenders. We drag it up onto the deck, and lay it next to the 12 mm wire cable we'd scrounged earlier.

A few hours later and our first prop-fouler is assembled. The wire cable is wound through the rope every two metres, and big orange buoys are tied off on the end. The cable has added quite a bit of weight, and would sink the fouler in the middle, probably beneath the propeller depth, so we've tied off several smaller buoys along the length to keep it afloat.

'You reckon this will work?' asks Jimmy, eyeing up his handiwork. He's made a neat job of the cable splicing.

'I don't know bro. The whaling vessels will have cutters on their props, and these will scythe through small cables. But 12 mm cable is getting up there. We're certainly in with a chance.' I have a think about what we could add. Ideally, we'd have 20 mm cable or more. You'd need quite a few buoys to support it I guess, but it'd wreak havoc on their drive-train. To cut that away would be such a difficult job as well. We take another look through the rope locker, scrounging up the gear for a second prop-fouler. Jimmy gets to work, keen to get it all done before the next bout of bad weather hits.

I wander back inside. The Hammer is passing around the latest news articles from around the globe. One quotes a Dutch maritime expert, who believes that the *Shonan Maru* is clearly at fault, and its captain should face charges.

'You'll be interested in this one,' the Hammer says, handing me an article from New Zealand. I scan down the page, and there is a quote from Murray McCully, the New Zealand Foreign Minister. He's quoted as saying that Sea Shepherd went down to Antarctica looking for trouble... so what did they expect? These comments are a green light for the whalers to continue sinking any small vessels that might stand in front of their illegal activities. With five Kiwis on board, and the vessel being registered in New Zealand, you'd think there might have been at least a small amount of support from the government there.

McCully, though, in my opinion, wasn't interested in supporting us and he took the easy option and supported the Japanese. It doesn't surprise me, though. His team has done little to oppose whaling since they got in office.

Interestingly, I'd called his office six months earlier to tee a meeting up with him. I was told very nicely that he was too busy to meet with me in Wellington. He's also my electorate MP, so I suggested I'd meet him in his Browns Bay office instead. Again he was too busy to spare the time. So I left the message that we were going down to Antarctica to stop Japanese whalers, and it would be nice to have the Minister's support.

Two days later, Maritime New Zealand Ship Registrations called us up, suggesting that we no longer qualified for New Zealand registration, and that we should make plans to have the *Ady Gil* (in those days called *Earthrace*) registered elsewhere. Of course, this was far from what we planned to do. I believe the government pressured Maritime New

Zealand. They denied all this, of course, but when asked why they had suddenly made the call to us, they couldn't answer the question. In the end we managed to keep the registration.

New Zealand used to be at the forefront of environmental action. It stood up to the Americans in banning nuclear ships from its shores. It stood up to the French after they bombed the *Rainbow Warrior* in Auckland. And yet, today, a New Zealand-registered vessel with five New Zealanders on board has been deliberately rammed in international waters by Japanese whalers, and the government is basically saying we got what we deserved. No mention is made about the illegal whaling that continues on our back doorstep. There is a total lack of political leadership on this and other environmental issues. New Zealand should stand up to these thugs. Instead we let Japan bend us over and shag us.

Standing up to Japan, an important trading partner, might jeopardise our exports there. Trade, tourism, foreign investment, they all take priority over some whales that few people ever see anyway. Whaling also has no easy solutions and so our elected leaders become gun shy. They just hide under the covers and hope the problem will go away. Politicians, however, have a role to provide leadership and solutions. The only reason Sea Shepherd is forced to go to Antarctica is because our governments have failed us.

Part of the challenge is that no agency is charged with enforcing the ban on commercial whaling. Nor is any government prepared to stand up to the Japanese by sending a patrol boat down here. I'd much rather they were here and we could be off chasing shark finners or tuna poachers. But in the absence of any official or government involvement, we are the only ones standing in the way. And it really pisses me off to hear people in power saying we got what we deserved. If all six crew were killed, perhaps that would also be what we deserved. A few metres' difference and death would most certainly have occurred.

The last few days my mood swings have swung very easily. I wake up happy to be alive, and then I start dwelling on things and wishing our situation was different. What has happened, though, can't be undone. *Ady Gil*, the boat that is, won't come back. She lies on the bottom of the Southern Ocean. But there are still many positives to be thankful for. There is a job to be done here and we can still make a real contribution.

In our record attempt in 2008, I remember hitting a massive log off the coast of Palau. It did so much damage that I thought any hope of the record was lost. We limped all the way to Singapore on one engine, and arrived to a seemingly hopeless situation.

I remember dwelling on the problems. We had so many that it just seemed pointless continuing. Fiona, my CEO, pulled me aside and gave me a good sharp talking to. 'Look Pete, you need to sort your shit out. This team needs you to lead us — not to dwell on what might have been. We need to fix this boat and get it going as quickly as we can.' She was like one of my old school teachers giving me a good bollocking and, in this case, she was quite right. 'It is what it is, get over it,' were her final words to me as she headed off in search of something.

She was quite right, of course. Get over it. The challenges were many, and individually each one was not insurmountable. It was just that in their entirety they seemed colossal. We had a broken propeller, split P-bracket, bent driveshaft, smashed gearbox, smashed engine mounts, smashed rudder, and a four-metre gouge down the side of the main hull. But each problem individually wasn't so massive.

The first problem we had to overcome was just getting the boat pulled from the water. No boatyard in Singapore had spare capacity — there was a two-year waiting list. Similarly, there were no options in Malaysia or Indonesia. The nearest yard willing to lift us was Australia, but to go there would leave us no chance of the record. So Tino, my chief engineer, gets in a little inflatable boat and starts driving all around the island of Singapore and asking for help.

The most promising place is a jack-up oil rig. I'd worked on these in the North Sea, and they always have a substantial crane, and if not drilling at the time, plenty of space. Tino ties his boat on one leg of the rig and clambers up the ladder.

'Sure we'll help ya,' says the company man. 'This rig is idle for another month until our refit starts.' Tino wanders around, checking the crane, and ensuring our 24-metre hull will squeeze on.

It's all looking good, when the company man comes back out. 'Um, I'm really sorry to do this to ya. But I just spoke to our owners in London. It would seem we have a problem.'

'And what might that be?'

'Well, we are an oil rig right. And we work for oil companies. Now your boat is promoting biodiesel that is in direct competition to petroleum products. Any help we give you would be viewed very poorly by our customers.'

Tino puts on his most charming smile, and explains that we can just do it low profile — no one need ever know. Our profile in Singapore, though, is already considerable. Images of the world's coolest boat, running on biodiesel, and under repair on a jack-up oil rig, would most certainly traverse the globe. The irony is not lost on the London owners, nor will it be lost on media. He's right I guess, but it's still immensely disappointing that he turns us down.

Tino gets back in his little boat and continues pottering around Singapore. He finally comes across a crane overhanging the water, and a small section of concrete, not really big enough to seat our boat. But when you're desperate you'll try anything.

'Sure we'll help ya,' the boss of Posh Semco says. He's got a thick, working-class East London accent, and a slim, young African lady hanging off his arm. He barks a few orders and suddenly there's a dozen Malaysian Chinese running around setting things up. By four o'clock on Friday afternoon, I limp *Earthrace* beside the Posh Semco wall, and we start rigging up the crane.

It's 5pm in the afternoon when Fiona finally secures a three-inch, five-metre-long piece of stainless steel for our driveshaft. It took us four weeks to secure such a piece in New Zealand. By nine o'clock that evening

Earthrace is pulled from the water, and we start on repairs.

A local boat builder comes down to give us some advice. He looks at our list of repairs and the damaged sections and shakes his head. 'You'll need at least three weeks to get all that done,' he says. He then starts listing the times for different jobs. We don't need a pretty job, though. Nor do we need it to be bulletproof. We just need it to last until Spain, and the finish line.

He walks off half an hour later, muttering something about he'll be back in a week to check on progress. If it takes three weeks as he reckons, there's no way we'll get the record. As Tino says, 'We now need a small miracle.'

We gradually step through the repairs, prioritising them. Some have to go in order, others can be done anytime, and others needed certain periods to dry or cure. We end up with an array of projects and what bottlenecks lie ahead.

By far the biggest bottleneck is getting the driveshaft machined. At 10pm it seems hopeless. But at 11pm on Friday night we finally track down a Norwegian guy, in a pub, who owns a CNC machine shop that can do the work. By midnight he locates his man to program the machine. And by 1am on Saturday morning, they start machining our new driveshaft.

What follows is the most amazing job of my life. From then, everyone we ask for help agrees, every tool we pick up works, every nut we grab fits — everything we do just seems to work. My team works virtually continuously for three days, a few sneaking the odd hour of sleep here and there while waiting for composite to cure or paint to dry.

Tropical rainstorms come thundering down on Saturday morning, halting progress for a few hours while we rig up tarpaulins. A group of locals see us struggling in the wind and rain, and clamber up with their own plastic sheets to give us a hand.

On Sunday morning our new, shiny driveshaft is delivered, and by mid-afternoon, a crew is working in 45-degree heat and 100 per cent humidity in the engine room, connecting couplings and aligning things back up. On Monday morning, *Earthrace*, amazingly, is dropped back in the water.

The job sure isn't pretty. The split P-bracket has the bodgiest looking bit of composite work the world has ever seen. The smashed rudder I just remove. We have two anyway, and the boat can steer OK on one, especially at speed. The gouge down the side is repaired but it never gets the final paint. All in all it's is a quick and dirty repair. But I don't need perfect.

'Do you reckon it's all sorted?' Fiona says to me, as I clamber back aboard *Earthrace*?

'Of course it is,' I say confidently. Secretly, though, I'm worried about many things. There could easily be leaks in some of our composite work. There could be a vibration in the drive-train somewhere. Maybe we've overlooked something. So many things nag at me as I start the engines, and idle away from the Posh Semco yard.

'No leaks,' yells Tino, grinning from ear to ear. 'Rock on baby.' He starts dancing in the helm, but he's like a praying mantis, long limbs flailing everywhere.

We're still in the five-knot zone but no one here seems to heed speed limits anyway. I gradually ramp the speed up, and the drive-train is silky smooth. We cruise up to 30 knots with no sign of any vibration, the parameters are all good, and we are back in business.

An hour later and we're refuelling at the 1-15 Marina, and preparing to leave. My team are all spread out on the dock and they are shattered from exhaustion and lack of sleep — except for Tino, who continues to be on an energy drink high. Or maybe he's just high on life. You never know with Tino.

'What you achieved here is a small miracle,' I say to them proudly. The many onlookers are probably wondering what I'm on about, but I couldn't care less. Right now, all I care about is this outstanding group of volunteers who made something amazing happen. We achieved in three days what should have taken three weeks. No one moaned, no one bitched, no one snuck off. They all just delivered. All it would have taken was one person in this team not to deliver and we wouldn't be there. And yet there we were. I will possibly never have such a job like that again in my life. And I'll be OK with that, because I have been part of something special.

From there I knew we'd get the record. We were so far ahead of the old record that I didn't need to push the boat any more. We cruised the last few legs, arriving back in Spain in one piece, and smashing the old record for circling the globe by over two weeks.

It was on our second attempt, but looking back on it, we never deserved the record on our first attempt anyway. We made too many mistakes, we were ill prepared, and my decision-making and leadership were not the best. On the second attempt, however, our whole team delivered — every one of us, and especially in Singapore. And we definitely deserved the record.

Funnily enough, the guy John Walker who held the trophy prior to us refused to hand it over, despite UIM, the governing authority for powerboat events, and Guinness World Records, both sanctioning our time. We'd actually considered some drastic measures to get the trophy back for the handover ceremony in Italy. 'We could start legal proceedings,' Fiona had suggested. Tino wanted us all to turn up on his doorstep. 'He sleeps with the trophy as a teddy bear,' he'd said, 'so we know it'll be somewhere handy. Probably tucked up on his pillow I expect.' And a few of our supporters who lived in theUK had offered to go down and, in their words, 'rough the pompous git up a bit until he hands it over'.

We never did the record to get a trophy — we did it to promote biodiesel. We'd already had enormous media and publicity surrounding our record, and having a trophy on the mantelpiece at home wouldn't make any difference now. 'He can keep my trophy,' I'd said, after he refused for the third time to hand it over. 'The trophy obviously means a lot more to him than it does to me.' I'd figured it was time to move on and do something new, like helping a team stop whaling. Spending time and energy in chasing a trophy wouldn't make the world a better place.

I learnt many lessons on *Earthrace*. One of them was to focus on what was important. In this case, the trophy wasn't. Another more valuable lesson was that you would get dealt a crap deal from time to time. Just deal with it. Crap happens. What happened in Palau when we hit that log could so easily have scuppered our record attempt, and yet it didn't. An amazing team of talented people rallied around and achieved something special, and I was privileged to be in the middle of it.

Well it seems right now some crap has happened. The *Ady Gil* has been sunk. Get over it! Sea Shepherd still has the *Bob Barker* and the *Steve Irwin*. We still have the jet-ski and some RIBs. And we still have a job to do down here. I get up and head outside for some air, promising I'll stop bitching about my boat being rammed, and all the other things pissing me off recently.

A few days later our plans are changed, and the *Bob Barker* heads north, with the *Shonan Maru* still on our tail. An eerie mist descends over us as we cruise into the main harbour on Kerguelen Island in the southern Indian Ocean. A French territory, populated only by researchers and scientists, this island is classed as the fifth most remote piece of land anywhere in the world. By what measure they come to this conclusion I don't know, but it certainly is hard to get to. It sits half way between Australia and South Africa, and deep into the roaring forties.

As we pass up the channel, a group of Commerson's dolphins come and greet us, surfing along on our bow wave, and enjoying some company for a change. This island gets just four boat visits a year, so the dolphins, as well as the scientists, will all make the most of our presence here.

Mikey comes up onto the bow where I'm busy watching the dolphins playing beneath me. 'Man, they're a cool looking dolphin,' says Mikey. They have a large white body, but with dark heads, tails and dorsal fins. What sort of Darwinian quirk led to that colour scheme surviving I'm not sure, but they do look interesting.

'You know where these dolphins are found?' I ask Mikey.

'Um. Here,' Mikey says. I'm not sure if he's serious or not.

'Actually, here, and Patagonia. And that is it. Amazing, really.'

Mikey smiles. He's been much happier since he found out the *Steve Irwin* was returning to Fremantle. Their chopper has been down for a few days, and they've decided to head back and get it fixed. So Mikey and the rest of us all get to head back — although I've decided to stay on the *Steve Irwin*, along with Larry, until the end of the campaign.

One of the dolphins makes an acrobatic leap in front of us, and there's a rush of clicks from several cameras. 'You know Mikey, nature is amazing in its ability to find little niches for animals to survive in. But you gotta wonder how the heck they got here from Patagonia. Did one of them one day go, "Hey, I have a brilliant idea. Let's swim 5000 kilometres where there's a great little tropical island for us to chill out on for a while." Or did a pregnant female get swept all this way in a storm?'

'Maybe they used to be all along Antarctica, and now all that remain are these two populations, the others all having been wiped out through competition or climate change.' I look over at Mikey a little surprised. Sometimes I think of him as not the sharpest tool in the shed, and yet at others he seems quite clever.

'Well, whatever it is Mikey, we're lucky to see these little buggers. Very few people ever do.'

Mikey nods his head. 'Hey, thanks for sorting out getting me back home,' he says, changing the subject.

'Wasn't me, mate. I think you threatening to rip Chuck's head off helped, and the fact that the chopper needed repairs. Also, the *Bob Barker* only has a day of oil left so had to meet up with the *Steve Irwin* anyway.' Really, I could've done a lot more to help Mikey, but in the aftermath of the ramming I got so tied up in media and other things that a few jobs, like getting Mikey back home, slipped through the net. The good news is now he's heading home, and he's much happier for it. Thankfully, Chuck gets to keep his head.

A buzz suddenly goes round the boat, and the *Steve Irwin* emerges out of the mist. People on both boats are jumping up and down and waving at each other furiously. There are many friends spread over these two vessels, and aside from the Gill-billies, this is the first time most have seen the other vessel.

I spot Larry lounging around the crane. He actually has a slight tan, no doubt from a few weeks chilling out in Hobart. He's been eating well too by the looks. His belly is slightly swollen from too many burgers and fries, and there's a contented look about him. 'Wasup my homie?' I yell down at him. 'Hey, you've been eating well, haven't ya?'

'What did you do to my boat ya useless prick,' he yells back indignantly.

An hour later and the two boats are tied together, and there's a long session of 'I'll show you mine if you show me yours.' Boat, that is. People wander backwards and forwards between the two. A group of French scientists emerge, from which boat I'm not sure. There's a continuous dialogue of blah blah blah and hand waving, as only the French can do, as they are escorted around the two vessels.

Sea Shepherd enjoys a good relationship with the French. Their President recently hosted Paul, and his vessels are always welcome in the various French territories that dot the Pacific, Atlantic and Southern Oceans. I look up to the *Steve Irwin* mast and the French flag has already been raised, albeit hanging limply in the lacklustre breeze.

A few lucky crew are ferried ashore for a quick tour. This is ostensibly a wildlife sanctuary, and human presence here is limited. As a result, the wildlife is extensive, and it doesn't seem to mind if it occupies a rock ledge or the one road, a stream or a man-made drain.

The penguins are especially intriguing. They get intimidated by people standing and will shy away, but as soon as you lie down they get interested. They waddle over, eyeing you up suspiciously, before settling down beside you. It's almost like they enjoy your company, and once the first penguin arrives, others will shortly follow suit. Polar bears of course are limited to the Arctic circle in the northern hemisphere, so the penguins down here have no natural land predators. At sea they get eaten, whereas up here away from the water's edge there is safety.

Fuel, oil, water and food is all transferred to the *Bob Barker*, and the following morning the Gill-billies are all safely aboard the *Steve Irwin* and heading for Fremantle.

'I'd like you to look at this photo and tell me what you see,' Paul the New Zealand Maritime Safety Investigator says slowly. He's flown to Fremantle to interview my crew, but all he seems to ask about is the initial skirmish between the *Shonan Maru* and ourselves, which was a couple of weeks before the ramming.

The photo he hands over is of Jimmy pointing the spud gun, presumably at the Japanese. It's similar to the many other images of us hassling the whalers. I remember back to that day, which was just a few weeks ago, but that now feels like a year. It was a great morning I reckon. A slight smile crosses my face as I remember the whalers all running for cover once Jimmy started firing the spud gun. There's little point in us arguing about it, though. Images and video of this are plastered all over the Internet and media now.

'Look mate, I'm not disputing that we deployed prop-foulers, lasers and spud guns against the whalers. That was our job. If you really want I can show you footage of what happened that day. Or just wait until *Whale Wars* comes out in June and you can watch it then. None of this is in dispute. What is in dispute is the ramming.'

The investigator waits a few moments as he considers his words. 'Look Pete, we've received a complaint from the Japanese about what happened on this day, and we must investigate it.'

'Well, don't bother investigating it any more. I'm guilty as charged, and I've got the footage to prove it.' There's an awkward silence between us as I sit there glaring at him. 'Tell me Paul. Did they also complain about the ramming?'

'Um. No. Well, not that I know of. The original complaint didn't come to us directly, though.'

'So how did the complaint come to you?'

Paul shifts in his seat uneasily. 'The complaint came through the Foreign Ministry.'

'You mean Murray McCully's office?' I can just imagine the minister sitting at his mahogany desk fielding a phone call from the Japanese Ambassador, and promising to rein us in.

'Tell me Paul, what information have the whalers provided you with?'

'Well, concerning the initial encounter they have provided quite a lot.' His pile of papers and images are testament to this.

'And the ramming?'

Paul looks at me for a few moments, and sighs. 'Actually, Pete, they haven't provided any information concerning the collision. Yet. We have requested data from them but it goes via the Foreign Office, and as yet we have had nothing back.'

'And what will you do if they continue to provide no information on the ramming?'

'Well, we can request an interview with them, but they are under no obligation to submit to the interview, because they are a Japanese vessel. It would be up to the Japanese Foreign Office to force them to be interviewed.' With the whaling industry well entrenched through Japanese political circles, there is no way they'll force the *Shonan Maru* captain to do anything. And with New Zealand's current regime I can't imagine any pressure being exerted. I explain this to Paul, who sits there listening politely.

Eventually, he opens his hands as if to say he gives up. 'Pete, I am just doing my job here. We are investigating both the initial incident, as well as the collision. What happens after this is not up to me — it is up to my bosses and the New Zealand Foreign Ministry.'

In fairness, as he says, he's just doing his job. As am I. He's a nice bloke really, and in a difficult situation. I'm sure, like most other Kiwis, he's no fan of Japanese whaling, and to sit here grilling one of the few people standing up to the whalers I imagine is not what he wants to be doing right now.

We continue talking for another four hours, moving onto the ramming and final sinking. I'm about to leave, but I decide to ask one last question. He's asked me enough. 'Paul. I want your honest opinion. Tell me roughly what your findings will be?'

'I cannot answer that question until I have all the facts.'

'Well you've interviewed me and all my crew, you've seen video from four different angles, and you've seen hundreds of photos leading up to the ramming. Surely you can give me an idea.'

We sit there in silence, neither of us wanting to talk first. Finally, Paul starts to speak. 'I cannot give you an answer to that. I am an investigator, and I do not have all the facts yet. Therefore I cannot give you a professional opinion. What I can do, though, is give you my personal thoughts.'

'And they are?'

'I don't think the captain of the *Shonan Maru* wanted to sink you. I think he just wanted to cross your bow really closely . . . or maybe just give you a little nudge. But he misjudged it and hit you.' That is all he is prepared to say. I get up and shake his hand.

7
Foul tactics

As I wander along the dock back to the *Steve Irwin*, I can see Chris busy lashing down his prized helicopter. It's all repaired and ready to go I hope. Crew member Erwin is sorting fresh drums of oil and fellow crewman Pedro is deep in discussion with some random officials. Larry, who has decided to stay on with me, is helping load supplies.

A short time later we say our final goodbyes and the *Steve Irwin* undocks and plots a new course for Antarctica. Jason and Mikey are both flying back to New Zealand later today, and Laurens is heading to Thailand for a week or two of leisure. It feels like something is now missing. They were an awesome bunch of lads, and I'll miss their company. The *Steve Irwin* now seems eerily quiet.

I'm certainly happy to have Larry back. I did miss his input on the *Ady Gil*, and I imagine things might well have been different had he been with me. Things generally happen for a reason, though, and maybe Larry breaking his ribs and not being there, and us then getting rammed, is part of some bigger picture that I don't see yet. And maybe we never will. Whatever, I'm happy to be heading back for another crack at the whalers, and with Larry to give me a hand.

A few days ago a plane spotted what we think was the whaling fleet, but it was a long way west and in fact nearly beneath Africa. So our voyage to catch up with them will be a long one. The *Bob Barker* we believe is closing in on their last known position, but locating them without a helicopter will be a real challenge.

The days drift by as we head south-west. The intel dries up and so with nothing new to go on, the *Bob Barker* just starts running grid patterns, much as we did on the *Ady Gil*, while we head in their general direction.

A few days later I'm in the foc's'le with Larry, working on what we originally termed Plan F. 'How much did these cost?' asks Larry, holding up one of the rapid-fire igniters for the oxygen lance. He rolls it over in his fingers. It looks a bit like a metal shotgun shell with a safety clip on one end.

'About 50 bucks each,' I reply. Our last effort at lighting the lance under water involved flares, but it ended in a complete debacle, with Larry and me paddling around furiously after a parachute flare. We've since purchased 10 rapid fires, designed specifically for this job.

Following the instructions, we place the rapid fire on the lance end and hit it on the ground. There's the telltale sound of the glass vial breaking, but no sign of any heat coming off the unit. Larry looks at the rapid fire in disgust. 'Must be a dud.' He grabs a second one and the result is the same. Similarly, the third and fourth ones fail to fire.

'Maybe the rod is dodgy,' he says.

'Surely not. It's just a metal rod.' I pull off the last rapid fire and examine the rod. It's hard to imagine it being dodgy. It's just metal tubes after all. 'Hey, maybe we should light it on the grinder. That'd at least tell us if the rod is stuffed.'

So we turn on the grinder and I push the rod end into it, while Larry cranks up the oxygen pressure. It takes a few seconds, and the lance then suddenly bursts into life. I throw the visor down on my welding mask and line up the lance on a two-inch thick piece of plate steel held in the vice. There's a hissing noise as the lance starts cutting, and molten metal gets splashed all over the workshop. Simeon has sparks all around him, and he beats a hasty retreat outside, while the onslaught of molten metal continues.

The steel is finally severed in half, and I turn off the trigger. There are flames on rags and bits of plastic, and Larry scuttles around stamping on them, while I just sit there admiring the damage.

'Man, that is unbelievable,' I say. The two-inch piece of plate has been completely cut in half in just 30 seconds. The bit left in the vice has a jagged edge down the side where the lance cut it, and the bottom section is still glowing red hot.

'Wow,' exclaims Larry, who by now has sorted the fires. Simeon sneaks a look inside, then steps gingerly back into the workshop. 'Is it safe yet?' he asks, half jokingly, as he looks through the haze of smoke.

'What the hell are you doing?' yells the bosun, as he comes barging through the doorway. I explain to him we're just testing the rapid fires for the oxygen lance, but, unsurprisingly, he looks like a deer in the headlights. Finally, he heads off moaning about keeping him informed. Then the phone goes, with the bridge control upset that we hadn't informed them of our activities, and concerned about the fire risk of what we're doing. Next one of the officers comes in, also expressing their reservations about our activities.

'Just think of it as welding,' I'd suggested to him, although the oxygen lance is far from just a welding tool. It's more like oxygen-fired destruction.

I pick up the chunk of metal off the floor. The oxygen lance is certainly an amazing tool, once lit. I reckon we'd need just a few minutes under water to disable one of the harpoon vessels with it. Of course, first the harpoon vessel needs to be temporarily disabled or stationary. This does happen with prop fouling, or when the vessels refuel or transfer supplies. Either way, though, I think we only have a tiny chance of getting a vessel in such a state. But the reason it is attractive to us is that with just a few minutes' work we could potentially disable one vessel completely, then a second vessel would be needed to tow it back to Japan. So, two vessels would be taken out of whaling for the rest of the campaign.

Try as we might, however, we're unable to get the rapid fires to light the oxygen lance. And obviously we cannot take a grinder under water to do the lighting. So in the end Larry and I decide to abandon it.

'What other tactics do we have left?' asks Larry. He's in a sombre mood. The oxygen lance had been our most promising tactic, albeit a long shot.

'Well, there's the laser. We're still allowed to steal any whales from the Japanese. There's still the option of me going back to Japan aboard one of the whaling vessels. And Paul has promised we can continue to use the spud gun. I'm sure a few more bottles of butyric acid on the *Nisshin Maru* wouldn't go amiss.'

Larry wrinkles his nose up. 'Sea Shepherd has been throwing butyric acid for four years mate. I'm sure the Japanese have got a decent cleaner for removing it by now. And if you're a whaler, and you spend your days disembowelling whales, you think you'd really care about some smelly old butter?'

Larry has a point. Although there is the possibility of it tainting the meat as well, I guess. I don't know if this is a fact or not, really.

We start cleaning up our mess, which is considerable, and I eventually head off, leaving Larry to finish up. 'We need some new tactics, bro' Larry says as I head off. I look back at him and nod. 'Yeah. Let's work on it, eh.'

It's 2am the following day and I'm halfway through my watch on the *Steve Irwin*. I shift around in the driver's seat and look around the bridge. It's a spacious area this. Things are all nicely laid out. It's like some person with obsessive-compulsive disorder worked on this in the early days and made sure it all fitted together perfectly. Someone spent a lot of time laying this helm out I reckon. And someone since has done a great job in upgrading everything. I look down at the new radar screen. There's a bright blob showing up at the 12 nautical mile mark. Probably an iceberg. I make a note to keep an eye on it.

After the incident with the oxygen lance, the officers decided to give me a second four-hour shift. So eight hours of driving per day. Perhaps they've decided I'm a liability with all the spare time on my hands. Not that I have much spare time, as most days are spent writing a book and preparing things for when we do finally catch up with the whalers.

Vincent, my watch partner, wanders back into the helm and sits his ample frame down in the navigator's chair. He'd pass for an American most probably. Cowboy boots, a big belt buckle, blue jeans, pony-tail — he looks like one of those US baby boomers who buy a Harley-Davidson when they hit 50.

'You own a Harley?' I ask nonchalantly.

'Sure. I've owned several. I love ma bikes.' There's a strong Australian twang in his voice — a bit like he's holding his nose when he speaks. He rubs his hand down his grey beard and lets out a deep sigh. Someone enters the helm and takes a position up near the windscreen, their dark shape just visible in the low light. I finally recognise the shape of Larry.

'I can't sleep,' he says finally. He stands there looking out. 'What time you on till?'

'Midnight till four.'

'Hey, do you miss *Earthrace* at all?' He has struggled getting used to the name *Ady Gil*. He and I still occasionally slip back into calling her *Earthrace*.

I think about this for a while. The boat has been my life for the last four years, and it's been an amazing roller-coaster ride of highs and lows. I've had the best days of my life aboard her, but also the worst.

I think back to the last Pacific crossing we made from Panama to Australia. It was an incredible journey. We stopped at Galapagos, Tahiti, Fiji, Vanuatu and several uninhabited atolls. They were all such brilliant stops. But the best was the last one. I'd actually thought it uninhabited, but as we approached, there were three fishermen in dugout canoes. I was looking at my GPS navigating into the lagoon, and a few seconds later I looked up and the three fishermen were gone, which at the time I thought was a bit odd.

Anyway we anchor up in one of the most amazing pristine places I've ever seen. Coconut palms overhang stunning white sand beaches and beautiful blue water. I look off the transom step and there are colourful tropical fish swimming around on the numerous corals that cover the seabed. A large turtle comes swimming lazily by. He glances at us, then just carries on, ambling his way between the central hull and our starboard outrigger. I jump in the warm water with a couple of crew and we paddle around for a while, eventually getting the masks out and exploring things.

As I'm hopping out, I notice a little movement on top of a rock ledge on shore. A few seconds later there is more movement. I'm thinking it is a lizard or something, but I grab the binoculars to check it out. There, on top of the rocks, are two pairs of eyes watching us. I give them an uneasy wave, and a few seconds later the eyes disappear.

An hour later and a single bloke in a dugout canoe comes paddling out. He doesn't come straight up, though — he stops about 50 metres away and eyes us up suspiciously. He then comes a little closer and stops again. Finally, he reaches the starboard outrigger, and he runs his hands along the hull. 'Hoooooo,' he says in a soft voice. He then paddles to the main bow, ignoring our attempts at greetings. 'Hoooooo,' he says a second time, now running his hand around the tip. Finally, he reaches the stern and he looks up at us. '*Bonjour*,' he says timidly.

'*Bonjour monsieur, ça va?*' I reply, exhausting my French in just four words.

A hint of a smile crosses his face. 'Blah blah blah,' he replies in French.

It turns out he speaks French, some pigeon English, and a local dialect. We convince him to climb aboard, and there starts a slow and cumbersome conversation, but it gradually emerges that when the three fishermen saw us, they didn't actually know what we were, so they went and saw their chief. He saw us and concluded we were an invasion force, and ordered all the inhabitants into a cave on the other side of the island. When we never arrived, he sent out two scouts, who were the ones watching us over the rock ledge. They then returned, and the chief then sent out this guy, their fiercest warrior, to check us out.

Before he leaves, I run inside and grab him some posters and canned food. We load them into his wee dugout and he gives us a big white toothy grin, and paddles off.

Two hours later and we're just getting the barbecue going when a number of canoes come paddling out. It is the chief, several warriors, his wife and some daughters. They all climb up into the deck area and present us with flax trays containing all sorts of foods, including fish, pawpaw, mango, coconut and limes.

Adding their food to ours, we prepare a banquet, sit up on the roof, and have one of the most amazing evenings of my life with these wonderful people who exist in complete harmony on this isolated tropical paradise.

They are immensely curious about the outside world, just as we're curious about their life. It strikes me that they all want to travel and live overseas, while not really valuing this special place they already have. To some degree we're in the same boat, excuse the pun. We're on this amazing boat and travelling the globe, and yet we all look enviously at this island paradise, wishing we could live there.

It's late evening by the time we say our goodbyes. My crew and I are all bloated from the massive feed, and our minds are satiated with information from our generous new friends. They wave at us, shake our hands, kiss our cheeks, and climb back into their canoes.

I'll remember that day for the rest of my life. All of my crew will. I've been blessed to visit such awesome places and to meet so many wonderful people, and the *Ady Gil* was what got me there.

The satphone suddenly rings in the communications room, bringing me back to reality. 'I'd like to speak with Paul please,' comes the voice on the other end of the line. I look up at the clock, and it's 2.30am. Paul is OK with media calls at all hours, but he hates being woken otherwise.

'Can I ask what it is regarding please?'

'This is the captain of the *Bob Barker* speaking. We have found the *Nisshin Maru*. I think Paul would like to take this phone call,' comes the abrupt reply.

A few minutes later and Paul is up and manning the phones. After getting details from the *Bob Barker*, and putting the *Steve Irwin* onto a new course, calls are made to several Sea Shepherd people, and then the media calls commence. Paul is single-minded with media. He speaks in sound bites. The points roll off his tongue in a relentless barrage of facts, figures and opinion. 'The whalers are more aggressive than ever before, they continue to illegally hunt whales in the Southern Ocean whale sanctuary, and we are down here to shut them down.' I sit there listening to his impressive dialogue. He answers the questions he wants to and ignores the ones he doesn't.

Larry listens for a few minutes then heads downstairs to pass on the news. With 40 crew on board, all starved of information, word quickly spreads that the *Bob Barker* is on the tail of the *Nisshin Maru*, and the entire whaling fleet is heading directly towards us.

During the following day, additional snippets of information filter through. The *Bob Barker* and the *Yushin Maru 3*, a spotter vessel, are involved in a collision, with superficial damage to the *Bob Barker*. Shortly after, the *Yushin Maru 3* disengages from the fleet, but whether because of damage sustained in the collision or not is unclear.

The *Bob Barker* in an incredibly tough vessel. I was really impressed with her structures, which are enormously strong. It is possible the captain of the *Yushin Maru 3* figured they could damage the *Bob Barker* with a little nudge, but they came off second best. Which would be ironic, given what the whalers did to the *Ady Gil*.

Later in the day, my old friend the *Shonan Maru* joins the procession of vessels. Heading towards us then is the processing ship, two harpooners, a security vessel and the *Bob Barker* in hot pursuit. Thus far it seems the *Bob Barker* has the speed to keep up with the fleet, which is reassuring. The season is about to get very interesting!

Two days later and the fleet reaches us. Paul slots us in behind the *Nisshin Maru*, while the *Bob Barker* sits to port of us. A few miles astern, the harpooners and security vessel complete this angry flotilla of enemies. There follows a most bizarre situation — all these vessels simply driving around the Southern Ocean. No whaling. No actions. Simply a group at stalemate, but with no whaling occurring, each day costing the whalers dearly in terms of lost revenues.

I've just finished my afternoon watch, and I head down to the mess for some company. Larry is sitting sipping coffee as I plonk myself down in a comfy chair next to him.

'Wasup my homie?' I say cheerfully.

Larry looks up and sighs.

'I'm just bored. This campaign wasn't quite what I was expecting. 'We've been following the whalers for days now and we've done nothing to them.' He takes a sip of his coffee and savours it, but the frown remains etched on his face.

'Yeah, well as long as we're on their tails, they ain't whaling,' I reply. 'Every day like this is a good day.'

'Yeah I know. I just wish we were out there in the RIBs giving them some stick.'

Larry's not the first to express these sentiments. Many of the crew are anxious to do more than play 'follow-the-leader' around the Southern Ocean. Paul has mentioned that the small boats might be launched in the next patch of good weather. I explain this to Larry, but he remains sombre.

'The trouble is Pete, all they're gonna do is throw those bottles of butyric acid and ya gotta be bloody superman to get them over the net. Or they're gonna try the prop-foulers, but they're only shitty old bits of rope. There's no way any of them can stop a harpooner.'

'So what are you suggesting?'

Larry takes a final mouthful of coffee and puts the empty cup down on the little table.

'What I'm suggesting is that we need some new tactics. I don't think the Japanese will mind if all we can do is throw stink bombs and toy prop-foulers.'

'Maybe we resurrect a couple of the tactics we had planned for the

Ady Gil?' I leave the questions hanging. Larry nods his head and a smile creeps onto his face for the first time.

'Yeah, like boarding the *Nisshin Maru*?'

This was one of our gutsier proposals. I'd always thought of it as a long shot, but it remains somewhat alluring, if only because of its sheer audacity. The plan was to shoot a lightweight grapnel and rope using my bow (as in bow and arrow) and get it latched over the net of the *Nisshin Maru*. Three crew climb up the rope and onto their deck, then wreak some havoc.

'Do we still have the bow and grapnel?' Larry asks.

'Nah, the grapnel was lost when *Ady Gil* was rammed. The bow and arrows are all here, though.'

Larry nods his head thoughtfully. 'I could probably make a new grapnel . . . there's no carbon on board, but fibreglass would work OK.'

'Let's run it by Paul first and see what he says. Now, what other tactics have we got?'

It's a productive three hours of brainstorming that follows, with various crew stopping by to add their opinions. We end up with a handy list of possibilities to take up to Paul.

He's sitting behind his desk typing away on a Panasonic Toughbook as we enter his office.

'Hi Paul, you got a minute?' I say, grabbing a seat in front of him.

'Sure guys. What's up?' His words are polite, but I can tell he's busy. He always is. I run through a quick explanation of the *Nisshin Maru* boarding plan. He pulls his glasses apart in the middle and lets them hang, a lens dropping down on each shoulder. He leans back in his chair while he considers our proposal.

'Pete,' he says finally, 'I think you should concentrate on boarding the *Shonan Maru*. They sank your boat so you have legal justification for boarding theirs.'

I nod my head slowly. He's right in what he says, appealing as the *Nisshin Maru* is as a target. I move on to the next proposal.

"You remember that idea of the bow and arrow and shooting

chemicals into the whale? Well . . .'

Larry scowls. 'I'm not sure we'll still get permission for that one, bro. People are a bit sketchy about using a weapon in broad view of the whalers.'

'Yeah but what if we use a different device? Maybe a massive hypodermic needle or plunger. We pull in close to the dead whale and pump it full of chemicals in one quick hit.'

Larry's eyes narrow and he stares at me for a few seconds. 'What sort of chemical do you have in mind exactly?'

Now there has been much debate about this and stretching back at least twelve months. Suggestions have included mercury, poison (both real and fake), butyric acid — even radioactive isotopes. I think I've come up with the ultimate though. I glance at Larry who's got a wry little smirk on his face.

'Actually . . . I reckon we use human blood.' Larry looks confused for a few seconds and then a big smile emerges on his hardened face. 'If they process a whale that has human blood in it,' I continue, 'well, they can't tell it from whale blood. The Japanese will absolutely freak out.'

Larry moves forward in his chair and laughs. 'And whose blood do you propose stealing for this?'

'Well, bro, I hadn't really gotten that far. Perhaps you could volunteer. Or maybe we take 50 mils from each crewmember and make a blood-bank from hell. Or maybe we just suck a litre from the sickest crewmember on board . . .' Suddenly another option lights up in my mind. Menstrual blood. I decide to keep this one to myself for now. Perhaps asking the hamsters to each make a donation will be just a little too weird.

'We're not finished yet Paul. There are a couple other proposals. The first is we want to shoot bottles of red paint onto the side of the *Nisshin Maru*.'

'Why?' Paul scowls at us.

'Well . . . we want to have red splashes all over the word 'research'. It symbolises whale blood. It also has us highlighting that the research is bogus. Finally, it'll mean that the boat will have to be repainted in Japan, which will cost them.'

Paul agrees to this, plus a new kind of prop-fouler that Larry and I have been working on, and we're 'happy campers' as we leave his office.

As we wander back to our room, I reflect on Paul Watson. The way he treated us was typical of him. He grasps ideas quickly, makes his decision then moves on. His personality is polarising; people love him or hate him, but seldom in between. In many ways, he's a visionary leader. There's a presence and charisma about him that's intoxicating, and while it doesn't convert all people, those who do come under his spell become incredibly loyal, and I'd be one of them. He provides the goals, and people like me, his disciples, carry them out. In another life he could well have been a prophet.

There's a definite machiavellian streak in him, too. When people have served their purpose, they can be callously discarded. There's a certain ruthlessness in the way he pursues things. This trait, though, is found in many great leaders. Sentimentality will not block their goals, which in Paul's case is marine conservation. He cares about little else, and certainly not people's feelings.

He has outstanding recall and a prodigious memory, especially in history, geography and politics. One evening in a game of Trivial Pursuit he barely missed a single question, while the rest of us struggled to beat him to a single answer. I've watched him many times in the company of others; it's like he holds court. He dominates proceedings if the topic interests him and, if not, he changes it or retires to his cabin. Many of his arguments are well rehearsed. He's used them so many times that they come out in an orchestrated barrage of facts, figures and theories. It makes him a formidable opponent in any debate, as journalists who tackle him discover.

But the thing I like most about Paul, and it's one of his greatest strengths, is his ability to empower people. He readily delegates responsibility and ownership to those around him. He never micro-manages, he works on big pictures and ideas and the rest of us buy into them; and, hopefully, make them happen.

I believe Paul will go down in history as one of this century's great leaders. It is incredible that he has been doing this now for 30 years and he still holds fast to his ideals. He has made an outstanding contribution to marine conservation and he has made the planet a slightly better place. I consider myself fortunate to have worked for him. Like most people in Sea Shepherd, I feel blessed to be one of his disciples.

The following day, Larry and I are on the back deck working on the new prop-foulers. We remain in the grasp of an ugly low-pressure system and the venomous Antarctic wind bites into our exposed skin.

'Be miserable out there on the *Ady Gil*,' says Larry, as he stares out at the angry sea. White caps scour the horizon and every now and then the spray from one hurtles up over our work area.

Prop fouling is something we'd neglected until now, and yet as engineers we should have made the effort to develop a couple of foulers on the *Ady Gil*. The concept is relatively simple; to get something wrapped around the propeller of a whaling vessel. Historically, Sea Shepherd has relied upon ropes thrown from RIBs; as the harpooner drives over them, the ropes get sucked into the propeller, causing either vibration, or loss of speed. Or, potentially, stopping the vessel completely.

They've had limited success. In 2006, the *Kaiko Maru*, an underpowered piss bucket, was hamstrung for a considerable period. Then in 2009 one of the harpooners was disabled for an hour or two. Considering the effort expended, however, this represents scant reward.

Part of the problem is the sheer size of the machines you're trying to disrupt. Harpooners put out over 5000 horsepower, delivered through a driveshaft at least 500 mm in diameter. It takes considerable force to arrest such beasts.

The second challenge is the rope-cutters deployed on the whaling vessels. These are a pair of shallow blades that slide against each other once per driveshaft resolution. If a rope is entangled, as long as the propeller keeps rotating, the cutters will progressively work their way through and sever the rope.

'What do ya reckon?' says Larry, pointing at his handiwork. He's weaving six steel cables, ranging from 10 mm to 15 mm in diameter into one large cable.

'It's hardly a thing of great beauty,' I say to him, as I pick up the completed end. It resembles an orgy of eels all twisting in mass copulation. Larry looks up at me with mock offence.

'It's not meant to be pretty my bro. It's meant to be functional.'

I move the cable backwards and forwards then bend it back on itself. 'I reckon your twisting is too tight. It's making it rigid. Maybe loosen it a bit to keep it flexible.' His eyes narrow and he looks down the five metres of cable he's completed. 'Hmmm . . . I'll see what I can do.'

'When ya finish with Sea Shepherd, you can always get a job doing macramé in a commune,' I say hopefully. He ducks his head down as a spray of freezing salt water comes galloping over us. He is too slow and his face cops a lash on one cheek. He manages a faint smile.

'Well, whatever I do after Sea Shepherd, it's gotta involve warm weather.'

It's late evening by the time we finish — two of the ugliest prop-foulers the world has ever seen. They are heavy — maybe 100 kg each and only 15 metres long with 150-litre buoys tied on each end. They keep it afloat, but more importantly they'll guide it along the harpooner. So once deployed, as long as we get a buoy on either side of the bow, it will be aligned when it passes the stern, regardless of what turns the harpooner attempts.

The length of the cable is the key to the working — too long and it will pass under the propeller, too short and it will catch on the keel. But we think 15 metres will be about right and we can always shorten it later. The steel will resist the rope-cutters and the weight of the device will make vibrations in the propeller more excessive. Once entangled, it would be a big mission to get it removed. We don't know if it will actually work as planned, but it'd be fair to say we're quietly confident.

We clean ourselves up and head to the mess where Nodge, one of the chefs, has opened up the bar. Sea Shepherd vessels for the most part are dry; that is, no alcohol. Only on special occasions will Paul agree to a few bottles being quaffed. Well, the special occasion today is Larry and I need empty bottles for paint bombs.

Two slabs of Victorian Bitter lie on the bar, and a scrum has formed around Nodge as she starts handing them out.

'And what may I ask is this in aid of?' asks Pedro, as he slumps into a chair across from me. His speech is slow and a monotone, and the tone almost resembles that of Kermit the frog. When I first met him, I thought he was slightly retarded, and yet he's incredibly intelligent. God does this to people; he evens things up. If he makes them super clever like Pedro, he'll then add in a few quirks to their personality. Maybe it's so no one gets all the good stuff. Well, in Pedro's case, God gave him a funny voice as well.

'Well, Pedro,' I reply with a flourish. 'You get to drink one bottle of free beer. You give the empty bottle to me. I'll put some tape on it.' Pedro raises his hands, stopping me.

'But why do you want tape on a beer bottle?'

'So it can fit in our potato launcher.' I point at Larry who is busy sliding a finished bottle down the barrel of our launcher.

'Well, why do you want it to fit in there?'

'So we can fire it at the evil *Nisshin Maru*.'

His eyebrows come together in a frown. 'But what's the point in that? I don't get it. Hmm . . .' Pedro is deep in thought. 'In other words, I am a guinea pig to give you an empty beer bottle so you can have fun painting the *Nisshin Maru*.'

I shake my head in resignation. 'Pedro, you don't have to drink beer if you don't want to. It's not as if there's a shortage of people wanting to drink free piss,' and I point over at the bar where a dozen crew remain crowded around Nodge.

'You do get to write a message on the bottle,' Larry adds. 'Like, a message to the whalers.' He holds up a completed bottle with black writing scribbled on the tape.

'Oh, can I see?' Pedro's interest is piqued with this latest revelation.

The bottle is handed to Pedro, who starts reading aloud: 'Eating whale meat will not make your penis any bigger . . . or harder.' Larry and I both crack up laughing, but Pedro looks perturbed.

'You can't write that. It's horrid.'

Larry stops laughing. 'Well, you can write something nice on yours, and I'll write something horrid on mine.'

Pedro spots Paul Watson on the couch.

'Paul,' he yells out above the din, 'These people are writing naughty words on their bottles.'

'I don't care,' says Paul without looking up. 'They're going to be smashed on the *Nisshin Maru*, anyway.'

'Think of it as democracy in action,' I say to Pedro, who looks annoyed at Paul's indifference. 'What you write on the bottle is like casting a vote. You can vote for the Pope, or you can vote for Timothy McVeigh, or anyone else for that matter. But you don't get to tell others who to vote for.'

'Hey, I like that,' says Larry approvingly. 'This is democracy in action.' He grabs another empty bottle and starts wrapping it in tape.

'Yes, well I don't.' Pedro's demeanour resembles that of an impatient school teacher. 'I don't think you should be implying the Japanese have any issue with erectile size or dysfunction. I'll be writing something intelligent on mine.'

'Yes, but that's a liberty intelligent people such as yourself can take,' I reply. 'Simple creatures such as Larry and me don't have that luxury.'

Pedro snorts, rises from his chair and glides over to the bar to collect his beer. He returns to his seat a few minutes later and Vincent is waiting for him.

'Hey Pedro,' he says innocently. 'Can you just try this hat on? I think it'll look really good on you.' Before the bewildered Pedro can answer, Vincent has wrapped a red and white Arab scarf around Pedro's head. Now Pedro, being of Portuguese descent, it'd be fair to say he's darker than a good tan. In recent weeks, as his bushy beard has flourished so too has his resemblance to a disgruntled Arab. Now that he's sporting Arab headgear, well, let's just say if he were sitting next to you on a United Airlines flight to Washington, you'd be starting to sweat. Larry hands him the potato launcher and Pedro leans it on his shoulder like he's about to fire an RPG rocket launcher. The transformation from Second Officer to Osama Bin Laden is now complete. The resemblance is, in fact, most remarkable and Simeon, until now just hovering around us, swoops in for the 'money-shot'.

'That'll be in *Whale War III*, won't it?' Larry chirps.

Simeon gives a little wink and smiles, 'Ya gotta get the shot when it's on offer.'

8
Battle stations

The seas flatten out through the night, and it's a rolling two-metre swell and moderate breeze that greets us the following day. By lunchtime, word from Paul filters down that the RIB is to be launched in the afternoon. Amazingly, the *Steve Irwin* has been on campaign for over two months, and yet this is their first small-boat activity against the whalers. For many, this is why they came to Antarctica, even if they're not in the RIB itself. The lifting in spirit is palpable. Mustang suits, gloves, dive hoods, thermals and all manner of gear are all dusted off and made ready for action.

It's nearly 3pm when Chad and I wander out to the RIB to check on progress. Chad is our navigator on today's voyage. He's a typical activist; tattooed arms and back, large holes in his earlobes, long hair and an artistic bent. He heads over to the Animal Planet crew who are busy loading in their sound equipment and cameras.

I find Larry in the back of the RIB strapping down a dive bottle.

'I'll show you ya toys for today,' he yells out, when he spots us eyeing up his handiwork. 'You have 24 paint bombs in here,' and he points to a plastic container on the floor, 'six butyric acid in here,' and he points to another container, 'and six of these things,' and he hands over some kind of flare.

I raise my eyebrows, 'What, pray tell Mr Routledge, am I expected to do with these?'

Battle stations

Larry shrugs his shoulders.

'Well, your instructions are to throw them on the deck of any whaling vessel. What you do with them is entirely up to you.' I roll the canister over in my hand. According to the label, it's a hand-held orange smoke flare. The odds of me ever throwing it over the net of any whaling vessel are slim indeed. I guess it might make us feel good to try. I hand the flare back to Larry, who tucks it away.

'How's the potato launcher?'

'Yep . . . nearly ready.' Larry connects up the airline between the dive bottle and the launcher. There's a reassuring hiss as he opens up the valve and air pumps into the accumulation tank. 'I'll just test it,' he says with a smile, and he places the launcher on his shoulder, lining it up with the *Nisshin Maru* a few miles ahead of us. He pulls the trigger, and there's a loud thump as 150 psi of air comes exploding out the device. Half the deck-crew cower down with the noise, and a few give us angry glances. 'She's all charged and ready for action,' Larry chuckles. He quickly ties the launcher down with a bungy cord and jumps down.

Shortly after, the crane lifts our packed RIB and lowers it into the water. Various deck crew handle lines to keep it from swinging. Our crew today is four: Bosun the skipper, Chad our navigator, a cameraman and me. Even with just four of us, the vessel has a cramped feel.

Our 150-horsepower outboard is kicked into life and we're off. The ride is surprising. Our narrow bow cuts a good clean line through the chop, and as we get airborne over a couple of waves the landing is smooth and nicely balanced.

Minutes later and we're pulling alongside the *Nisshin Maru*, albeit keeping well out of reach of the tentacle-like water cannons. Six of them patrol each side of this massive vessel, and their strategic location and reach make for a formidable defence.

'Is this close enough?' Chad yells at me.

I look over at the giant ship and frown. 'The launcher will reach OK, but it's so far away I'll have no accuracy.'

'So how close do you need to be?'

'About half this distance,' I say, realising this will probably be a difficult encounter. Chad and Bosun start an animated discussion, while I get the first paint bomb ready. I grab one of the bottles and slide it down the barrel, ensuring it reaches all the way to the base.

'We're going to try and dodge the water cannons,' Chad yells at me in his smooth American accent.

'Just take your chances and shoot whenever you can.' I just nod my head back at him. 'It could be a rough ride so hang on . . . and it's gonna be wet as well.'

I smile up at Chad. 'Well, we're not here to take photos, are we?' He returns my smile, and we start our run.

Each water cannon has a man controlling it, but their adjustment is slow and cumbersome. It is possible to weave around and mostly avoid them, but it's a risky game. If we get nailed in close to the *Nisshin Maru*, there's a good chance of damage to both ourselves and our gear. A number of previous crews have ended up with black eyes, bruises and smashed electronics from encounters such as this.

Bosun suddenly turns to port and we come racing in on our first pass. We skirt under a jet, and leap neatly into an open area some 30 metres away. I line up the barrel on the 'R' in 'Research', and pull the trigger. There's a solid whack into my shoulder as the bottle goes hurtling out the barrel. Its trajectory is impressively flat, and we watch anxiously as it smashes into the giant black hull; a big red splatter mark suddenly appearing where it hits. It looks like a bullet hole. Or perhaps a harpoon wound. Either way it looks grand, albeit a few metres above the word 'Research', which was the target.

I line up my second shot and it too is high, but then we start to get pummelled with one of the water cannons. Bosun veers away, but then a second jet starts to get us.

'Hey Pete,' Chad yells, as I'm loading in my next round. 'We're gonna try the other side. It's possible all their water is diverted to just this side.' I nod my head, and we start a big double U-turn, then race along the port side of the *Nisshin Maru*.

Sure enough the cannons down here are off, and it takes the whalers several minutes to get them powered up. By then, we've fired two more rounds; the first just low, but the second right on target, with the 'A' in 'Research' now mortally wounded.

There follows one of the most exhilarating hours of my life. We pound through waves and dodge water cannons, we get smashed occasionally, and we leave our symbolic red marks down both sides of the *Nisshin Maru*. In the end I run out of paint bombs so we return to the *Steve Irwin*, bruised, battered, but grinning from ear to ear.

We then get instructions to transfer some goods between the *Bob Barker* and *Steve Irwin*. Not nearly as exciting! I'm thinking this will be our last action for the day, but then Chad turns to us with new orders.

'I just got a message from Paul. He wants the chopper to land soon, but he's worried about it getting hit by the water cannons on the whaling vessels.' Chad stops temporarily as he ducks from some spray. 'So he wants us to chase them away.'

Paul discussed this with us the previous evening. Once the chopper lands, it takes about 15 minutes to remove the blades before it can be pulled inside the protective hangar. While exposed like that, it's extremely susceptible to salt spray from water cannons, and in fact the *Shonan Maru* had attempted to hose it down on the first encounter of this campaign. Chris the pilot said a single hosing would be the end of the helicopter for this season.

We set off after the *Yushin Maru 2*, just a few hundred metres astern of the *Steve Irwin*. As soon as they realise our intent, they veer sharply off to port. We chase them for several miles then turn back.

Our next target vessel is the *Yushin Maru 1*, but it remains more intent on prowling around the *Steve Irwin* despite our presence.

'Let's throw some flares at them,' yells Bosun, as we cruise along their port side. I look dubiously at the box of flares sitting on the deck. I'm doubtful of our ability to lob them over the net as I pass one each to Bosun and Chad, and hang onto a third one for myself.

'You'll need to get real close,' Chad shouts at Bosun, who is lining us up for a pass. As we ease alongside, each of us takes our turn in throwing, but all three hit the net and fall harmlessly into the water. It's not as though any of us are poor throwers, but rather a combination of a bouncing boat, no run-up, and a restrictive survival suit and lifejacket that render our arms all but impotent. Despite this, the Japanese crew, having witnessed our intent, think better of their strategy and veer away from the *Steve Irwin*. That just leaves my old nemesis, the *Shonan Maru*.

The piercing shriek of their LRADs greets us as we slowly approach. Chad starts yelling and pointing at the *Shonan Maru*, but his voice is swamped under the deafening noise. I follow the line of his arm. He's pointing at two crew who have silver tanks strapped on their backs. As we edge closer, I see both of them are holding impulse guns. We'd seen these on an earlier encounter with the *Shonan Maru*, and there ensued much speculation about what they were. An FBI agent in the US had eventually identified them for us. Normally, they're filled with pepper spray and used for crowd control. Today, it would seem, their role is to control us.

It's a careful path that Bosun weaves with our RIB. We dodge the water cannons as best we can, keep ahead of the impulse guns, and tolerate the constant howling from the LRADs. We finally make a run in and sling the last of our flares, but all we achieve is a solid pasting from their water cannons. Bosun steers back out to open water where we lick our wounds. The *Shonan Maru*, despite our pestering, remains obstinately just astern of the *Steve Irwin*. Chad looks down at me.

'Have you got anything else left Pete?'

I glance at the containers, most of them now empty. 'Not much. Just two bottles of butyric acid and that's it . . . We could always go and grab one of those new prop-foulers that Larry and I built,' I suggest.

Chad frowns at me. 'Paul wants these guys off his tail now. It'll take half an hour to sort a prop-fouler, and by then the chopper will be out of fuel.' I glance over at the *Shonan Maru*, which is now angling towards us. It feels like the hunter has become the hunted.

'OK then, let's go and hit them with this,' and I dig out one of the last two bottles.

The *Shonan Maru* is not an easy target, as nets surround almost all of its structure. Just the large exhaust stack and the upper bridge area remain exposed. 'I need you to get real close for this,' I shout at Chad. Bosun takes his time, dodging from side to side and keeping their anti-boarding crew moving. He makes two dummy runs on the starboard side, then deftly swings in astern and alongside them. We glide to just 15 metres away and I take my shot. The bottle hurtles up and shatters just beside the helm door, and we then veer off to port before the water cannons reach us.

'They fired their impulse guns,' Chad yells excitedly. I look back and three crew are busy scampering along the side. The *Shonan Maru* starts to drift and we pull away.

Chris in the helicopter sees his opportunity to land and comes hovering down onto the helipad, while we pull alongside the *Steve Irwin* ready for extraction. It's a happy team that climbs up the ladder and onto the safety of the main deck a few minutes later.

'Nice shooting, Pete,' says Chad, slapping me on the shoulder. He can hardly control the grin on his face.

'Hey bro, it was a good team effort. You and Bosun did a great job getting us in close.'

'I couldn't believe how powerful those water cannons were. I feel like I've done 10 rounds with Mike Tyson.'

I feel the same. My body is bruised, battered and fatigued, but it's also a glorious feeling. 'Yeah, but a lot of fun, though, eh?' I reply.

'You know Pete. That was the best fun I've had in ages . . . and what about that last shot of yours. You nailed them.' A crowd forms around us and we retell the stories of an amazing afternoon of activism. In the end we meander off to change, shower, feast and have a well-earned sleep.

The following morning our RIB crew is summonsed to Paul's office. We're thinking he's about to congratulate us, but the second I see his angry face I realise we're in trouble. There's a long silence as we move seats around and sit down in front of his desk. 'Have you seen this?' he says finally, handing me a press release from the whalers. I read the heading. *Three crew injured in violent Sea Shepherd attack*. I look up at Paul. He looks like the whole world is on his shoulders.

'No, Paul. This is the first I've seen of it.'

There's another awkward silence before he speaks.

'The *Shonan Maru* crew are claiming you injured three of them with a bottle of butyric acid.' I look over at Bosun and Chad who look as bewildered as I am.

I finally decide to tell him what little I know.

'Look Paul, I did land one bottle of butyric acid just behind the bridge, but I fail to see how it could injure anyone. The door was closed and no one was near where it landed.'

He sits there staring at us . . . at me mostly, and his fingers tap away nervously on his desk. Long seconds tick by, before Chad finally speaks.

'Actually, I think they might have injured themselves. I definitely saw them fire their impulse guns, the spray then engulfed them . . . and the next time I looked back, all three were scarpering away from the area and rubbing their eyes. I thought nothing of it at the time . . .' His voice trails off. Paul's demeanour shifts slightly, and he leans forward in his chair.

'Did we get this on film?' We all just shrug our shoulders. We rarely see any of the footage anyway. Paul dismisses us and we wander back to the mess.

I make a strong espresso and sit on the floor in front of the little bar heater. The warm glow of radiating heat is welcome, but the meeting with Paul has darkened my mood. I'm positive I never injured anyone. The more I think about the shot, the more convinced I become that I'm right. Or perhaps, as Chad suggests, they injured themselves. In which case, they're still wrong.

Battle stations

I think of Paul trying to manage this crazy juggernaut that is Sea Shepherd. I don't envy him his job at all. I ran *Earthrace* for several years, and yet my team was tiny — 30 at the most, and normally only 10 to 15. That was tough enough. Paul has got hundreds of volunteers, multiple boats, and campaigns against a determined and well-funded enemy, which, after today's press release it would seem, is also dishonest. It's almost like there are two wars going on — the first is fought down here on the water, a battle to physically stop the slaughter of whales. But there is a second war going on — it is fought through battles in images and video clips, sound bites and press releases.

It's an hour later that crew member Monica comes bouncing up to me with a cheesy smile spread across her pretty round face.

'I've got something for you,' she says cheerily, laying her laptop down in front of me. She clicks the play icon, and a QuickTime movie starts to roll. It shows three crew on the *Shonan Maru*, two of them holding impulse guns. They fire the guns, then a few seconds later all three crew scamper forward, disappearing out of frame.

'Now I'm going to show you a close up,' she says, 'and I want you to watch what happens just after they shoot.'

I watch the video several times, and with each playing, my mood improves. The two crew holding impulse guns are facing forward. As they fire, a fine mist shoots out, but then it comes back over them, enveloping them temporarily in a small cloud. As it does so, all three appear to experience some discomfort. One of them bends over, as if in agony, while the other two both start frantically rubbing their eyes. 'There's your three injuries,' says Monica with conviction. 'They shot themselves.'

'Has Paul seen this?'

Monica nods her head.

'A-ha. He's working on a new press release as we speak. Let's just say his day is much improved.' Monica picks up her laptop and heads off, leaving me to reflect on what's been a crazy 24 hours.

Paul will land a few good hits with his press release and video —

a few more salvos in this ongoing media battle. It is a shame to see anyone injured down here, regardless of what side they're on. Whatever was in those guns, though, was intended for us, so perhaps they've only got themselves to blame.

Later that evening and I'm back in the mess thinking about things when Larry comes sauntering over.

'What ya working on?' he says cheerfully.

'Just mulling over how to board the *Shonan Maru*. Paul is still keen on the idea. But, today. Man, we couldn't even get close. With water cannons, nets, spikes and now pepper spray, it'd be a small miracle to ever get aboard that thing.' Larry just nods his head as he chews something. 'I'm starting to think that the only way will be to sneak up on them after dark.'

Larry raises his eyebrows.

'Boarding a vessel, at night, and while it was moving, that'd be a big ask.' He struggles getting the words out because he's so busy chewing.

'What are you eating, bro?'

There's a furtive glance as he scans the room. He then whispers in a conspiratorial voice, 'Check this out,' and he pulls from his pocket a half-eaten packet of biltong. This is dried beef favoured by South Africans, and while such products would be OK on most other boats, on a Sea Shepherd vessel, they're strictly forbidden. Larry slides the packet back into his pocket.

'I'm South African, right. And in South Africa even chicken is a vegetable. It's just against our genetic makeup to go vegan. I was moaning about this to one of the Animal Planet guys and he slipped me this biltong.' There's a sly little grin on Larry's face.

'You get caught by one of the chefs with that bro and you're dead meat, excuse the pun.'

'Look. It was God who put man at the top of the food chain. I see no point in going against his wishes and climbing to the bottom of it.' He pulls out a sliver and dangles it at the front of my nose. 'You wanna bit?'

Battle stations

It feels like being back at school and one of the kids has snuck a bottle of their dad's whisky into the class. You're offered a swig and the appeal is more in the fact that it's forbidden rather than the actual taste of it. I look at the sliver, but Larry suddenly says, 'Too slow,' and shoves it into his expectant gob.

Larry chews his cud for a bit and then starts mumbling, 'Going back to the *Shonan Maru* boarding, what are you thinking?'

'Well, I figured we'd go when it's pitch-black and use the night-vision goggles so we can see what we're doing.'

Larry nods, 'Jet-ski or RIB?'

'Mmm. Not sure, really. Probably one of the RIBs.'

He ponders this for a bit while he chews. 'You know, the trouble with those RIBs is the big metal frames sticking up in the air. As soon as we get close, they'll start clanging against the spikes down the side of the *Shonan Maru*. We may as well just take a big bell and start clanging it as we approach.' He pauses for a few seconds.

'The other thing with the RIBs, I reckon, is they'll pick us up on the radar. All that metal. You're probably only going to get one crack at this, and for my money it's gotta be the jet-ski. They definitely won't pick us up on the radar, and we've also got a chance of slipping between or under all those spikes . . . still not easy, but . . .'

We sit there in silence for a bit. Various crew are coming and going through the mess, and Larry has decided he's had enough biltong, or perhaps he's getting twitchy about being caught.

'Oh I nearly forgot,' he says suddenly. 'Check this out,' and he hands over the knife he's been working on.

The blade is about 25 centimetres long, with the biggest serrations I've ever seen. It curves in on itself, a bit like a sickle, except the end is rounded so you can't spear anything with it; a ferocious rope-cutter that was made by Schrade in the US specifically for Sea Shepherd. It came with no handle, though, so Larry has spent the last three nights beavering away on it in the workshop. What he's made is quite remarkable. He's fashioned two brass plates to mate against the blade base, with wooden surfaces that mould onto the plates and then has it all held together with neatly recessed stainless steel bolts.

'A work of art, Mr Routledge,' I say, as I roll the weapon over in my hands.

'I've just gotta oil the wood and she's all finished.'

He's a talented lad, young Larry. At times, in fact, he more resembles a gnome. Not a garden gnome, though . . . maybe a workshop gnome . . . and a very practical one at that. Lately he's been wearing his 5XL Sea Shepherd sweatshirt, which is about five sizes too big for him. His stumpy arms can hardly poke out of the end of the sleeves even when they're rolled up. He's wearing the hood over his head, and as I pass the knife back to him he's looking just like the Grim Reaper — or maybe the 'Gnome Reaper'. I give him my thoughts on this, but he's unmoved, preferring perhaps to be thought of as a bull elephant.

'Hey, any news on the new *Ady Gil*?' he asks, changing the subject.

'Nah, nothing recently. I'm not actually sure Ady has the coin to fund a new boat. The initial budget was five million, but with it being a boat you can bet that'll blow out to at least seven or eight.'

Larry frowns.

'Wow! Big money. Maybe you should tee up some appointments with a few billionaires and pitch it to them.'

'Nah mate. I don't connect with them.'

Larry looks bewildered.

'Hell, you can sell bloody ice to Eskimos, 'course you can sell it to them.' Larry puts the knife down on the table between us.

'Here's the thing, bro. I actually don't like the lifestyles that most squillionaires lead. They spend their time owning and consuming as much of the world's resources as they can. He with the most toys wins: five cars, private jet, private helicopter, superyacht, three houses. All that resource tied up to maintain their lifestyle and I hate it. So on the very rare occasion that I get to meet such people, I can't help myself from telling them what a greedy bunch of bastards they are.'

'Couldn't you just pretend you like them?'

'Nah, but I can't. My true feelings always come through. I'm just the wrong guy when it comes to selling to fat cats.'

'Yeah, well what about Ady Gil?'

'He's the exception. He is loaded, but he's also got a massive heart, and he really does care about the planet, which is more than I can say for most people in his league.'

Larry smiles, 'Hey remember him peeling those spuds when we crossed the Tasman?'

I laugh at the memory. He'd joined us on the Auckland to Hobart leg and he was as crook as a dog for the first few days. On day three, I told him that he was cooking dinner, but it was still pretty rough and every time that he got going, a wave would smack us and all of the food kept going on the floor. Eventually, he decided to just work on the floor. There is a classic photo of him sitting down in the galley, naked aside from a manky old pair of Y-fronts, peeling potatoes. He looked like a bloody punkawallah. I remember thinking at the time that all of his dignity was gone — what remained was the essence of the man. All the money in the world didn't matter. He was just the same as the rest of us . . . for a few days at least. Boats can be great levellers like that.

'I tell ya Larry, if all of the fat cats had hearts like Ady, the world would be a better place.'

'Yeah, be a damned mad house too, though,' and he laughs.

'Back to those fat cats bro, most of them just don't care about the planet. They're just too busy buying stuff. I remember when we took *Earthrace* to Palma, in the middle of the Mediterranean. We were docked smack in the middle of the biggest, fattest, most ostentatious bunch of superyachts I've ever seen. A journo came down to see us and there were the usual questions. Then she asked what we did that was environmentally any better than any other boats. Even a blind weta with no feelers could spot lots of things. Anyway, I rattled off a list of about 20 things, and the last one I mentioned was recycling . . . we had four recycling bins on the boat you see. She was dubious if this was anything special and so I made a wager with her for a dozen bottles of wine that less than a quarter of the superyachts there would have any form of recycling bins on board. Well, the silly tart took me up on the bet, and we spent the next couple of hours traipsing through all these gin palaces. There was a total of 20 that let us on, and amazingly, not a single one had any form of recycling on board. Not one!

'These are not small boats either. The largest was 90 metres long and employed 47 people. The amount of crap that goes through these boats in a day is amazing, but sadly, most of it just ends up at the tip. I already knew few of them had any recycling on board. The marina manager had proudly shown me their recycling facility and it was actually pretty sharp. They had bins for metal, glass, plastic, paper, organic and rubbish. And they were all empty except for the rubbish bin — which was overflowing with glass, cans, paper and plastic. The point I'm making is that the owners of these yachts just don't give a toss. If they did, they wouldn't own a superyacht in the first place.'

Larry is deep in thought.

'Well, when the revolution comes, they can be the first ones lined up against the wall,' he says.

'I'm not sure the revolution will involve guns and tanks, or your knife for that matter, but sooner or later we gotta realise that the way we're treating this planet is unsustainable. I had a decent chat to the first mate on that monster boat. Apparently, they travelled to the Caribbean and back, and all so the owner would have a weekend entertaining four mates and a few high-class Miami hookers. The voyage used two million litres of fuel and all for a few beers and some slap and tickle. It's just obscene.'

A couple of crew have decided to sit down and listen to me ranting. I'm in full swing, though. And I'm talking to the converted.

'I reckon the owners are starting to realise there's a problem, but instead of reducing their habits, they just hide within this new state called 'Richistan'. It has no borders, aside from the barbed wire fences and security guards that surround them in their exclusive marinas, airports, resorts and tax havens around the world. The only contact they have with ordinary people is the slap on the arse they give their personal stewardesses who are unfortunate enough to have to serve them. It's a club full of billionaires with hidden identities.'

'I remember a few years back a famous sportsman had a new boat built. It was some super flash behemoth. He pranced around this thing in Sydney Harbour and all the TV crews filmed him, and the public ogled at his ostentatious display of success. In years to come, we won't be photographing people like that . . . we'll be throwing rocks at them . . . and rightly so. Although maybe we'll never get near them, because they'll be hidden behind security fences.'

'Maybe we can ram them from a Sea Shepherd boat.'

'Consumption today is based on economic right. If the super rich have the money to buy millions of litres of fuel for their superyachts or 747s, no one questions it. In the future, though, we will also ask the question as to whether or not they have the moral right to do so. And if you ask me, that day can't come soon enough.

'The trouble that the squillionaires have is they have the most to lose with such a shift. If it is no longer acceptable to have all their toys, they'll have their wings severely clipped, whereas for your average bloke in the street, consuming a little less may not be so onerous. So it is perhaps understandable why the fat cats hate this talk of the environment. And that, Mr Routledge, is also why when I meet said fat cats and I try to get them to start thinking about the planet, or perhaps parting with a little of their riches, I invariably fail.'

Larry picks up his knife and he's about to leave.

'So did ya get ya wine off the journalist in Palma?'

'Nah bro. She pissed off and I never saw her again.'

He laughs and scurries off. I look up at the clock. 'Oops, I'm late for my shift.'

It's two minutes after midnight as I clamber up the stairs towards the bridge of the *Steve Irwin*. The entrance is lit with a single dull red light bulb. Locky looks at his watch and frowns as I enter. He's already started the handover to Vincent.

'Here's the *Nisshin Maru*,' he says, pointing at the radar 'Here's the *Bob Barker*, and this up here is a big iceberg,' and he points to a big blob about 20 miles away. 'So watch out for "growlers" as we get close to it.' Locky then disappears, leaving Vincent and me to take care of the next four hours.

'What kind of music you into?' says Vincent, as he pulls out his MP3 player and plugs it in.

'Dub, house, electronic, trance,' I reply.

Vincent scowls. 'There's none of that crap on here mate,' he says with a thick Australian drawl. 'How about Credence Clearwater?' Without waiting for an answer the music starts. He saunters back over to the captain's chair and his ample body moulds into it. His head starts bobbing around.

He's a big man . . . maybe 120 kilos and 195 centimetres tall. Some would probably call him big-boned. He's wearing black cowboy boots that give him a few extra centimetres in height . . . like he needs it! His black jeans are held up with a black belt and a big Texan buckle. His black skivvy is tucked into his pants, which are pulled up way too high. I've noticed a lot of men pull their jeans up in proportion to their age. Looking at Vincent, his will be buckled above his ample bosom in a few years. I chuckle at the thought, but say nothing.

'Hey, you still thinking about boarding the *Shonan Maru*?' he asks, breaking the silence. I nod my head at him.

'If you actually manage it, you realise they'll probably lock you up and throw away the key, that's assuming the *Shonan Maru* crew don't kill you in the meantime.'

'You trying to cheer me up or what?'

'I just want you to know what you're in for. Prison is not some hi-de-hi holiday camp for the elderly you know . . . and especially not in Japan. Have you ever been locked up before?'

I look over at Vincent who has a concerned look on his face.

'Yeah I was locked up in Libya for a short time. And also in Guatemala. So I don't think that Japan will hold too many surprises for me. How about you?'

Vincent starts laughing. 'Actually, I was locked up briefly last year. It's all because I've got a big head, you see.'

Vincent starts explaining to me his last run-in with the law. Apparently, his head is big. Looking at him, it's not just big, it's massive, made to look even bigger with the scruffy beard he's sporting. His head is so big, in fact, that there are no motorcycle helmets big enough to fit him. Now last year, Vincent bought himself a big Harley, no doubt the bike of choice for baby boomers wearing black leather jackets with tassels and their jeans pulled up to their bosoms. So he's riding around town and gets pulled over by a copper who doesn't believe the 'big-head' story. So Vincent gets all lippy and the next thing he finds himself behind bars. Thankfully, when it got to court, someone managed to produce a tape measure and it was confirmed that, yes, Vincent does indeed have an extremely large noggin. Not that I would have thought a tape measure was necessary.

'I don't think you've got a big head,' I say to him cheekily. 'It's perfectly in proportion with ya belly.' I laugh at the joke. Vincent just smiles and pats his stomach affectionately.

'How'd ya get so big on a vegan diet anyway?'

Vincent winces. 'I'm not vegan mate. I'm vegetarian. I love my chocolate and cheese too much.'

'Well, even vegetarians would struggle building a belly you've somehow managed to pack away. I bet there's a well-worn path between your front door and the local fish'n'chip shop.'

'Not a chip shop. A pub more like it. And while I might be big, at least I'm not a "sheep shagger".'

It was only a matter of time, of course. Australians can only take stick from Kiwis for so long before they'll resort to their old favourite.

'Well, you should know, you've got three times as many sheep as we have,' I reply.

'Yeah, well we've got five times as many people as you, so per capita, you lot are the kings of sheep shagging.'

I look over at Vincent. He has a smug look on his face and his head is still bobbing a little to the music; although now I think it's Johnny Cash.

'Well, here's a question for you then Vincent. Apparently, your koalas are dying from chlamydia, a sexually transmitted disease that for some reason in Australia has made the jump from man to marsupial. Now how do you think that happened?'

'Oh that's a cheap shot,' he replies. 'Actually, joking aside, our koalas are in real trouble. That disease is continuing to spread and there are worries about the population being wiped out.'

'Well, of course it's continuing to spread. The promiscuity of the Australian male will ensure that the disease spreads to all corners of your fair land.'

'Oh, turn it up.'

I wander over to the MP3 player and start scanning down the Artists, but nothing grabs me. I'm about to give up when I spot a lone iPod tucked away against the windscreen.

'Easy there, Pete,' says Vincent immediately. 'Nothing too radical.'

I scan down and it's a treasure trove of goodies, relative to Vincent's 'Solid Gold Hits' of the '60s.

'It's gotta have a guitar, bass and drums,' says Vincent, as if to remind me, 'no electronica.'

I settle on Muse and press 'Play', and Vincent immediately starts moving around excessively in his chair, almost in time. I'm not quite sure if he's taking the piss or not. He'd be a funny dancer, I reckon. Thinking about it, he probably doesn't dance any more. He'd stand by the bar with his tasselled leather jacket, an old dark beer that needs chewing before ya swallow and a staunch look on his face. And in his younger days, his dancing would have been limited to dry-grinding the odd slapper.

Not that I can boast about any dancing prowess in nightclubs. I remember many years ago when Sharyn and I were in London and we went out on a crazy pub-crawl for my brother's birthday. We ended up in some underground club at 3am and someone filmed us all dancing. Now, I'd always thought I was a 'super-cool' dancer, but after viewing the video footage the following day, I was somewhat horrified to discover that I was totally useless. My arms and legs were all over the place, and my head moved like it was on another body altogether. You could also just tell that I was left-handed. Somehow it just all looked wrong. Since then, I've decided I don't care, and I imagine that, these days, I look even worse.

Vince stops his seat-dancing and looks at me disapprovingly.

'None of this electronic crap. I'd never be seen dead in a club playing this shite. The place would be full of gay men in pink lycra trying to pick me up.' He then shakes his head as if to say, 'No thanks.'

'Look Vince, I don't think you'd have anything to worry about. Gay blokes seem to like clean-shaven bodies with a bit of muscle tone, whereas yours looks more like a wombat looking for a Weight Watchers' clinic. And with that big engine of yours, not to mention ya big head, I just don't think there will be a big queue of blokes lining up for your affections.'

'Yeah, well let's hope not. Although it seems you're the expert in this field.'

'Actually, Vince, there'll be one bloke with an eye for ya. He'll be wearing black leather shorts with the bum cut out, no top, a studded dog collar, and a leash . . . and a billiard ball strapped into his mouth.' I start laughing before I've finished and it even warrants a chuckle from Vincent.

We sit there with the music for company and the miles tick by. At 2am, we pass the iceberg. It's pitch-black, though, so a blob on the radar is all we see of it. Vincent decides he wants his ancient music so puts his player back on.

'Hey, going back to this *Shonan Maru* boarding, when are you looking at doing it?'

I haven't really figured that out yet. I wander over to the weather computer and look at the long-range forecast. There's a big high coming in a few days and it might extend down far enough to give us some decent weather.

Forecasting for Antarctica is tricky, though. There are only a few weather stations, so forecasters have limited data to work on. It's also very volatile down here and there are numerous mini-systems that the forecasting programs are unable to predict with any degree of accuracy. For what it's worth, however, it looks pretty decent.

'Well, Vince,' I finally answer him. 'I reckon in three to four days, you'll be looking for a new quartermaster to complement your copious abilities.'

'And you'll be strapped out on the deck of the *Shonan Maru* with a big Japanese bloke spanking your arse. Ha ha.'

The following day, Larry and I are in the mess taking a closer look at the forecast.

'This high here,' I say to Larry, pointing at an anticyclone on the screen of my Acer laptop, 'may just give us a brief respite in the weather.' The high should scrape over us in two days, but it's followed by a nasty depression that will stir things up for some time.

'When do you reckon it'll pack up?' says Larry. I click 'Play' and we watch the simulation several more times.

'Three days maximum I reckon.'

'Well, best we get rid of your sorry little arse in two then, eh?'

We start going through the Animal Planet video footage of the *Shonan Maru*. The hardest part seems to be finding a place to board without getting speared by the anti-boarding spikes.

'What about here?' says Larry pointing at the port stern quarter. I watch the vessel roll, and the spikes stay well above the water, so at least we wouldn't get speared in the process. There's no visible foothold, so I'd have to climb up, initially just using my arms. Under normal circumstances this would be OK, but I'll be restricted by the dry suit, as

Earthrace becomes the *Ady Gil*. How to make the coolest boat in the world even cooler.

Ady Gil being lifted back into the water after the refit.

The helm of *Ady Gil*. More like a race car than a boat.

Ady Gil on her way to the Poor Knights Marine Reserve in New Zealand.

Trying to look cool in Hobart before leaving for Antarctica. The Mustang combat suits were the best pieces of kit we had. From left: Me, Larry Routledge and Mike Smith.

Xavier Rudd plays at the Walk Against Warming march in Tasmania, Australia. A 'hamster' dances in the foreground.

Mike Smith comes to grips with cooking vegan meals.

Simeon Houtman

This little guy landed right next to the *Animal Planet* cameraman and hung around for half an hour. Towards the top of the iceberg you can see a dark line, probably ash from an eruption thousands of years ago.

Jason Stewart

We ran out of fresh water, so we started picking up pieces of ice and melting them. The pieces pictured here are from the main ice shelf and probably date back 10,000 years.

Mike Smith having his weekly bath. Water temperature was -1°C. Thirty seconds was too long.

Three humpback whales play around the *Ady Gil* for half an hour. An amazing day for all the crew and something we will always cherish.

Mike demonstrating how NOT to hold a bow and arrow.

James Burrowes lines up the *Nisshin Maru* factory ship with our potato launcher. The whalers hated this device and it was confiscated by the police when the *Steve Irwin* arrived back in Australia.

The lads at work . . . towing a prop-fouler and using the laser.

Ady Gil crew preparing the prop-fouler with the *Shonan Maru* in the background.

Hassling the *Nisshin Maru*. If you can keep near this vessel, whaling stops.

Waving goodbye to the *Bob Barker*, just minutes before the ramming. In the background is a *Yushin Maru* harpoon vessel.

Ady Gil and the *Shonan Maru* just before the ramming.

Ady Gil seconds after the ramming. Note the bow of the *Ady Gil* on the right side of the image.

Recovering gear off the *Ady Gil* just after we were rammed.

Ady Gil sliced in two. The *Shonan Maru* crew in the background check out their handiwork.

Ady Gil under tow from the *Bob Barker*.

The 'Gill-billies'. We're like cockroaches — you can squash us but you can't kill us. From left: Mike Smith, Laurens de Groot, James Burrowes, me, Jason Stewart and Simeon Houtman.

The Gill-billies celebrate being alive after the ramming. From left, and clockwise around the table: Jason Stewart, James Burrowes, Mike Smith, Laurens de Groot and me.

Bob Barker in pursuit of the whalers in Antarctica.

Launching one of the RIBs on the *Bob Barker*. Fiona McCaig is clearly happy about something.

The wildlife in Antarctica is incredible. The *Steve Irwin* s behind the iceberg and the *Delta* is in the foreground.

The *Delta* being launched for action from the *Steve Irwin*.

Helicopter crew removing the blades with the *Shonan Maru* in hot pursuit. The whalers tried to hose the chopper down several times.

Getty

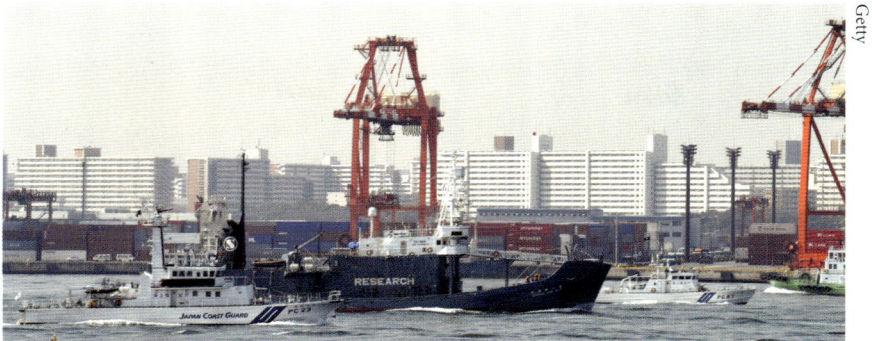

The *Shonan Maru* — with its special piece of human cargo — coming into Tokyo Bay under coastguard escort.

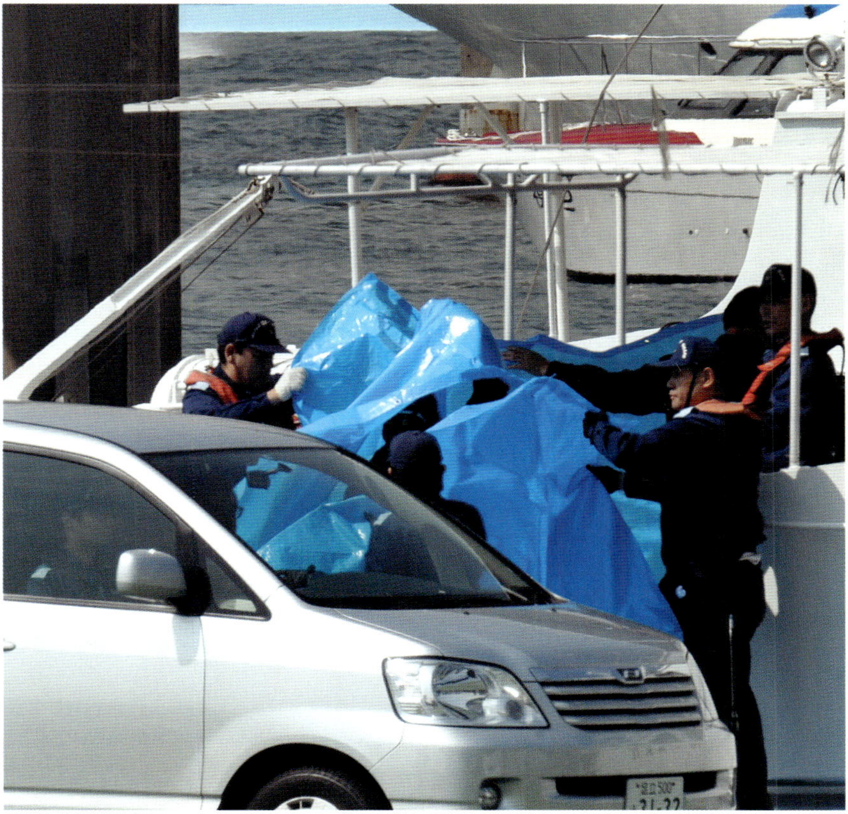

Getty

I'm escorted off the *Shonan Maru* under the 'tarpaulin tunnel'.

This placard says it all . . .

Fronting the media in Auckland after being deported from Japan.

well as weighed down with all my gear. I frown and explain this to him but, sadly, it seems like the best place.

We move on to the last video clip, which was shot the previous day by Chris in the helicopter.

'Aha,' says Larry. 'Look at this. There's a spike now missing down the port side.' Above the spike is a big Yokohama fender.

'What's the bet they removed the spike when they refuelled last time and they forgot to put it back. That gap looks about four metres, and our jet-ski is only three and a half metres long. So, with a bit of luck, I could squeeze us alongside there.'

We look at the location from several different angles and we go back over the old footage. It's a tight fit, but it seems like our best and only option.

'This is it, Pete,' Larry says finally.

'Yeah, but what if they've put the spike back since the footage was shot?'

Larry pauses for a few seconds. 'Then you'd need to be Spiderman to ever get aboard that thing.'

I sit there looking at Larry and, for some reason, the memory of him falling off the log and breaking his ribs comes back to me.

'I hope you can drive the SeaDoo better than you straddle logs.' I say to him.

He laughs. 'I got the easy job. You just worry about how you're gonna climb up that thing.'

Larry scurries off to get himself a coffee while I start working out timing for our wee adventure. At the moment, despite being a long way away from it, we are actually on Fremantle time, which has sunset at 4am and sunrise at 7am. In two days we'll be some 600 nautical miles further west so all of these times will be delayed by about an hour.

Larry comes back with his mug of espresso.

'How does six o'clock departure sound?' I say to him.

'Based on what?'

'Well, we leave the *Steve Irwin* at 6am, which will have me aboard the *Shonan Maru* at about 6.30am, which should be the darkest bit of the night.'

Larry nods, taking a wee sip from his mug.

'What about the moon?'

'No. Won't affect us. The moon sets at 3am.'

'Well, then 6am kickoff it is.'

The final bit we work on is a list of gear, and as we dissect the mission, it steadily grows. Dry suit, Weezle undersuit, thermal top, thermal pants, thermal socks, night vision goggles, lifejacket, hand-flare, strobe light, torch, knife, dive boots, gloves, hood, GPS tracker, VHF radio, Epirb.

For Larry it's an even bigger list. In addition he'll have a video camera strapped to his helmet, an emergency radar transponder and a secure VHF radio. He'll also have a hand-held device that will give him direction to my location if I should fall into the water and then back to the *Steve Irwin* once he's dropped me off . . . and the SeaDoo, of course.

We sit there for a while, trying to think of anything else.

'Mind if I join ya?' says Vincent, and he plonks himself down beside me. He's got two bananas with him. He places one on the table and starts to peel the other one. I frown at him and shake my head.

'What!' he says indignantly.

'Bananas are bad luck on boats,' I reply seriously.

'Oh piss off,' he says and proceeds to stuff the banana into his mouth. Although if his mouth is in proportion to his head, I expect that he can fit an entire box of Chiquita bananas in there.

There's actually a small amount of logic behind boats and bananas not mixing well. Back in the eighteenth century, scurvy was a common disease among mariners who spent sustained periods at sea. Their diet often consisted of little more than biscuits, canned meat and rum. They didn't realise it at the time, but it was the lack of vitamin C and a few other elements that was causing the disease.

Now Captain Cook, incidentally one of the greatest mariners of all time, discovered that if his crew ate fruit and vegetables, the scurvy disappeared. So the boats then started loading up with all manner of fresh produce and, in the tropics, this included bananas. Most fruit as it ripens emits gases. Which is OK, except those coming from the evil bananas made all of the other fruit ripen too quickly. The result was many boats suddenly found that all their food had rotted, and instead of having scurvy as a problem, now it was starvation. Of course, scurvy would be the lesser of the two evils. Captain Cook, being the man that he was, figured all this out, too, and so bananas were banned from his boats. Since that time, a great many captains refuse to allow bananas on their boats and, even today, the superstition of bananas bringing bad luck remains.

On *Earthrace*, I've always banned bananas, but occasionally some overzealous crew member, or a sneaky one, will ferret a few on board. Of all the terrifying experiences that we had, a number of them occurred when the 'devil's fruit' was at hand. Some Colombians opened fire on us thinking we were drug runners, and we ended up with a few bullet holes in the hull to remind us. We also had Somalian pirates open fire in our direction as we headed into the Red Sea. And off the coast of Guatemala we had a fatal collision with an unlit fishing skiff and I was detained under armed guard in a military camp for nine days. Granted it's not an entirely scientific study, but I still hate bananas on boats.

I explain all of this to Vincent, but he remains unmoved.

'Never heard that before,' he says as he's peeling his second banana. He finishes his snack and heads off while Larry and I work on completing our list.

At midnight I head up to the bridge for what I'm hoping will be my last watch with Vincent. The time passes incredibly slowly, though, and I'm a happy camper as I finally slide into my scratcher just after 4am.

Sleep doesn't arrive. I toss and turn as the excitement and tension surrounding the boarding grows in me, and at 8am I just give up and head down for breakfast.

Most of my day, thankfully, is spent getting everything prepared. By dinnertime, I'm ready to rock. The only niggling worry I have is about the batteries on our night vision goggles. We're on our last pair, having used the others up while looking for icebergs on the *Ady Gil*.

After dinner I head back to my room and there's an animated discussion between Larry and one of the cameramen from Animal Planet. Larry looks up at me.

'The only cameraman willing to go tonight is this big "doofer",' he says pointing at Joe.

Now I had perhaps foolishly agreed to take a cameraman, but both Larry and I have concerns about it. Three lads on a jet-ski is a tall order, so I'd requested the smallest person they had.

'At 190 centimetres and 105 kilograms, Joe, you are hardly the midget cameraman we asked for.'

Joe shakes his head wearily. 'The others have all backed out. I'm the only one prepared to go.'

'Then we'll go without a cameraman,' I reply. 'I don't really care if you film it or not. And, if anything, taking even a small cameraman was pushing it.'

'But I thought the SeaDoo was some super grunty top of the line beast?' protests Joe.

'Look bro, that thing pulls like a schoolboy. It's got 260 horsepower cranking out. Horsepower ain't the problem. It's stability. Three of us make it top heavy, especially with a big bugger like you perched on the back.'

Joe shakes his head and wanders off mumbling, and a few minutes later he's back, but this time with Monica in tow. I'm not actually sure what her role is with Animal Planet, although it would seem her present role is to charm Larry and I into agreeing to take Joe.

'He's too bloody big,' I say to her before she's even opened her mouth. 'Send ya smallest cameraman.'

She puts on her soft purring voice. 'Look Pete, the cameramen are all worried sick about this mission, and frankly I don't blame them. Right now, Joe is the only one prepared to go. If you don't take him then we don't get the footage.'

'Yeah, well I got no problem with that.'

'Yes, but Paul has already agreed to taking the cameraman.' Monica is leaning forward, and her ample breasts are bulging out the front of her top. She looks at me pleadingly then back at Larry.

'Look Monica, Paul will back me whatever my decision is on this. If I don't want to take Joe, he'll accept it.'

She sits down on Larry's bunk and sighs. What he'd do to coax her in there for a night, I wonder slyly.

'Pete. This story will be really important in the TV series. Next to the *Ady Gil* ramming, it'll be the biggest story we have. I'm begging you to reconsider.'

'Monica, my job tonight is to board the *Shonan Maru*, not to film a TV series. Taking Joe just jeopardises the whole mission.'

'Please Pete.'

I let out a sigh and sit down on my bunk. I look over at Larry, but he's too busy perving at Monica.

'I tell ya what I'll do. When we load the jet-ski, I'll take Joe for a couple of minutes and see how it handles. If it's OK, I'll take him. If not, I'll drop him back. And if I do drop him back, you gotta promise me you wont bitch and moan about it.'

A big smile erupts on her face.

'You and Animal Planet both owe me on this, OK? . . . And Joe, no eating anything from now, and you gotta have a big dump before we leave.'

He smiles nervously. The two of them gather themselves up and they wander back down the hallway. We watch them, deep in discussion about camera gear, no doubt . . . or perhaps liability insurance.

'She's got a dodgy back,' I say to Larry.

He frowns at me. 'What ever makes you say that?'

'See how she walks. It's kinda lopsided. I bet she's got some problem with her spine.'

'Well, I don't know much about her spine, but she's got a good rack,' Larry giggles and we cram back into our cabin.

'She had you wrapped around her little finger, didn't she, Pete?'

'We are but simple creatures, Mr Routledge.'

Larry picks up a VHF radio, and starts strapping it to his buoyancy vest. 'Hey what do you reckon about taking Joe?'

'I think he's too big. More to the point, I think he's soft. First sign of trouble and he'll be whimpering for us to call it off. He'll crap himself so much he'll probably end up with no footage anyway.'

'Hmm. My thoughts, too. Let's do this. We'll take him out for a couple of minutes on the jet-ski and if either of us decides we don't wanna take him, we drop him back — no questions asked. OK?'

Larry nods his head and goes back to his radio. I start doing one last check of my gear, when Larry turns to me.

'Hey did I ever tell you about my mate who did some time in a Japanese prison?'

'No. What happened to him?'

'Well, he got sentenced to six months in some hellhole in Tokyo. And on the first night, he was really worried about getting molested or something. He was placed in a two-man cell, with some big, fat sumo wrestler on the bottom bunk, and my mate was on the top. Anyway, about half an hour after lights out, my mate is just starting to relax a bit, when this sumo wrestler suddenly says, "Hey, you know what happens at night in prison eh?" My mate is all worried, of course, and he's not quite sure what to say. Eventually, he replies, "Umm . . . yes." The next thing the sumo wrestler says is, "Well, do you wanna be Mummy, or do you wanna be Daddy?"

'My mate is now crapping himself, but he decides if he's forced into anything, he'd rather be Daddy. "Umm . . . I'd rather be Daddy, thank you." The sumo wrestler then leans out from under his bunk, looks up at my mate, who is terrified, and says, "OK then Daddy. Come down here and suck Mummy's c**k".' Larry bursts out laughing. 'Honestly, Pete, it's a true story.' And he carries on laughing.

'Come on bro, you're supposed to be cheering me up.'

Battle stations

But Larry can't stop laughing.

I have one last check of all my gear and then clamber into my bunk to chill out. There's no point in trying to sleep, so I just lie there mulling things over. At 3.30am, Larry heads off to get the SeaDoo rigged up to the crane, and with nothing better to do, I decide to go and abuse Vincent, for hopefully the last time.

'Still got ya banjos playing?' I say as I wander into the helm. Vincent is leaning back in the captain's chair like he's King Muck. His MP3 player is putting out some dreadful hippy track from the '60s. I plonk down in front of the radar.

'I'm gonna miss you, ya skinny little prick,' he says finally.

'I'm gonna miss you too, ya fat bastard.'

An engine room alarm sounds and Vincent hurries over to the control panel to reset it. He then collapses back into his chair. We sit in silence as the sun disappears behind the horizon.

'Hey, I've been so busy abusing you this last week bro, and yet I don't even know what you do.'

'What do you mean?' replies Vincent.

'Like, for a job. I'm assuming you've got some form of employment somewhere.'

Vincent looks somewhat surprised. 'Have a guess.'

'Hmm. Well, you ain't no ballet dancer, I'll wager dollars to doughnuts. Although with that big engine of yours, you could well be a belly dancer for Arab men. I hear they like a bit of meat on their men.'

'Oh turn it up,' he replies with feigned indignation.

'Seriously Vince, I wouldn't have a clue what you do. Other than being a bouncer at some night club catering to blokes in pink lycra suits, and where ya can solicit the occasional stray drunk at closing time, I wouldn't even hazard a guess.'

'Another cheap shot! In actual fact,' and there's a long pause, and Vincent looks at me, 'I'm a violin repairer.'

I burst out laughing. In a million years, I'd never have guessed that.

'You know Vince, you are one unique individual. I guarantee that you are the only 120-kilo violin repairer in the world, with a noggin the size of a beach ball, and a penchant for leather pants with the buttocks cut out. It does, of course, beg the question how on earth those cucumber-like fingers of yours ever manage the intricacies of repairing a finely tuned violin.'

'What's wrong with my fingers?' he says, holding up his hands and looking at them. His fingers are fat and stumpy, and the ends look like they were all cut off in a band-saw accident when he was a meat worker's apprentice.

'I'll bet ya Vince, and assuming ya digits have always been thus shaped, that ya mum gave up trying to teach ya to tie your own shoelaces. She decided it was easier to just tie them for you, until such time as puberty finally kicked in, and she then levered you out the front door and changed the locks. And since then you've been prancing around in your Daniel Boone cowboy boots, which of course have no laces.'

'Nonsense,' replies Vincent. 'These fingers are finely tuned machines. They are an extension of my mind.'

'Yeah, well, ya mind can do with all the extension it can get I expect.'

Vincent chuckles. 'You're awfully flippant tonight. Make the most of it, because this time tomorrow you'll be doing the bidding of Japanese security forces, with guns pointed at ya head . . . and it'll be you with the bottom cut out of ya pants.'

I just nod, not thinking of any witty retort.

'Hey, did you ever carry guns on *Ady Gil*?'

I climb out of my seat and wander over to the windscreen to check out the weather. 'When it was *Earthrace*, I always had a .308 semi-auto sniper's rifle and a couple of assault shotguns, but when it became the *Ady Gil*, I got the hard word from Sea Shepherd to ditch them, which pissed me off at the time. As the captain of a vessel, having a gun or two just gives you another option in protecting you and your crew, but ya hope ya never have to use them of course.'

Vincent nods his head. 'Well, did you ever use them?'

'Hmm . . . kinda. We've been shot at a couple of times. The first time, the Colombian Navy mistook us for drug-runners. They fired a few rounds into our hull. After that episode, though, I was always more careful in ensuring I had a couple of weapons on board. Then a while later, we were heading up into the Red Sea. There's this narrow gap between the Yemen and Somalia, and it's well known for piracy. Just as we reached the narrowest section, a little skiff with two 150-horsepower outboards started following us. As they pulled alongside us, they started signalling us to stop. It was five skinny little blokes. I put my foot down, but this little skiff was actually faster than we were, and they started coming right in close to my window. Next thing, they pulled out four AK47s and one of them fires a whole magazine clip above our heads. I could hear the Clap! Clap! Clap! as each round fired. I started weaving around, but this little skiff was way more manoeuvrable than we were. Then another one of them opens fire, emptying his magazine in the water beside us. There were these little spouts of water jumping up about a metre or so from the hull. Then the skiff came right in close to my window and I was looking down the barrels of four AK47s. I was just crapping my pants.

'I grabbed my navigator and we ran out the back with the G3 semi-auto and one of the shotguns, and as soon as they saw the firearms, they veered off. They followed us from about 100 metres away for a few more miles and then stopped. I tell ya, it was one of the most terrifying experiences I've ever had.'

'So ya never shot any of them?' Vincent sounds disappointed.

'Nah, but I'm sure that if I didn't have those guns on board, the outcome would be different.'

'Yeah, fair enough.'

'That's also why I felt a bit naked on the *Ady Gil* with no firearms.'

'Yeah, well, that hardly matters now of course, with the *Ady Gil* resting beneath two kilometres of water.'

'Indeed.'

I finish off my last session abusing Vincent, although it probably ends in a draw. Eventually, I shake his hand and head down to check on Larry.

'And don't come back ya sheep shagger,' Vincent yells as I walk out the door.

9
Boarding the enemy

It's pitch-black as I climb out the forward hatch and over to where Larry is busy with the jet-ski.

'Nearly ready,' he whispers to me as he connects the last strop onto the crane. I glance astern at the *Shonan Maru*'s lights a couple of miles away. 'In an hour I'm going to be sitting on the deck of that,' I reflect.

I walk over to the railing, and look out at the cold, black night. It sure looks uninviting. A breeze is now coming across our port side. Maybe 10 to 12 knots, which isn't that much, but it's the start of the depression that will be hitting us any time now.

'I hope this weather holds off another hour or so,' I say to Larry, but he's busy barking orders at the deck crew.

I pull my night vision goggles down over my eyes, and the black deck transforms into a green ant-hive of activity. There are at least a dozen people all frantically finalising things for us.

The jet-ski is hoisted beside the outside rail of the *Steve Irwin*, and Larry, Joe and I clamber on. A few seconds later, we're unceremoniously dumped onto the frigid Antarctic water. A quick blip on the throttle and the 260-horsepower SeaDoo roars into life and lifts us out onto the plane. Seconds later and we're astern of the *Steve Irwin* and heading for the *Shonan Maru*. It's a lumpy ride, with the waves and swell conspiring against us. I look back at Joe, who clings precariously onto the stern as we bash our way along. He's already given up all hope of filming by the looks.

The green glow of the *Shonan Maru* gradually grows in my night vision goggles.

'She's turning away from us,' yells Larry.

'Hopefully, just reacting to the *Steve Irwin* slowing,' I reply. 'I'd be amazed if they could pick us up on their radar in these conditions.'

We continue smacking our way through the waves for another 10 minutes, before finally catching up with the vessel that a month or so ago rammed and sank the *Ady Gil*. I scan the various deck levels, but there's no sign of life.

Larry gradually edges the SeaDoo towards the side of the *Shonan Maru*, but it's become the ride from hell. The wake from the boat is interacting with the waves and swell, and I can tell that boarding this boat is going to be tricky indeed. The *Shonan Maru* is rolling from side to side, and the dangerous metal spikes along her side rise and fall by several metres. I scan over our entry point where, thankfully, one spike is still missing. It's going to be a very tight fit squeezing in there.

Larry is lining up for the approach, when suddenly my goggles go blank. I switch them back on and the screen lights up for a second and then dies again. The cold here drains the batteries so quickly. I pull the goggles off and pass them to Larry.

'Look after these, bro.'

I look grimly at my entry point. In the darkness, it now just resembles a black hole.

'How am I ever going to manage this now?' I wonder. Even with the night vision it was a big ask. Larry does his best in battling the waves and we bash and bump our way closer to the behemoth beside us. I duck under one of the spikes, and there's a loud clunk as we smack into the side. Seconds later and we're tucked into the gap.

Well, it's now or never, and I stand up and lunge into the blackness. Reaching out with both arms, my left hand clutches onto something, while I kick away with my legs trying to get purchase on the side. The *Shonan Maru* then rolls back and a wave comes rushing up, grabs me and tears me away. I hurtle into the frigid waters and a short burst of cold sears down the back of my neck.

Suddenly, it's all very quiet as the *Shonan Maru* glides away. I'm gripped with fear as there's no sign of the SeaDoo. If Larry is still following the *Shonan Maru*, I could be in real trouble. I pull up the dog collar on my life vest and check it's still working. The little red LED blinks at me reassuringly. I then grab the emergency strobe light from my left arm and am about to turn it on when I hear the welcome rumble of the SeaDoo rotax engine idling towards me.

We lose a further minute or two as I clamber aboard, and for the second time tonight we're playing catch-up. There's a fear nagging the back of my mind, but it's not a fear of injury or falling, but rather of letting people down. Half the crew of the *Steve Irwin* have been working to get me into this position and now it's my turn to deliver. My first attempt wasn't even close.

Larry lines up our entry point again. I watch the *Shonan Maru* rolling in the swell. Up, up, up, down, down, down . . . and I leap. My left foot locates a ledge, while my arms reach out into the blackness. All feeling in my hands is gone, so I have no idea if they've grabbed onto anything or not. The vessel starts to roll back and for a second time, I start falling away from the boat. Then I suddenly feel a slight resistance on my left arm as the net pulls tight and, to my amazement, I stop falling. I cling there grimly, waiting for the roll back the other way. When it comes, I quickly get my left hand onto the steel beam behind the net, while with my right hand I grab the knife from the sheath on my right leg. On the next roll, I hack a big opening in the net, and then on the next roll, I step aboard the now infamous *Shonan Maru*.

I crouch down to keep hidden, then whisper into the VHF radio, 'The Kiwi has landed,' and it's a strange emotion that wells up inside me — a combination of relief in not letting the team down, exhilaration at having achieved something difficult, and trepidation at what now lies ahead of me.

The dark of the lower deck envelops me in a welcome embrace. I remain kneeling for several minutes, just watching and listening. The only sounds are the waves lapping the hull and a distant drone from the engines deep beneath me. I place the knife back in its scabbard then methodically go through my gear. My right glove came off when I fell in the water, but aside from that everything else is there and working.

I slowly creep forward to the ladder, stop for another minute listening, then ascend to the main deck. As I reach the top, there's a distinct smell of cigarette smoke. I stand there frozen, peering forward, but there's no sign of any activity. The smell is definitely fresh, so I patiently wait there trying to work out the source. I finally decide that it must be the air vent a few metres in front of where I'm hidden. Inching forward, I poke my nose (some would say of ample proportions) into the vent airstream, and sure enough the scent of cheap roll-your-own cigarettes floods my nostrils. I continue working my way forward, being careful to keep in the darkened areas.

I remember when I was a kid that the darkness could be quite intimidating, but at the moment it's like my best friend. There's a certain confidence in sneaking around in shadow, safe in the knowledge that as long as you're patient and careful, no one will find you.

The next ladder leads me up to bridge level and it takes several minutes to creep the last 10 metres to the helm doorway. My heart is thumping as I slowly raise my head and peek into the bridge. I feel like I'm a naughty boy perving into the girl's changing sheds.

One guy is standing looking at a chart table with a dim red light glowing above his head. Then there're three people in a row, one looking at the radar, one looking aimlessly ahead, and a really short guy who's but a metre from me, holding a pair of binoculars. I sit there patiently watching them. Every few minutes Shorty raises his binoculars and checks out the Sea Shepherd boat, now some three or four miles off to our starboard side.

As he lifts the binoculars for the fifth time, I test the door and, to my surprise, it's actually locked. Having seen enough, I retreat to the next doorway, and it too is locked. A few metres past this is a large hatch. I sit there studying the handles, and conclude there's just one holding it closed. I turn the handle and slowly open the hatch, but there's a horrible squeak from one of the hinges. I stand there peering through the small gap, ready to bolt, but no one appears. There's a light from the helm in the distance, a couple of closed doorways, then a stairway leading downstairs where there's a faint murmuring of voices. I close the hatch and climb to the upper deck.

Finding a dark corner, I pull out my little diver's torch and start going through my gear again. My right thumb is bleeding and, try as I might, I can't seem to stop it. In the end, I cover it with a few layers of duct tape and decide to ignore it. Both hands are frozen anyway. My jaw is also starting to ache. I don't remember injuring it, but I must have given it a smack when I fell off and into the water.

Next I remove the knife and scabbard from my right leg. There was much discussion about my knife on the *Steve Irwin*. Some even suggested I shouldn't be taking a knife — how I was expected to then cut through the net, I'm not really sure. Others had opined I should have thrown it overboard by now. It was a gift from my girls, though, and has been with me almost continuously for the last four years, so there's no way I was just going to chuck it away. But I also don't want to go barging in on the *Shonan Maru* crew with an obvious weapon. So in my infinite (some might say misguided) wisdom, I decide to hide it. I figure I'm in enough trouble already anyway and getting caught with a knife isn't going to make much difference. Crawling around the upper deck, I find a suitable box that looks like it's been undisturbed for a long time. I slide the knife under it, being careful not to leave any smears of blood in the vicinity.

I then fossick around the upper deck looking for a place to hide. In the end I settle for the Institute of Cetacean Research (ICR) banner, which is strung about 30 centimetres above deck level. I crawl underneath it, lie on my back, and close my eyes. I figure by now that Larry will be back on the *Steve Irwin*, so I give them a call on the VHF radio.

'Steve, Steve, Pete, Pete, over.' This is our elaborate code system with 128-bit encryption that the Japanese will never decipher. Steve is the *Steve Irwin*, and Pete is me, of course. Brilliant, eh? Shannon's sweet voice comes purring back on the radio, and it's like a breath of fresh air.

'Hey, we're all really worried about you Pete. Are you okay? Over.'

'Yeah, I'm fine. Hey, can you give us an update on Larry and Joe. Over.'

'They're fine. We're just retrieving the jet-ski now. Oh, Paul says "Well done", by the way. Over.'

'Roger that.'

There's a period of silence and then Peter Hammerstedt from the *Bob Barker* comes on. 'Hey, Pete, we just want you to know that we all support you, and we're really proud of what you've done. And our thoughts are with you.'

'Roger that.' As I click the transmit button on my radio, it's making an audible click on the whaler's radio. They've got a speaker on the upper deck here somewhere, and it's loud enough to make me nervous. I decide to stop the transmissions. The whalers have probably got a scanner and sooner or later they'd pick up our conversations, which we don't want.

I lie there soaking up an extraordinary experience. I still find it hard to believe that I am actually here. That moment when the net pulled tight on my second attempt was when I realised that I'd made it. I'll remember those few seconds for the rest of my life — from utter despair to total relief and all it took was a couple of frozen fingers clinging to a net that I couldn't see. For the last six weeks, I've been working on getting to this point and now finally I am here. Although I'm the one on the *Shonan Maru*, it was a real team effort to get me here — especially Larry who was outstanding. And Joe, much to my surprise, never moaned once. He maybe missed getting any footage, but he never caused us any grief either. I take it all back what I said about the big doofer.

As for Paul, I've finally had a 'well done' out of him. I know he's Spartan with his praise, so it's nice to finally have him pleased with my efforts. He was also fantastic in just letting me run the mission and making sure that everyone on the *Steve Irwin* just supported it. I feel privileged to be here in an odd kind of way.

An hour later and I'm still tucked up snugly beneath my banner. I've squeezed both hands underneath my black buoyancy vest and life has gradually returned to them. My jaw, though, is starting to really throb. Each pulse of blood sends a little shot of pain coursing through my nervous system. I doubt it's broken, but a little cracked maybe? Not much I can do about it, however, so I just try to ignore it.

There's the faint sound of a door closing, then scuffing noises on the lower deck. Inching over to the ledge and looking over, I see one of the crew wandering around. He checks various ropes and fittings. Probably just doing his morning rounds, I think to myself. He stops by their little Zodiac and looks up towards me. His face is round with a drooping moustache and a pointy beard dangling below his chin. He resembles Genghis Khan, with strong Mongoloid cheekbones and a warrior-like face. I lie there completely still as he scans the deck around me. Finally satisfying himself, he wanders off, back to the warmth inside the vessel no doubt.

The winds have increased. It's a good 15 knots, and the occasional gust to 20 knots. I look down at the waves and white water. No way could we do the boarding now. The weather, thank goodness, held off just long enough.

There's a low crackle over the radio, 'Pete, Pete, Steve, Steve. Over.' It's Shannon's cheerful voice again. She must be nearing the end of her shift.

'Hey, Pete, just letting you know that the chopper is on its way. Should be with you in a few minutes. Over.'

'Roger that.' There's a few seconds silence.

'Hey, and good luck there, Pete. We are all supporting what you have done.'

'Roger that. Thanks heaps. Over.'

There's the distant thud! thud! thud! of chopper blades as the little Hughes 300 comes racing towards me. My plan was to wait until first light before confronting the crew here. If I barged in during darkness, I'd scare the hell out of the crew. So, hopefully, with it being light now, they'll take it all OK. It's also given me the chance to have the chopper present. I figure they're less likely to do anything really crazy like beat me up, or throw me overboard, with the chopper watching. Finally, it gives Animal Planet a bit more footage to use. I don't really care for the TV series, although I know it's been very beneficial to Sea Shepherd. Not in terms of cash. In fact, Animal Planet pay virtually nothing for being here, but in terms of profile, it's been great for Sea Shepherd.

The chopper is hovering overhead when I climb out from under my banner. Surprisingly, none of the *Shonan Maru* crew has ventured outside. It's a biting cold Antarctic wind, so I guess with no small boats on their radar, they figure they're safe.

I walk down the stairs, along the side towards the helm door, and I glance up at the chopper. The cameraman is leaning out, filming.

'Monica, you owe me big time for this,' I mutter to myself. Seconds later and I'm in front of the door. We'd actually joked on the *Steve Irwin* that at this point I'd say, 'Hey is Peter Hammarstedt here?', look around and suddenly say, 'Oh sorry, wrong boat,' and run off back to the stern. Instead I just stand there looking in at them. Shorty is still on watch, and he jumps back as I appear in his binoculars. There's a mad rush of bodies scampering around, and a few hurried shouts from several crew members. They look like headless chooks, with no one really knowing what to do.

One of them with big popping eyes glares at me angrily, while the rest of them, for the most part, look terrified.

A little wee man, maybe in his fifties, comes timidly over to the door.

'Go away,' he says, and he tests the door to make sure it's still locked. I hold up to the window my Japanese note that explains I am unarmed and I am there to see the captain, but he just ignores it.

'Go away,' he says a second time.

'Look, if you don't let me in I'm just gonna go to your upper deck and start destroying all your electronics. And then I'll just wander in through one of your hatches anyway.' I stare at the little man. He looks at the crew behind him, back at me, and then shakes his head in disbelief. I wait there patiently for several more minutes before he finally unlocks the door and lets me in.

The helm is smaller than I had expected; less than half the size of the *Steve Irwin*'s. There's eight people all squeezed into the tiny space. Popeye continues his aggressive glare at me, while the rest of them glance around nervously and look at the floor. Funnily enough, I'd been really worried about this moment. I'd had visions of being beaten up, or pissing my pants in fear, and yet standing here, I'm hardly worried at all. The crew here have arrogantly chased our boats around the Southern Ocean and destroyed mine as part of their aggressive campaign; in person, they're a bunch of pussies. It's easy to be tough when you're on the helm of an 800-ton whaling vessel with water cannons and LRADs pointing at your enemy — not so easy when they're on your boat staring you in the eye. No one says a thing.

'Who's your captain?' I say, breaking the impasse. The little man who'd opened the door steps forward.

'I Captain,' he says slowly, looking at me anxiously. He's only about five feet tall with skinny little arms and bowed legs. His face is gaunt and unshaven. I hand him my note. 'I'm the captain of the *Ady Gil*, here are my instructions.' He takes the package reluctantly, holding it by the corner as though it's poisonous.

Their radio suddenly crackles with the voice of the Japanese translator aboard the *Steve Irwin*. The captain, somewhat surprisingly, answers it, and there follows a five-minute conversation with the translator doing most of the talking. Her instructions are basically the same as those contained in the note. These are as follows:

First, I am arresting the Captain for the sinking of the *Ady Gil*, and I am requesting that he accompany me back to the *Steve Irwin*. (Of course, there is little chance of him doing this. In any case, I can only legally arrest him if I am on a New Zealand-registered vessel or in New Zealand territory. So unless he comes voluntarily, which he won't, I'm legally unable to enforce the arrest warrant.)

Second, if he won't come with me to the *Steve Irwin*, then I will refuse to leave his vessel. He sank my boat, so I am requesting he take me to either New Zealand or Australia. He is unlikely to agree to this either. He'd be in big trouble if he ever set foot in either country. So his options are to drop me onto another vessel — perhaps from the Coastguard or Customs of New Zealand or Australia, or to take me to any one of a number of countries. In the note, I've said that I refuse to transfer to another vessel, though, and Paul Watson will be making this clear to various authorities. His realistic option is to drop me off in Indonesia, Malaysia, the Philippines or Japan. Politically, the first three would pose diplomatic challenges. They'd be calling in big favours of these countries to have them accept me. It would also open up the possibility of protests there, which I'm sure the Japanese would rather avoid. A 'right can of worms' really! So if I were a betting man, I think he'll take me all the way back to Japan, which is what we're hoping for anyway. It won't be the captain's decision of course. Word will come down from the big brass in Tokyo.

Third, we are asking for US$3 million to build a new *Ady Gil* (which they will also refuse).

All of this puts them in a right pickle. They will refuse all three of our requests, but they have a Kiwi on board their boat, and they must do something with me. What makes it worse for them is they rammed and sank my boat and regardless of what spin they try to put on it, the *Bob Barker* video footage is damning of them. On the surface, you might say, all we did was get a man onto their boat, which doesn't really mean much, but it has in fact placed them in a real conundrum.

The translator finally finishes and I look around the crew. They all look disappointed. The significance of my presence is now dawning on them. The captain finally throws my note on the floor, stamps on it, then storms out of the bridge. A few minutes later I can hear him yelling on a satphone. Shortly, he returns, picks my note up off the floor, and heads back to what I'm assuming is their communications room. There are more one-sided conversations, followed by the slinging of something against the wall.

For quite a period of time I just sit there in the helm quite content really. I watch them working away, taking note of various things. On watch they are extremely thorough. Two radar screens are constantly monitored and Shorty continues to scan the horizon with his binoculars every few minutes. Amazingly, though, they haven't even searched me. I could be hiding an Uzi and five grenades under my vest, and no one has even bothered to check, nor have they made any effort to restrain me.

A while later, and Popeye returns to the bridge with a piece of paper. He comes storming up to me and thrusts a picture under my nose. On it is me in one of the RIBs holding a potato launcher.

'This you?' he says questioningly.

I smile at him. I can hardly say it's not me. There I am in all my glory, looking at the camera and smiling.

'Yep, that's me alright.'

Popeye suddenly erupts into a rage and starts ranting in Japanese. This continues for about a minute until he gets more and more worked up. He keeps pointing at three crew behind him. Finally, I start to understand what he's on about. The three crew are the ones who injured themselves when they fired pepper spray at us. Somehow it seems they have deluded themselves into thinking it was the butyric acid that stung their eyes.

Finally, I've had enough of his belligerence, and I stand up and face him.

'Look, these three shot themselves with their own guns. It was their own incompetence that led to their injuries, not me.' My face is about an inch from his now, and I can smell stale tobacco on his breath. There's real venom in his voice. It's a low growl, and a couple of bits of his spit land on my face. I don't know what he's saying, but I do know he's seething with anger. I figure he's about to take a crack at me. I glare back at him, turning just fractionally so he can't knee me in the balls. If I were him, my next best move would be a head butt, although unless you're a real brawler, it's not really an instinctive move you'd make. This guy doesn't look like he's had too many fights outside an East-end pub after closing. So if he's going to start a fight, he'll swing a punch. With my dry suit, undersuit and vest I'm actually pretty well protected apart from my noggin, and connecting with someone's head is not easy.

I stand there keeping my stare going. The crew are all deathly quiet, preferring to keep well clear of us. The captain appears in the doorway and barks a sharp order at Popeye. He glares at me for a few more seconds then reluctantly backs away. I'm tempted to tell the captain to tell old 'psycho chicken' to keep away from me, but bite my lip. I'd probably just wind him up for no good reason.

Eventually, fresh crew arrive in the helm and they strip me off, taking note of all my clothes and gear. It's a sizeable little pile that sits on the floor once they are finished. I'm then given a pair of underpants, some overalls and sandals. Shorty bandages my cut thumb, and I'm ordered into one of the rooms on the lower level.

Over the last few days I've had little sleep, and it suddenly catches up on me. I crawl into the small bed, and despite my aching jaw, within a few minutes, I'm asleep. Through the day I wake a few times, shift around a bit, contemplate my good fortune and drift back to sleep.

By late afternoon I get up and check out my room. I was so knackered I'd hardly noticed it when I came down. It's a three-man cabin, although the other occupants have all made way for me. It's about three metres wide by five metres long, with a basin in one corner. I have a look at my jaw in the mirror. One side has all puffed up. It looks a bit like I've got mumps.

Hajimoto, the first officer, comes in.

'Ban-gohan [Dinner],' he says cheerfully, and I follow him into the mess. Two big chefs are there waiting, and they bow their heads courteously as I enter. I sit in the corner and am served five different bowls of food. Cabbage soup, rice and fish all look familiar, but the other two look a bit suspect.

'Um . . . not wanting to be rude or anything, but what are those two?'

Hajimoto smiles, 'This one is jellyfish, and this one here . . .' there's a pause and he thinks of the words, 'is . . . um . . . raw fish guts.'

I smile back at him.

'What about if I was to say I was vegan?' I say looking back at the rice and cabbage soup and not really finding it that appealing on its own.

'Then I think you will be very hungry on this boat.'

I feign a smile, and try the jellyfish. It feels like someone else's snot sliding down my throat. The fish guts is equally as delectable, but the rest of it is fine. My jaw is a constant throb, and I swallow it all with a minimum of chewing. As soon as I'm finished I'm led back to my room, which has two crew stationed outside to guard me.

Most of the following day is spent being interviewed by Hajimoto. He remains sceptical that I boarded at night from the jet-ski, believing instead that the chopper dropped me off. In the end, though, I don't care what he thinks, so I let it rest. In the end, I ask him 'What's going to happen to me?'

'Hmm . . . we haven't decided yet,' he replies.

'Am I under arrest?'

He puts his hand on his chin, as he thinks about this. 'No, but you are our captive.'

'Well, if I'm your captive, I would like to request one hour of exercise outside per day, and a pen and paper to write with.' He nods his head.

'I will have to ask *Senchou* [Captain], but I think it will be OK.'

'Also Hajimoto, can you tell me what our heading is?'

He frowns at me, and makes a cross with his hands.

'No information,' he says sternly. Which I think means he won't tell me, rather than he doesn't know. He's the first officer so of course he'll know what our heading is. He heads off to speak with the captain, then returns to my cabin a few minutes later.

'The *senchou* has agreed to your exercise. You can have from 10 until 11 in the morning. But I am sorry, you are not allowed a pen.'

'Why not?'

He shifts uneasily on his feet. 'Well . . . a pen could be used as a weapon.' I look at him in disbelief.

'Come on. If I really wanted a weapon, take a look around. The mirror there. Just smash it and ya got 20 blades ready to go. The safety pins on the quilt, the metal fittings holding the hatch in. If I really wanted a weapon, there're many other things I'd use before resorting to a pen.'

He studies me for a few moments. 'I am sorry. The *senchou* has made his decision. There is nothing I can do.'

He looks at his watch. 'It is time for your shower.' He heads me into a small cubicle. It's one of those low-slung shower heads suited to dwarfs, midgets or Asian people with a penchant for squatting. I turn it on, get the temperature right, and clamber under. It would be fair to say I've spent an inordinately large amount of time thinking about showers, due mainly to the lack of them while in Antarctica. It went from none on the *Ady Gil*, one per week on the *Bob Barker*, two per week on the *Steve Irwin*, and, well, apparently one every day on the *Shonan Maru*, and there is no shower monitor banging on the door when your three minutes is up.

A big smile erupts on my face, as the warm water slides down my shoulders.

'For a shower every day, I got no problem with squatting like a Chinaman,' I say to myself. It's a good 15 minutes later when I emerge from the shower, bright red from the heat, and sparkling clean from all the scrubbing.

As I'm led back to my room, Popeye is removing the mirror. He sneers at me as I walk past him and climb into my bunk. I glance at the quilt, and the safety pins have all been removed, as have the fittings from the hatches. 'Nice one ya tosser,' I say to him. He ignores me and continues his work.

At 10 o'clock the following day, four guards escort me outside for my exercises. I lead them to the upper deck where my knife is hidden.

'This is the best place,' I say confidently. I just mix it up with press-ups, chin-ups, sit-ups, and a bit of clambering on the stairs to give my legs a bit of work.

Between sets, I scan the horizon, but there's no sign of any other boats. I look at the sun and work out where north is. An SAS mate of mine taught me how to do this and it's quite a handy little trick. You imagine an analogue watch and you point the 12 at the sun. Next you find the midpoint between the hour hand and the 12. So at the moment, it's 10 o'clock. I point the 12 at the sun and the midpoint between the 10 and the 12 is 11, which is north. As another example, if it is 4pm, point the 12 at the sun, and the midpoint between the 12 and the 4 is 2, which is north. Pretty cool, eh? It only works in the southern hemisphere. Also you need to know the time, and it's only approximately accurate with things like daylight saving screwing it a little, but for a rough indication, it's brilliant.

I quickly work out that north is directly on our port beam, so we're still heading in an easterly direction, and by the looks of it, we're doing about 11 knots. So I expect we remain near the fleet, but keeping out of range so they don't get any other stray visitors in the night.

Over the following days, a pattern in my routine emerges. Breakfast is at 7am, exercises at 10am, shower at 11am, lunch at midday, and dinner at 5pm. Outside of that, I'm just left in my room with a couple of crew keeping an eye on me. A boring existence perhaps, but not uncomfortable in any way. The crew seem fine with my presence as well. Most of them nod when they see me, except for Popeye who continues to hate my guts.

On day five, though, things change. The crew all seem very frosty. Then while I'm exercising, I notice we're now heading north-east, which is away from Antarctica.

'We've changed heading,' I say to Hajimoto that night over dinner. 'Are we heading back to Japan?'

'No information,' he replies, crossing his hands.

'Look, I know we're now heading north-east, so you might as well tell me.'

He glances around the mess, then whispers to me, 'I cannot tell you anything about what our heading is, or where we are going.'

I pick up my bowl of miso, and slurp it noisily, while Hajimoto gets to work on his fish. He pulls up the entire fillet with his chopsticks and takes a bite. I decide to change the subject.

'Hey, there's a few crew who've been really grumpy at me today. Do they still think it was me that hit them with the butyric acid?'

Hajimoto frowns. 'There is now some doubt. None of the crew has seen your video. Perhaps it wasn't you. Me, I don't know.'

'Yeah, well, I've seen the video, and it's as clear as day. They fire their spray, it comes back onto them, and they start rubbing their eyes. So you can tell them to stop being so angry.'

'There is something else. I am not saying we are going back to Japan. But if we were, it is a month early, and that would have many crew missing out on a month's pay.' I sit there looking at my miso. I almost wish these lads were less likeable. In fact, Popeye aside, they're a great bunch. In many respects, they're just ordinary blokes doing a job.

'What about Popeye? Is he angry because he's missing a month's pay?'

Hajimoto looks puzzled. 'Popeye?'

'Ya know — the angry guy, with the poppy eyes.'

'Ah . . . him. No. You need to understand, this boat provides security to the fleet. We're expected to protect the other boats, and yet we were unable to protect even ourselves. You boarding this vessel at night has brought great shame to this crew. It was especially embarrassing that you were on our boat for several hours, and we never even knew. The man you call Popeye, he is like our security person, so for him, the shame is even more.' He picks up the fish again, and holds it in his chopsticks.

'I do wish you had never boarded our boat. It has made things very awkward for us.'

'Yeah, well, I wish you'd never sunk my boat. That made things very awkward for me.'

He just frowns, and continues eating his fish.

Over the following days, our voyage north-east, and away from Antarctica, continues. This should see us crossing above Australia, and passing close to Indonesia. I try to piece together the Asian geography in my mind, but I'm not really sure what bit of land we'll come across. If I were to guess, I'd say Bali. Either way, I'm confident that in another week or so we'll pass some land.

I turn the numbers on my phone into a calendar, placing little pieces of tape on them and moving them around each day. Then, during exercises, I check our heading and speed. It's day 13 when we finally sight land — a low island off in the distance on our port side. Dark storm clouds hang over it, and the land is covered in a lush tropical forest.

'Is that Indonesia?' I say to Genghis.

He just crosses his hands — no information.

'It's Bali, isn't it? I can tell.' In fact I can't, but a big smile erupts on Genghis' face, giving it away.

'I cannot say anything,' he says, laughing at me. We stand there admiring our first view of land in several months. I am about to start my exercises when Genghis starts talking excitedly in Japanese, and pointing forward. We all run to the lookout station and look at where he is pointing. A mile or so ahead is a big fish thrashing around on the surface.

As we get closer, I can make out the dark shape of a marlin. As it struggles it drags a couple of long-line buoys with it, but it's gradually tiring. By the time we pass him, he's lying on his side. He senses the boat, and makes another desperate surge for the surface, but he's getting tired.

I'm not a fan of long-lines any more. We've passed hundreds of them in the last few days, their evil webs indiscriminately catching birds and all manner of wildlife that we should just be leaving alone. That poor marlin we've just passed will continue in agony for hours yet, until he finally dies of exhaustion — a sad ending for such a magnificent creature.

I remember when *Earthrace* arrived back in New Zealand in 2009 there was a plonker on the wharf weighing in a really small marlin. It was about 75 kilos, and the angler was posing for photos like he was some kind of hero. The captain of the charter boat was skulking in the background, so I went over to have a chat.

'He wanted to keep it,' he said to me defensively. 'There was nothing I could do.'

'Well ya could've told him to piss off. You're the bloody captain.' I shake my head and wander back to the crowd that has gathered. Scanning around the people I can see most of them are angry. The people here know the guy has killed a baby marlin, but amazingly no one says a thing. They all just stand there watching, while the wanker poses like we should somehow admire his achievement.

Finally, I step forward.

'You should be ashamed of yourself, bringing that marlin in here.' There's a few nods and murmurs from the crowd. The guy turns to me angrily and blurts out, 'This will feed my family for a month, so don't tell me what I can and can't catch.'

'Yeah, well I hope you all choke on it,' I spit back at him.

Later I found out that he owns a carpeting franchise and is 'loaded'. The charter boat had cost him $2500 for the day. If he really needed to feed his family he'd other options.

Looking back at it, there were several things that upset me about that incident. Firstly, the guy taking the baby marlin and then gloating about it. Also, the captain allowing it to happen on his vessel. The worst bit, though, was the crowd, all appalled at the man's actions, and yet none of them stepped forward to say anything.

I love Kiwis. Being one of them, that's natural I guess. There are many traits in Kiwis that are most admirable. One of our flaws, though, is we are so averse to all forms of conflict (unless it involves an oval ball and two posts at either end of the field). We shy away from situations when we should be making a stand.

I use that story about the marlin when I'm fortunate enough to talk in schools. I tell the kids, if they see others, be they children or adults, doing something that is wrong, to step forward and say something. Don't sit there twiddling your thumbs waiting for someone else to do it. Have some respect and stand up for what you believe in. In many ways that's what I've done in boarding the *Shonan Maru*. There's a great Maori saying that sums this attitude up beautifully — Kia kaha, kia mana: Be strong, and stand up for what you believe in.

I stay with the *Shonan Maru* crew until the marlin and long-line have disappeared in the distance behind us. I then finish my exercises and head back to my room. Now that I know our location, I'm determined to track our position all the way to Tokyo. With so much idle time on my hands, it becomes my daily obsession.

The earth's rotation causes what's termed a Coriolis effect. One result of this is the weather — it's what makes high and low pressure systems rotate. In the southern hemisphere, for example, a high-pressure system rotates anti-clockwise, and a low-pressure system rotates clockwise. In the northern hemisphere, the same thing happens except the direction is reversed. Then there's this weird thing that happens near the equator where there's no rotation. It's one reason for the doldrums, a zone of water around the equator that for much of the year is dead calm.

The same acceleration also affects the water emptying from my sink. It acts like a low-pressure system, rotating clockwise south of the equator, and anti-clockwise north of it.

At the start and finish of each day, my routine includes a quick fill up and empty of my sink. On day 18, the rotation doesn't show until the water has almost totally drained. By 11 o'clock it's even less apparent. At midday, Hajimoto wanders into my room and watches me. 'What are you doing?' he says curiously, as I pull the plug for the sixth time today. The crew perhaps are wondering if captivity has finally addled my mind.

'Watch the water,' I say to him. 'As it empties, there's now no discernable rotation at all. It just drains straight out.' Hajimoto, though, doesn't get it. He just stares at me blankly.

'No rotation,' I say. 'We are on the equator.'

He looks puzzled for a few seconds, then his eyes light up.

'Aha... *Wakarimasu* [I understand]. Very good, but I cannot confirm,' he says with a chuckle. I continue with my sink checks and by 2pm the direction has reversed.

I know we are now at zero degrees latitude (the equator) and Tokyo is at 35 degrees north. Each degree of latitude is 60 nautical miles. So there remained 2100 nautical miles to travel in a northerly direction before we reach Tokyo. Looking at the water pass us I can get a rough idea of the speed, and using the sun I can tell our approximate heading. Those two bits of information allow me to work out how many miles in a northerly direction we travel each day. And I just keep a running tally as we work our way towards Tokyo. It all sounds rather clever really, but I've got so much time to think about things. Perhaps it'll stop me going mad having little mental challenges. I also see it as defiance against the captain and Popeye, who have been petty in not revealing where we are going or when we will arrive.

The days and miles tick by and I get to know many of the crew. They're actually a really nice bunch of guys. Over lunch one day, the bosun comes and sits down beside me. I've been calling him Genghis, because he's the spitting image of Genghis Khan. I'd first seen him when I was hiding on the upper deck. There's something very genuine about this guy. I've noticed, too, when he blinks his whole face is involved, rather than just his eyelids.

'What's up Genghis?' I say cheerily.

He still doesn't like the name, although none of them can tell me their real name, so he accepts it I think.

'When we think "Sea Shepherd",' and he pauses while he thinks of the words, 'we think "terrorist". But you not terrorist. Maybe you almost normal,' and he chuckles.

'Look Genghis, if we were terrorists we'd have blown ya boat up, and shot the lot of ya, but we're not. We're just ordinary people in many respects, just like you.'

He nods his head slowly.

'I've been lucky on this campaign. I've crewed on all three Sea Shepherd boats, and now I've been a . . . um . . . "guest" on the *Shonan Maru*. And all the boats have good people with good hearts. At the moment there are two sides bashing themselves together . . . and it's no good. But what can we do?'

Genghis thinks about this for a while.

'Well you could stop bashing us, and then we would stop bashing you.'

'Yeah, but we did that for 18 years. And you kept coming down each year, and hunting whales. If we leave you, you just continue to hunt.'

'But why you want to stop us? Whale meat very important to Japanese people.'

'Yeah, but you don't need it. You catch over 25 per cent of the world's fish already. You eat more seafood per capita than any other country even without the whale meat. Stick to your squid, seaweed and fish guts.'

Genghis screws his face up.

'Fish guts, I don't like so much.'

'Yeah, me neither. The point I'm making is you don't really need to eat whale any more. It's just a delicacy for the wealthy anyway.'

He's remains unconvinced, but maybe I've given him something to think about.

He pours himself a cup of green tea from the pot.

'There is something you should know Pete. When we get to Japan, you in big trouble.'

'Hmm . . . have you heard something?'

He looks around, and checks that no one is listening. 'I think as soon as we arrive in Japan, you be arrested. You be charged with many things. And I think you spend long time in Japanese prison.' He shakes his head.

'I very sorry, Pete. I don't want you in trouble. I know you good person. Maybe not quite normal,' he smiles, but his mood is sombre. He finishes his tea, and heads off for his watch, while I ponder this.

Until now I figured they'd avoid a trial because of the publicity it'd cause. I was thinking they'd hold me for a few days, slap my wrist with a wet bus ticket, and boot me out under their immigration laws. If they charge me and hold me for longer than a few days, I'll become a festering sore and PR disaster for them. My captivity might play out well in Japan, but overseas it'll cost them dearly.

If Genghis is right in what he says, I'm in line for a period in prison, which is unappealing indeed. One of my nephews managed a bit of free accommodation compliments of Her Majesty. I remember his theory on the prison food chain.

'At the bottom,' he'd said, 'are the druggies and the old men, then pacifists and white collars, then your ordinary criminals, then violent offenders, and organised crime at the top. When ya first get into prison, everyone sizes you up to see where ya fit. And the higher up the food chain ya get, generally the easier your life will be.'

'So what'd you do?' I asked him, quite intrigued.

'On my first day I got into some fights, and I went absolutely psycho. If anyone so much as looked at me, I went for them. After that I was mostly left alone.' His final bit of advice I'd laughed at when he told me, 'If anyone messes with ya, get the first punch in, and make it a good one.'

Thinking about my situation, it doesn't sound like good advice. If I go getting into fights, I'll probably just end up in more trouble. Shaun seemed to think violence in prison is inevitable unless you're right at the top. Everyone beneath the gangs gets smacked around. It's a depressing evening I spend in my little cabin, with dark thoughts of brawling inmates and broken bones occupying my mind.

I keep having a vision of me sitting with a bunch of inmates, and they're all revealing what they're in for. Manslaughter, murder, extortion, grand theft, and then they look at me.

'Um . . . I boarded a boat without permission.' Of course, they all laugh at me, realise I don't belong there, and beat me up. There's an even worse vision in the showers, with a bunch of big sumo wrestlers slapping my bum, and taking turns on me. Getting to Japan was always part of the plan, but getting locked up with a bunch of hardened criminals certainly wasn't.

Worrying thoughts of incarceration continue to plague me as the days drift by. I keep counting the days and miles, as we ply our way relentlessly towards Tokyo. The voyage has become a valuable intelligence-gathering exercise. I've gleaned all manner of useful information that perhaps one day will benefit Sea Shepherd. This is despite Popeye's best efforts to keep me incommunicado. The electronics have surprised me. Their radar and navigation hardware, for example, is a generation or two behind that deployed on the *Steve Irwin*. They've got a satellite communications system, although much of their ship-to-ship traffic is an old HF system. I'd assumed they ran twin engines, when in fact they have a single 5000-horsepower beastie grinding away in the bowels. They have a large single propeller, and for the size of the vessel, a massive rudder. Considering its age, this boat remains an engineering marvel — fast, extremely manoeuvrable and with a massive range. It's a shame really to think the bulk of its working life has been spent slaughtering whales.

The food continues to be an eye-opener. Almost all of it is seafood, and virtually no red meat. Much of it is served raw, and while it's not spicy, like much of Asian cuisine, I'd certainly call it *oishii* (tasty). The seafood served has included seaweed, kelp, squid, octopus, oysters, mussels, scallops, yellowfin, bonito, sauri, shrimps, prawns, clams, whitebait and a whole assortment of little fish that in most countries you'd never even bother with . . . . oh, and the jellyfish . . . and the fish guts, of course. No whale or dolphin was served, although I made it very clear to the captain that I'd cause him much trouble if I saw it being eaten while I was there. If you removed seafood from the diet, they'd return to Tokyo looking emaciated I expect.

As we near Tokyo, I start to ponder my knife. The box I hid it under hasn't been moved, so I know it's still safely tucked on the upper deck. If I hand it over to the captain, he or Popeye will probably confiscate it for good. Or they'll run a media blitz about it, and make up some piss-pot story about me trying to knife them. I can just picture Paul Watson spitting back in his coffee when the ICR press release crosses his desk. A heading like: '*Ady Gil* captain attacks *Shonan Maru* crew' will jump out at him, and below will be my mug-shot and a picture of the knife. With little news of late, media would lap up such a story.

If I leave handing it over until Tokyo, the story will hopefully be buried in with all the other news surrounding my arrival. Thinking about it, I'll hand it over to the police or customs, or whoever comes to arrest me — one final embarrassment for Popeye before I head off. Assuming Genghis is right about me being in heaps of trouble, possessing a knife probably won't make much difference anyway.

So the following day during exercises, I decide to retrieve the knife and store it in my room. I start my routine at the back of the deck doing press-ups while three of the crew watch on silently. Genghis and Popeye then join them, the pair leaning back against the railing. I bow to Genghis deferentially and I scowl at Popeye. I've noticed when there's five crew guarding me like this, they're less attentive; perceived safety in numbers, I guess.

I move over near the box, and start doing chin-ups. This is part of my normal routine, so the guys don't seem at all wary. I hiss and grunt towards the end of each set. I've found the crew dislike this and it tends to keep them away. There's now a wall separating us. I pull off my black T-shirt, duck down to the box and grab out the knife. I slide it quickly into the shirt, but it catches on a fold. Not wanting to be hidden too long, I dump it on the floor, and stand up. Popeye is eyeing me up suspiciously. He wanders over towards me, while I jump up for my last set of chin-ups. I grunt even more than usual, but he gets right up to the wall and looks down at me. I drop down from the bar, blocking his view, and he stares at me.

'Wasup my homie?' I say insolently. He just snorts, and looks away. I peek down, and just a little of the handle is poking out, but it's not obvious against the T-shirt. I wander over to the stairs, and start my leg exercises, and Popeye's bulbous eyes follow me. He's definitely suspicious about something, but he's not sure what. The rest of the crew just look on casually. I finish the set, grab my shirt and knife, and slide them into my towel.

'*Ikimashou* [Let's go],' I yell at Genghis, and I hurry off down the stairs. Popeye, meanwhile, starts looking around where I've just come from. Too late, I think to myself. Ha ha.

Two days later and, by my calculations, we are almost in Tokyo. Hajimoto joins me at dinner.

'Tomorrow I think we arrive in Tokyo,' I say to him.

He's busy slurping his soup. 'No information,' he says. There are a few other signs of impending arrival too. Half the crew are sporting new haircuts, and the washing machines have been running almost continuously. Most of the crew seem happy, with even Popeye smiling a bit between his cheap cigarettes.

'Hey, can you tell me what's going to happen to me once we arrive?'

Hajimoto puts his soup down, and looks at me through narrow eyes. 'You will be arrested as soon as we arrive, and you will be taken to coast guard prison.'

'And after that . . .?'

'Hmm . . . I don't know. I think you in serious trouble. I also think you are now famous in Japan, but not in a good way.'

'What do ya mean?'

'Your arrival here has become a big story, and the police are expecting protests against you.'

10
Arrested, charged, incarcerated

It's mid-morning the following day when we idle into the wide Tokyo Bay. An overcast sky greets me as I sneak the curtain back on my porthole. Also there to greet me are six coastguard vessels and a small flotilla of other boats all jockeying for position around us. Everyone seems to have a camera at the ready; although the Japanese hardly need an excuse to get their little Nikons fired up, of course.

Our passage in is slow and meandering as we navigate the various channels, shipping lanes and traffic. It turns into sheer chaos as we approach the dock — several boats block our entry and officials are running around yelling and pointing, while a few captains take the liberty of blasting their horns in frustration. Eventually, some coastguard vessels get stuck in and barge the offenders out of the way. It's a good half-hour later before our engines are finally switched off. The *Shonan Maru*, for the first time in over a month, is suddenly eerily quiet — on the inside at least.

Outside, though, it is a different matter. The chaos on the water has now moved onto the dock. It looks like a scout jamboree; there are so many blokes with uniforms and badges running around, whistles are blowing, people are scurrying and arguing and flailing their arms in the air.

Arrested, charged, incarcerated

'You sure this isn't Italy rather than Japan?' I say to Popeye. He's standing sulking in the doorway, but he just ignores me.

There's a team of about 20 people erecting what looks like a fence. It's half built, but then an official comes barging over, ranting at them, so they pull it to bits. A short time later they start building it in another location.

There are choppers buzzing all around us; maybe seven media and another three that look indeterminate, although all seem to have cameramen hanging out, filming the mayhem that is unfolding beneath them.

'Hey, looks like we're famous,' I say to Popeye. He snorts at me. He's now busy watching the procession of officials who are filing past him and up to the bridge.

Genghis comes bounding into my cabin. 'You look happy,' I say to him.

'Ah Pete-san, it is good to be home.' He shaved his beard off last night and he looks a lot less fearsome now. His generous eyes seem to dominate his face. He sits down on the bunk opposite me and looks outside.

'Have you seen this?' he says, chuckling and pointing at the officials still struggling with the fence.

'Yeah, but I'm not sure why they need a "Great wall of China", though.'

'Ha, ha! It is not a wall Pete-san. It is a tunnel . . . for you.'

'And why do they think I need a tunnel?'

He scratches his chin. 'I think it is for your privacy.'

'Well, Genghis, unless they intend trundling me out in the buff, I'm not sure I warrant any privacy. Don't they know I'm from Sea Shepherd?'

He nods his head and chuckles.

The officials are now tying tarpaulins onto the fence, but the rotor-wash from the choppers is blowing them everywhere. One becomes a kite and shoots across the dock, before draping itself over a scabby old trawler. A second one scoots along the ground and wedges itself under a truck. What a circus!

I look over at Genghis who is still scratching his chin.

'I'm gonna miss you, Genghis,' I say to him. 'You've been very kind to me.'

He looks down, like he's embarrassed.

'I will miss you, too.' He's deep in thought.

'When you get to prison,' he says, finally, 'you be very careful. Japanese prison very dangerous.'

'I'll be fine, bro.' I try to sound confident, but it's unconvincing. Thoughts of a long incarceration continue to nag at the back of my mind.

He looks at the Maori tattoos on my arms.

'Do those mean anything?' he says, pointing at one of them.

'Yeah. Some of it is my family. This here represents my two girls,' I say, pointing at the koru spirals on my right arm.

'It's a bit like my family tree, I guess. And a bit about where I'm from.'

He nods his head but frowns.

'Maybe, while in Japan you should not show. Normally, only Yakuza have tattoos. I think if you show those in prison . . .' his voice trails off.

'Yakuza?' I ask, raising my eyebrows.

'Hmm. Same like Mafia. Only Japanese. You see any Yakuza, you keep clear!'

Genghis takes another look outside and starts laughing.

'Look at this,' he says, pointing at my tunnel. They've run out of tarpaulins, but the tunnel is only half-covered. So they have a couple of teams practising walking the tarpaulins along beside the tunnel, but the choppers are blowing them all over the place. It could be a long day! A group of officials start peering in my room, so Genghis says his goodbyes and heads off.

'What an awesome bloke,' I think, as he weaves his way through the growing mass of bodies.

It takes an eternity for all the officials to get in position. Eight of them squish into my little cabin, while dozens more are crowded in the hallway, galley and mess. An older man finally steps forward.

'I am Masaka,' he says in heavily accented English. 'I from Japanese Coastguard and I arrest you for trespass.'

The words come out like he's rehearsed them several times. He's clearly nervous. His hands are shaking and sweat is pouring down his brow.

'Very good,' I reply. 'I have something to declare.'

He looks at me blankly, so I'm not sure if he understood. Not worrying about it, I reach down and pull out my knife, handing it over to him handle first. Popeye, who is wedged in the corner, gasps when he sees it and his eyes nearly pop out of his head. Masaka is not really sure what to do now; he never rehearsed this bit. He holds the knife, just staring at it, then finally starts a little mini-conference with a few of his colleagues. I look over at Popeye, who is furious. I give him a cheeky little wink then return my attention to Masaka. They finally decide it is safer to have the knife elsewhere, so someone volunteers to take it outside. Popeye follows him out, probably wanting to see what had eluded his various cabin searches.

'Next, you handcuffed,' says Masaka.

'Look, there's no need for all that,' I reply, but no one is listening. A short, stumpy man steps forward and cuffs my wrists, but the right cuff refuses to lock. Another small conference kicks off, before yet another officer in a different uniform is summonsed from the galley. He locks the cuff in two seconds.

'You guys don't get to do this too often, do ya?' I say to no one in particular, but my attempt at humour is lost in the sea of blank faces. Next comes some kind of blue bib that is tied around my chest, followed by a matching blue cover for my handcuffs. How thoughtful!

'You must also wear a hat,' says Masaka, but what they produce hardly resembles a hat, unless you're a white supremacist from Alabama. It is a tall peaked hood that is only missing the cut-out eyes and a KKK on the back.

'I'm not wearing no hood,' I protest indignantly.

'But it stops photos,' replies Masaka earnestly.

'Yeah, well I don't mind photos. In fact, I like them. What I do mind is wearing that thing,' and I cock my head towards Stumpy who is waiting patiently with my next bit of attire.

This starts the third mini-conference, before Masaka finally turns to me.

'I am sorry. You must wear.'

I shake my head in resignation.

'Whatever.'

Stumpy goes to put the hood on, but discovers that my bib is on back to front.

It's half an hour later before they have me all kitted up and ready for the adventure. The hood means I can't see a thing. I'm also shackled to a guy in front and another guy behind me, but there's so little slack that we have to bump and grind our way along. Maybe I'm glad of the hood, lest I be filmed in the middle of a three-man *frottage*.

We shuffle our way through the galley, over a gang-plank and into the tunnel, but each obstacle becomes a mission unto itself. The helicopters have smelt blood by now and they come swooping down. Plastic sheets flap and tear around us and there are various voices yelling instructions. The racket is so loud that it sounds like one of the choppers is about to eat us. We finally squabble our way into some kind of vehicle. I sit there in silence for about 10 minutes and then my hood is removed.

I'm inside a mini luxury coach. Stumpy and another guy are sealed either side of me, and there are 10 other coastguards waiting patiently with us. A mini bus directly in front is being loaded up with more guards. Ten of them pile inside and it sags unhappily under the load. A few minutes later and the blue lights on its roof start flashing furiously and we're off — in convoy it would seem, with another loaded van following obediently behind us.

A stale smell starts to grate me and it's a while before I figure out it's Stumpy's breath. Each time he looks even slightly in my direction it gets worse. The smell is quite rancid, considering it's only a bloke's breath. It's like the stench of an old ewe that fell in the creek and died a few weeks ago, and being shackled to Stumpy, it's not like I can just hop into another seat. I put my head in my lap, preferring the smell of my loins to Stumpy's breath. I sneak a look at his left hand and there's a gold wedding band on his finger. 'His poor wife having to kiss that moosh,' I chuckle to myself.

Tokyo traffic is slow. A bit like 'bump'n'grind' but in vehicles, despite all our flashing lights. I sniff my lap all the way to the coastguard building where another half-built tunnel awaits us. Also waiting on arrival is the vulture-like flock of helicopters circling overhead. Stumpy sorts out my hood, our scrum forms for the second time and we maul our way out of the bus, through the flapping tunnel and into the hush of an air-conditioned office building.

I'm led upstairs to a small room with three people waiting patiently on the other side of a thick toughened-glass partition. This, it turns out, is the legal team that Sea Shepherd have appointed for me and they all bow down as I enter.

'Hi there,' I say and I attempt a small bow myself. The small man in the middle introduces himself as Miyake.

'Welcome to Japan,' he says with a warm smile. He looks much what you would expect of a wily defence attorney: slim and wiry, piercing little eyes and a tongue that flicks around his mouth as he speaks. Slicker than a sewer rat with a gold tooth — which is probably what I'll need to get out of him anyway.

'How was your trip?' he enquires.

'Um. It was good . . . I guess. It's nice to be off the *Shonan Maru* at least, although getting here was like a three-ring-circus, but just missing the elephants.'

He looks puzzled at the mention of elephants, but seems to dismiss it.

'Well, Pete-san, your arrival here has caused quite a stir. Media surrounding this has been extraordinary, but they have not really helped you at all.'

'Well, one of the reasons for coming here was to get media attention, so I'd see the coverage as a good thing.' Miyake furrows his brow.

'Unfortunately, they have portrayed you as a . . .' His eyes close and he tilts his head back as he thinks.

'... as an SAS terrorist,' he says finally. 'People in Japan think of you as a very dangerous man. So the authorities are being especially careful with you. The security detail for you today for example is over 100 personnel. That is more than most heads of state would ever get.'

I sit there mulling over his words. Me an SAS terrorist — I can't help but chuckle.

'Does it really matter that I am portrayed in a poor light?'

Miyake consults Fukuyama and Hiraishi, the other two lawyers with him.

'Well, we had originally expected the authorities would hold you for a couple of days and then send you home. There is no hope of that now. Photos and video of you are splattered across every newspaper and TV network in the country. Now the story includes a hidden knife. So because of the public interest, it is impossible for them to just send you home.

'Instead you will be detained in the maximum security block of the Tokyo Detention Centre. This is where Japan's most dangerous prisoners are sent. I am sorry, but this is not a nice place.' The three of them look quite forlorn, but I had been expecting a stint in prison after Genghis' revelations the other night anyway. Maximum security doesn't sound good, though.

'How long will I be detained for?'

'Well, we don't know. It depends on the prosecutor. We believe they will pursue the trespass charge as a summary offence, which would see you home in four weeks.'

I nod my head. I'd accept four weeks, I guess. It could be much worse.

Miyake goes on to explain the Japanese legal process, which is somewhat different from our own. The prosecutor can have me detained for up to 20 days without charge. Through this period he's allowed to interview me for eight hours each day with no defence attorney present. Once the 20 days have expired he must either charge me or let me go. If I'm to believe my lawyers, the odds of me just being released are slim.

'When do I get to meet the prosecutor?' I ask. There's another small discussion between the lawyers before Miyake turns back to me.

'We think you will be transferred to the Detention Centre shortly, and the prosecutor will then come and see you tomorrow. Get used to him as you will be seeing a lot of him over the next few weeks . . .' There's a pause while Fukuyama says something to Miyake.

'Oh, and don't sign anything without speaking to us first. The documents he produces will form the basis of his case, so we must all agree before you fingerprint any of them.'

'Fingerprint?' I enquire, raising my eyebrows.

'Ah, yes. In Japan we don't sign. We write our name, then put our fingerprint over it.'

I nod my head.

The lawyers eventually head off, although not before we exchanged a few more polite little bows. Stumpy then comes in with a less-than-inspiring lunch consisting of two bread rolls and a sachet of jam.

It's mid-afternoon before our 'push-me-pull-you' is strapped back together and we are back battling the forces of evil — helicopters and tarpaulin tunnels. I'm again seated in the bus with Stumpy at my left and, unfortunately, his breath continues to reek of that long-ignored carcass down the back of the farm. I sigh and poke my head back in my lap. Our blue lights are fired up again, the horns of our three vehicles all give a little toot and we're off.

It's an hour later that we pull into the massive Tokyo Detention Centre complex. It's a series of homogeneous tall buildings linked by a central star-like structure. My stomach knots up as I look at what will likely be my home for the next 20 days. Shaun's words start reverberating in my head. 'If anyone messes with ya, get the first punch in and make sure it's a good one.' As if! I sure don't belong here!

We pass through a checkpoint, then are waved into a drop-off zone much like an airport. I look out nervously, as my convoy slides alongside the curb. A bus ahead of us is busy throwing up its prisoners. They spew out onto the pavement, then assemble into a jagged line. It's my first glimpse of fellow inmates, but they're not at all what I was expecting — a motley bunch of pimply faced teenagers, overweight office workers, an old man, and a bum that looks like he's been dragged out of a London subway. No Affco meatworkers among them — perhaps I will emerge from here in one piece.

Our papers are handed over to one of the officers. He scans down the page then starts barking instructions at some of the guards. He orders me out of the bus, giving me a contemptuous little sneer as I hobble down the stairs. My posse assembles itself while I stare arrogantly at the other group of prisoners. There's the strangest set of emotions swirling around inside my head. It's almost one of power. The dozen inmates have but two guards between them and are dressed for a Sunday stroll, while I've got an entourage of dozens and am handcuffed, tied and strapped like a psychopathic killer. This must be what it's like to be really 'bad arse' and it actually feels quite good.

As we shuffle past the group I stick my jaw out and give each one an unsmiling stare. They mostly look down, but I can feel their eyes on the back of my head as I pass them. The last guy, a tall skinny kid with skunked hair, holds my stare.

'What you looking at?' I snarl at him. It actually sounds really vicious. I feel a bit like a dog that's been chained. You can bark and snarl like you're the most evil animal, safe in the knowledge that the chain, or in my case handcuffs, rope and guards, prevent you from having to actually follow through with anything. The kid looks away and I feel Stumpy behind me tense up, but we just continue shuffling along. Look out boys, Hannibal Lecter is coming through.

I'm led along a corridor and into a large, open-plan hall. A series of booths are scattered through the area, with little footprints on the floor indicating the path to follow. Each booth has a prison employee at it and there are a few prisoners working their way through what looks like an induction process.

An older man steps forward. 'I am your translator today. I will help you here,' he says.

I just nod. I'm still in my evil SAS Terrorist persona I've decided.

At the first station they take down my personal details, then my mug-shot, followed by fingerprinting. The next few are more medical in nature. I'm told to strip off and I stand there with about a hundred people all perving at me and chatting quietly among themselves. Maybe they just wanna see if it's true what they say about white fullahs. I've still got my coastguard posse following me, but they've been joined by what I'd later call the 'stormtroopers' — a group of guards that responds to any trouble in the complex. I feel more than naked as I remove my socks and underwear and place them in a basket.

I'm weighed and measured, then given chest X-rays. The translator then hands me what looks like a large pregnancy tester.

'You urinate on this,' he says, and he points me in the direction of a small urinal. This is rather welcome, as I've been dying for a piss ever since I met the lawyers. I saunter over to the urinal and grab my manhood, conscious of the many eyes watching me. It's a fair torrent that gushes out and my bladder breathes a sigh of relief as the pressure eases. Now I'm holding the tester in my right hand, aiming with my left as it were, and keeping an eye on the little urinal at the same time. As I move the tester into the stream, though, urine splashes everywhere and, in my panic, my left hand moves the stream away from the tester and, unfortunately, it then hits the edge of the urinal. I recover from there, but the damage has been done. Little droplets of yellow piss are scattered on the floor, on the wall and down my legs. I finally finish and turn around. All the spectators are looking in other directions. I scan around for a paper towel, but all that's there is an electric hand dryer.

'Um, sorry bro, but I've pissed on your wall,' I say to the translator. He wanders over and screws his face up at my handiwork. A bloke wearing green pyjamas is summonsed and he starts cleaning up my mess, while I hand the drenched tester over to what I'm presuming is a doctor.

With the piss test safely out of the way, I move to the next cubicle. Two men in lab coats and rubber gloves are standing there with awkward looks on their faces. The translator has a quick chat to one of the men then turns to me.

'Can you lift up your parts please?'

I look at him blankly. 'Which parts exactly?'

He looks down at my loins with a pained expression on his face.

'You want me to lift up my cock?'

'Ah yes. Your . . . um . . . cock.'

I lift it up, while the doctors, still a metre or so away, have a bit of a peek.

'And now the other parts as well please.'

'You mean my balls?'

'Yes. Your balls, please.' He seems slightly easier with this term. I lift up my balls and again the doctors have a look. I'm starting to get a bit angry at this. It's like I'm the freak show of the day.

'Now we need you to turn around please.' So I turn around and face the wall.

'Can you now bend over?' So I bend over. I stay there for about five seconds then stand up. The two doctors say something to the translator. He too now has a pained expression on his face.

'When you bend over . . . I very sorry, we need you to split.' I look at him blankly.

'What do you mean "split"?'

'Um . . . split you anoose.'

'My anoose?' And then suddenly I get it.

'You want me to spread my bloody cheeks,' I spit at him. 'Is that what you want?'

A half-dozen guards quickly enter the cubicle, glaring at me. The entire hall has gone deathly quiet. The translator looks at me.

'I think so. Yes.'

'You lot are winding me up, aren't ya? I bet these other prisoners don't have to do all this.'

One of the guards steps forward.

'Turn around and do it now!' he says. 'Is the same for everyone.'

So I angrily turn around, bend over and part my cheeks. I'm in the pose for a couple of seconds when a thought crosses my mind. I'm giving a 'brown-eye' to about a hundred cops, coastguard and prison guards. A big laugh comes rolling out my mouth. I bend over as far as I can and, with my hands, I pull my cheeks apart for all I'm worth.

'Um . . . thank you. That is enough,' the translator says quickly.

'No worries bro. I'm happy to stay like this all day. We get locked up at home for doing this, you know.' I start laughing again and I stay down for another five seconds. I stand up and turn around and there's a sea of faces staring at me with their mouths open.

'Was that OK?' I say. No one answers. They just stand there dumbfounded — perhaps wondering if I belong in a mental institution rather than a prison.

I move on to the next cubicle, where they take a series of photos of my tattoos, but it now feels like I've done myself a mischief with the 'brown-eye'. My cheeks were pulled apart so far that I think I have actually managed to split my 'anoose' as they call it, or the skin of it at least. I decide to just ignore it unless I see blood trickling down my leg.

I'm nearing the end of induction now — just two booths to go. At the first, I'm issued with my prison clothes — a white T-shirt, a black unbranded tracksuit and some green pyjamas. Then into the final booth, where I fingerprint a folder full of documents.

'You have now finished your induction,' says the translator, looking somewhat relieved it's over. You are prisoner 2406. You are in Block D, cell 1, floor 11. Do you understand?'

I nod my head.

Two guards then step forward and introduce themselves, but their names are both so complicated that they're immediately lost to me.

The first guard scowls down at me, his two eyes hidden behind perhaps the biggest nose I've ever seen. It seems to occupy half his face. It starts between his eyes, ramping out at 45 degrees, then curving into a big bulbous knob. It hangs right down to level with his mouth and its pockmarked and bright red complexion have it resembling some form of exotic tropical fruit. He starts talking and I'm most intrigued to see that the end of it actually jiggles. It's like this giant proboscis is in fact a separate organ. He could please most maidens with it, I think to myself. His mug is topped off with glazed yellow eyes and such an unhealthy pallor that I conclude he's either very sick or an alcoholic — or perhaps both.

Shifting my eyes to the second guy, he, too, it seems was absent when nature was handing out the genes of beauty. His face is squashed into a tiny area in the middle of his head. His eyes are nearly touching, yet despite this, a baby 'button' nose has miraculously been squeezed between them. Topping it all off is a narrow little mouth that would struggle accepting a nickel. The most startling thing about him, though, is the size of his head. It is so big it would be perfectly proportioned for the other bloke's nose. Unfortunately, though, it didn't get the bulbous organ, but rather the button.

I remember many years ago, thinking about babies with big heads. It seems a fair proportion of infants are born with large noggins and visitors to the maternity ward always say, 'What a lovely looking baby,' while secretly thanking the Lord their infants are more cranially blessed. But it's like the babies with the big heads disappear into the abyss, and I'd always wondered what happened to them. Well, I've found one of them at least. He grew up and became a prison warden at the Tokyo Detention Centre. Thinking about it; this is the second big-headed baby derivative I've met recently. The first, of course, was Vincent on the *Steve Irwin*, who'd failed to lever his head into Australia's largest motorcycle helmets. It'd be an interesting exercise to see which of them has the bigger head. I'd put my money on this bloke pipping Vincent by a centimetre or two. My mind wanders back to those midnight to 4am shifts with Vincent. It seems like a lifetime ago now. Yet it's only four weeks since I heard Vincent waxing lyrical about a pink lycra suit.

'What's your number?' The man with the big nose suddenly brings me back to reality.

'Um . . . I forget,' I say.

'2406,' he says impatiently.

'Right, 2406 . . . got it.'

He puts a new set of handcuffs on me.

'Now we take you to your cell,' he says. I follow along behind him and Big-head, with a dozen stormtroopers joining us for good measure.

We take the lift up to Level 11 and pass through a thick set of doors. Stretching in front of us is a long corridor, maybe 100 metres in length, with small cells along either side. Several prisoners are being ushered back into their rooms and there's maybe 10 other guards all busily working away. A prisoner inducted before me is escorted to his cell by one of the guards.

'You walk along white line,' Probus says, pointing at the series of white dashes in the middle of the floor. I'm led slowly along the corridor, and every cell, without exception, has a pair of eyes staring sullenly out at me. The eyes are blank and uncaring. It actually feels like a zoo, with dangerous caged animals on either side. The place is eerily quiet, with just the sound of guards' boots squeaking on the bright linoleum floor as we make our way along. A few of the guards glance at me as we pass, but no one says a thing. I'm in my 'assassin' mode, but it feels less convincing than my first attempt in the prison entrance.

There's a sense of relief when we finally reach my cell. I step inside and am instructed to sit on the floor. A new guard comes in and starts issuing instructions. It includes where I must sit, where I sleep and at what time, going to the toilet, brushing my teeth, changing clothes. It all seems very structured and organised. He eventually finishes and leaves. There's a solid clunk as the door is locked behind him and, for the third time in my life, I find myself in prison.

I would later learn that the walk to my cell was the best thing prison staff did for me. Most new inmates are simply ushered along with a single guard. I, on the other hand, had an escort of 12, plus I was still handcuffed and restrained. It painted me up as the most dangerous prisoner to enter the ward in a long time, and gave me instant credibility with other inmates.

I look around my humble abode. It's about 3.5 metres long by 1.8 metres wide. A toilet sits in the corner and a sink opposite, a shelf against one wall and a little writing desk with Japanese instruction papers. On the far wall is a single window.

'A room with a view,' I say to myself and a faint smile crosses my face. I wander over to look outside, but all you get are little peeks through security grates.

On the floor is a small pile of blankets. At 9pm each evening, I'm expected to make my bed — if you can call blankets on the floor a bed — and clamber in for a full 10 hours of kip.

There's a noise by the door and a hatch squeezes open.

'*Ocha* [Tea],' a little man in green pyjamas says. He passes in a small plastic pot of tea and the hatch is closed back up. I sit there watching the pot for a bit. Steam floats out the little spout and there are droplets of condensation on the inside. I pour some into my pale blue plastic cup and take a sip. That familiar taste of green tea — not amazing, but not bad either.

'*Ban-gohan! Ban-gohan!* [Dinner! Dinner!']' A deep voice resonates down the hallway and through the cells a few minutes later. My hatch is soon opened up once again and this time three dishes are passed through — a bowl of rice, a bowl of noodles and a bowl of nondescript soup. I drag my spoon through the soup and little shards of cabbage float to the surface. I tip the rice into the soup and eat them combined and it's actually quite tasty. I follow up with noodles.

A while later and some music starts up. I wander around trying to find the source. It's coming from somewhere in the roof where there must be a speaker hidden behind the grating. 'NHK Musica' I catch from one of the announcers. Then there's a half-hour sports show. Initially, I'm thinking it's football or baseball, but the cheering sounds different —

sumo wrestling perhaps, but I don't hear the sound of fat bellies slapping together.

Then it's news time and, lo and behold, I'm the lead story. I catch the words '*Ady Gil no sencho* [*Ady Gil* captain]', '*hogei* [whaling]' and '*saiban-kan* [judge]'.

'Hey, that's me,' I yell out excitedly. There are a few murmurs and grunts from a couple of other inmates, but then a surly guard appears at my door, indicating I'm not allowed to speak. It's actually a long item, taking several minutes before they move on to some government corruption scandal.

As the evening wears on I just sit in my designated spot and think about things. There's a damp chill about this place — concrete, steel, and a single window in each cell. No soft surfaces at all. It has a sterile feel about it — much like a communist hospital. I run a finger over a wall and it's slippery, like it's got some kind of Teflon paint to stop graffiti. It must work, I guess, because there are no marks at all inside my cell. It feels like it has no history of people before me — no graffiti, no pictures, no posters, no blemishes. Nothing at all — just a featureless box.

I remember the first time I ever got locked up and the cell was amazing. After I finished studying engineering, I got a job with a company called Schlumberger. With a name like that you'd think they made beds — in fact they are the high-tech side of oil exploration.

They sent me to Scotland for a few years where most of my jobs were on semi-submersible rigs in the North Sea. Then I was lucky enough to get transferred to Libya, where I ran a team in the central deserts.

I had this one job a long, long way south of our base and, halfway through it, this big gibley (sandstorm) came through, wiping out all the tyre tracks that you normally follow between locations. My crew left before me in the truck, while I finished the paperwork and met with the client. When I came to leave, all I had to go on was the compass on the dashboard of my four-wheel-drive, which I thought would be enough to get me back.

Some 150 kilometres later, though, and I was starting to get worried. I'd seen nothing at all familiar and the sand was getting softer and more difficult to negotiate. By late afternoon I crested a big dune and there, tucked in the valley before me, was a camp of tan tents, four-wheel-drives and various people ambling about.

I was going to just head down and find out exactly where I was, but the more I saw, the more uneasy I became. The tents were blended into the sand, and it all looked like a well-concealed military base of some sort. I slowly backed away, did a quick U-turn and headed back the way I'd come in.

Looking at my map, there was a large red square marked 'Restricted Zone' that I had possibly strayed into. This generally indicated one of Gaddafi's military areas where he hid terrorist training camps and other dodgy operations. It meant I was at least 50 kilometres off course, which was entirely possible. So I decided to head directly west for 50 clicks. Ten minutes later, though, I saw the dust of vehicles in pursuit and in half an hour they finally caught up with me.

Four guys climbed out of their vehicle and pointed AK47s at me. I tried to explain in my limited Arabic, but they just weren't interested. Two guys started rifling through my gear and, unfortunately, I had a case of explosive detonators with me. These were commonly used by Schlumberger engineers, but that didn't matter to these guys. As soon as they spotted them my heart sank and I knew I was in real trouble. They tied a shirt over my head and dumped me in the back of their four-wheel-drive with a stack of military crates.

It was a few hours later that we pulled into what I assumed was another military camp. I remember being shoved and poked into some kind of building and then into a room. My blindfold was removed and what I saw I'll remember for the rest of my life. I was in a prison and the first thing I noticed was five Arabs squatting and staring sullenly at me. This wasn't so amazing — what was incredible was the history contained within this place. It was the most ancient prison and it had humanity written all over it. The walls, floor and ceiling had untold stains and marks. Graffiti was everywhere; some of it recent and some from long since deceased prisoners I expect. Some of it had been carved into the walls. The bars had been cut, welded and repaired many times. Rustic shackles for chaining people lay buried into the walls and floor. The place had a foul stench about it, a mixture of urine, excrement, sweat, body fluids, food, stale water — dating from last night to a previous century at least. I remember thinking, 'This place could tell some amazing stories: from Shiites and Sunnis, Bedouins, Berbers and Rommel in the Second World War, this place would have seen the lot.'

Once I got over the shock of crapping in a tiny hole in the floor with five Arabs watching, and then squirting a bit of water up my bum to clean myself, life in there was OK.

In the end my team tracked me down a few days later, some baksheesh (bribe money) was paid and I was free to leave, albeit missing half the gear out of my wagon.

My lasting memory, though, is not of the military camp, the soldiers or the guns, but rather the prison cell and not because it was harsh, but because of the history that oozed out of every nook and cranny within those ancient walls.

The Japanese cell I now find myself locked up in is the complete opposite; a bare box with no sign of humanity whatsoever. It's like I'm the first prisoner to ever step foot in here.

It's just before 9pm when Probus comes back to my room.

'You make bed now,' he whispers through the little hatch. I start making it against the wall, but a few minutes later Probus is back.

'No, no, no,' he says. 'In middle.' Everything is so precise. The bed location, where your head goes, the order of the blankets and even how you lie in the bed. I finally piece it together to his satisfaction.

At 9pm, the two long fluorescent tubes turn off and a short single one flickers on. I crawl into my bed and lie back looking at the ceiling. My mind is still way too active to ever sleep, so I just stay awake thinking . . . and listening.

The floor is hard and the cold gradually seeps into my joints. I toss and turn trying to get comfortable. My pillow, about the size of a large brick, actually starts to feel like one. The thing that really starts to vex me, though, is the light. It's still relatively bright and my mind refuses to switch off with all the protons bombarding my eyelids.

I get up and grab a flannel and fold it over my eyes, but within minutes my little hatch is opened.

'No cover eyes,' the guard says politely. A while later and my nose is buried under the blankets, in part because of the light, but also to try to keep warm. This warrants another reprimand from the guard. Eventually, he's had enough. He unlocks my door and kneels down beside me.

'You are problem,' he says. 'Must sleep here, no cover eyes, no change bed, no change blankets. Must stay all night. OK?'

'*Hai, mondai ja nai* [Yes, no problem],' I reply, looking up at his stern face. He points a finger at me and frowns.

'From now, no trouble.' He closes the door and the sound of the lock engaging echoes down the corridor.

Sleep never really arrives for me — or not deep sleep at least. A combination of lights, cold legs, sore ears and hard floor all conspire against me and I'm somewhat relieved when at 7am the following morning, roll call is finally made.

'*Tenkin yo* [Transfer (ready for roll call)]' one of the guards bellows in the hall. His voice is deep and resonating, and it's like a brief baritone song. I sit in the designated spot and another guard steps in front of my window.

'*Bangou* [Number],' he sings.

'*Ni, yon, zero, roku* [2-4-0-6],' I reply. He bows his head and moves off to the next cell. I listen as he checks off all the inmates down my side of the hall, then back on the other.

Three men in green pyjamas then shuffle up pushing a cart. They look like hospital orderlies. The first passes in a pot of green tea, the second a bowl of rice and the third a bowl of soup. There's also a little portion of something akin to birdseed. I look down dejectedly at the soup. It's like a remake of last night's affair. The same bits of lifeless cabbage floating like dead bodies in a stagnant pond. I'm halfway through it when a guard opens the hatch and starts speaking to me in Japanese. Apparently, I'm not quite sitting in the right place, nor am I facing the right direction. It all seems awfully pedantic.

After breakfast I'm ordered into a room in the central area of the complex. A man and a woman are seated silently behind a large office table. The man gestures me to sit in the chair opposite him, which has been chained to the floor.

I sit down and cross my arms, which immediately incites a sharp rebuke from him.

'It is rude to sit like that,' he says sharply. 'You should be respecting me.'

I look at him, a little bewildered that crossing my arms would even be considered offensive.

'And you are who?' I enquire.

He leans forward, spreading his arms apart and placing his hands on the table. His voice is raised and there is a sharp edge to it. 'I am your prosecutor and you shall show me some respect.' There's a long silence as he glares at me. He's a handsome man, not heavily Japanese-looking, though. Maybe of Filipino descent I figure, with a little bit of something else thrown in. His hair is full and brushed back with a faint hint of a part down the middle. He's clean shaven and wearing a tailored suit and silk tie. His face is almost pretty, or perhaps effeminate is a better word, despite his aggressive demeanour. There's a certain arrogance about him as he continues to stare, without blinking.

I look down at his hands. No sign of a wedding ring, although he'd be in his late thirties. His fingers are long and delicate and the nails neatly trimmed. 'I bet he's never climbed a tree in his life,' I think slyly.

The faintest hint of a smile edges into the corner of my mouth and he's bellowing again.

'You find this amusing, do you?'

'Umm . . . no. I was just wondering if you've ever climbed a tree in your life.' His eyes narrow and his stare resumes. His eyes are nearly black, they're so dark.

'What I have done does not concern you, but what you have done is of great concern to me.'

I just continue to look back at him with my hands in my lap. The advice from my lawyers was to not sign anything, to not confess to anything and to not let him intimidate me. It seems the intimidation has started.

'I would like you to tell me why you boarded the *Shonan Maru* on February 15th.' He leans back in his big comfy chair.

'Well, I'm not saying anything about that without instruction from my lawyer.' I place my hands on the table and again there's a sharp rebuke from him. In addition to not crossing my arms or legs, I'm also not allowed to put my hands on the table or behind my head.

The prosecutor leans back smugly. He raises his chin and looks at the ceiling and then his eyes start to flutter as he speaks.

'You are not on the *Ady Gil* now, nor are you in New Zealand. You are in Japan in my company, and while here you will show me respect.' He raises both hands and clasps them behind his head.

'Well, it would seem, sir, that you are also showing me a lack of respect. It is OK for you to place your hands wherever you like, but not for me.'

A sneer crosses his face, as one nostril expands, lifting up the corner of his mouth. There's a long silence as we glare at each other, while the woman just looks at the floor. Finally, the prosecutor opens his mouth. He talks in a low growl.

'This is my office, not yours.'

I look around the Spartan office. It's clearly just an interview room.

'This is hardly your office. It's just one of many rooms shared by prosecutors and investigators, I expect.'

'That may be so, but you should understand that as your prosecutor, I have the ability to make life very easy or very difficult for you. And it will help your cause if you show me respect.'

'Look, as my prosecutor, your job is to charge me with as much as you can and to have me locked up for as long as you can. I'm already locked up in a maximum security prison, so it's not like you can send me to a worse place. I'm not your typical murderer or rapist who comes through here, and who are unhappy to be caught and desperate to be found not guilty. I went to great pains to be caught. I'm not even upset to be here. I will be accepting the things I've done and I'll accept whatever judgement the court hands down.'

The prosecutor's eyes narrow and he studies me warily. 'Does that mean you will accept all charges?' he enquires.

'Well, I haven't been charged with anything yet. But if you do charge me and I've done what you say, I'll probably be accepting the charge.'

'You are currently being investigated for boarding a vessel without cause. Do you accept the charge?'

'No, I do not.'

'Are you saying you did not board the *Shonan Maru*? Surely, this is hard to refute when we have photos and video of you on board.'

'I accept I boarded the vessel but I had just cause to do so. The captain of the *Shonan Maru* rammed and sank my vessel. Under maritime law he has an obligation to take me and my crew to his next port of call.'

The prosecutor remains motionless. He's a hard man to read. There's a small pimple on his chin and I can't help looking at it — the one visible flaw on an otherwise perfect skin. I bet he fussed over it this morning before leaving for work. I can't even remember the last time I saw my ugly mug in the mirror. On the *Shonan Maru*, I guess.

Finally, he replies. 'Well, if you defend yourself with that you will be found guilty.' There's a satisfaction in his voice and the sneer is back on his face. He takes a deep breath.

'You may not know this, but we have been studying your aggressive activity. You have been very evil in Antarctica. In almost all the vicious attacks against the Japanese scientists, you were involved. Prop fouling, lasers, acid throwing, flares and finally the illegal boarding; you would be the number one criminal in this campaign.' He taps the two blue folders lying on the table.

'I have in here,' he says slowly, 'enough evidence to put you away for a very long time.'

I try not to react, but I can feel my confidence evaporating. I was expecting the illegal entry charge and a deportation. If they're to pursue all these other things, I doubt I'll be going home any time soon.

The prosecutor continues his interrogation for several more hours. I'm totally sick of his sneering smile and condescending attitude. My arms feel like foreign attachments that I can't seem to get rid of. I'm one angry camper as I'm led back to Block D.

Lunch is another hearty two-course cabbage meal. I'm expecting more interrogation to follow; instead it's exercise.

I'd always envisaged a concrete area with weights, a basketball court and a field for running in, and perhaps half a dozen blokes bench-pressing 150 kilos and grunting like sows in a trough. What I'm led to couldn't be more different.

It's actually on the roof and rather than a little grassed area, it's a tiny little rectangle of concrete, painted green. No machines, no weights, no pull-up bars and definitely insufficient room to run in. What they do have is skipping ropes and little clippers for cutting your nails. And that's it!

'Skipping rope *kudasai* [Please give me skipping rope],' I say to one of the guards.

'No skipping today. Rainy,' he says. I look up at the sky. It's angry and brooding, much like me right now, but no actual rain.

'Where's the rain? I don't see it.' He points at a puddle on the ground.

'Danger,' he says.

I shake my head and scowl. I look around the yard and there's a little structure to provide shelter against the wall. Around it is a two-inch beam, easily strong enough for my weight. I jump up and start doing pull-ups from it. I get to about eight before one of the guards comes over.

'No, No! You cannot! Danger!' he says sternly.

'What! You mean doing pull-ups is dangerous too?' He nods his head. So they bring you up into that so-called exercise yard, but it's too small to run in, and they have no machines or weights. The only thing they do have is skipping ropes but they won't let you use them. It's all just a waste!

'Can anyone here tell me what you do for exercise?' I look around. There's half a dozen inmates just standing around, and a couple shuffling in circles. They stare at me angrily, sizing me up, wondering no doubt where in the food chain I fit relative to them. One is clipping his toenails. In the walkway are six fat guards, but they're doing their best to look the other way.

'What about press-ups then? Is that bloody dangerous as well?' The guard who told me off for chin-ups nods his head quickly.

'Press-up OK.'

'Well, thank bloody goodness for that,' I mutter under my breath. There's a fair bit of angst in me as I get down on the ground. This will help burn a bit of it off, although a punching bag would be better. I start with one-arm press-ups. It's not as though I'm particularly strong, but for some reason I've always been really good at press-ups. My fitness on them is pretty decent, too, having done heaps in Antarctica and on the *Shonan Maru*. I crank out 30 on my left arm and 30 on my right arm, with lots of grunting on the last few. I can feel the inmates staring at me as I crank them out.

As I stand up, one of the inmates looks at me nervously and holds my stare. He stands there fidgeting continuously; he scratches his hands, he shuffles his feet, his head twitches up and down and sideways, he looks away and then back at me again, he opens his mouth. It's not a smile, nor is it a scowl. The mouth just parts and his upper lip slides up, revealing an ugly array of grey teeth eroded away at the sides. Some have lost so much enamel that they resemble jagged little stalactites. His head continues to jerk, while his eyes for the most part continue to look at me with nervous suspicion.

'What you looking at?' I snarl at him. His mouth closes and he shuffles on, twitching and fidgeting as he goes. The way his head jerks reminds me of a chicken. He's a classic 'P' (methamphetamine) addict. The drug eats away at the nervous system and hardened addicts often end up with jerky heads. On top of that it erodes their teeth. That poor bugger will be in here doing 'cold turkey'. I switch over to normal press-ups and by the end of the half-hour I've done around 500 and am exhausted, in a good way.

Several guards then assemble and escort me back downstairs. Other prisoners seem to have a guard between several of them, while I have my very own posse. That's because I'm a particularly nasty and evil prisoner. Ha ha. The irony of this is not lost on me. The least violent person in the prison and yet I'm treated like I'm the meanest. As I reach my room, another guard comes up, informing us it's time for my bath. I've been nervously apprehensive about this, with visions of sumo wrestlers burying my head in a tub and slapping my little pink bottom. I'm somewhat relieved, therefore, to find the baths are individual, with no wrestlers in sight anywhere.

'You shower off dirt first,' says the guard. 'Then in the bath. Fifteen minutes only.'

It's another one of those dwarf showers where you squat down. I sneak a quick glance around to make sure no one's looking too closely, then I have a quick piss. Pissing in showers (and pools and baths for that matter) is a bloke thing. All boys do it. Some men apparently grow out of it, although I never quite made that transaction. There's some primeval neurological link between water and the male bladder. I'm not quite sure why man evolved with this trait. Darwin could no doubt explain it. He might also be able to elucidate why women never acquired the particular

DNA sequence for shower pissing. Well, I assume they never acquired it, but in reality, I don't know this for a fact. Maybe at the party we have when I arrive back in New Zealand, I'll ask some of the women there for an opinion, and of course, they'll assume incarceration has addled my feeble mind.

Moving right along, the piss is done, a quick scrub and I leap into the bath, which is scalding hot. My damaged butt-crack from yesterday's 'brown-eye' stings and it takes a good minute to sink in without screaming. I'm assuming the damage was from the brown-eye and not from some other nefarious prison activity I was unaware of during the night.

I sink right down so my nose is at water level and the warmth soaking into me is glorious. Not even the sprinkling of pubes on the surface can detract from one of the most wonderful experiences. I lie my head back and close my eyes.

It's a funny thought that enters my head. What is the technical name for your butt-crack? I'm sure it has a proper name, but I don't remember ever hearing it. Same for the back of your knee. What does the good doctor say when he's referring to this bit? My mind has hardly wandered from these musings when a guard is barking at me that my time is up.

I'm sparkly clean and pink from the heat as I clamber out and dry off. I'm just pulling my knickers on when there's excited shouting and cheering in the hallway. I wander out to find two inmates busy fighting — one short and skinny, the other short and fat. It reminds me of a fight between two girls I saw back at school. There's no real punches or violence. More, just pushing and shoving. It's odd that the guards don't step in and break it up. A minute later and I hear the stormtroopers heading our way; the thudding of dozens of boots shuddering along the hallway. The kids are oblivious. Skinny tries some fancy karate kick and it elicits a cheer from the inmates all egging them on. He's probably just watched a re-make of *Enter the Dragon* and figured he'd launch one of Bruce Lee's finest. Unfortunately, he loses balance and topples over. Fatty senses his chance and pounces.

Two seconds later, the stormtroopers swarm onto the pair, burying them in a sea of bodies. All that's missing from the ruck is a rugby ball and some mud. The two are separated and dragged off down the hall. None of the stormtroopers is big or intimidating, and a couple would look more at home in a florist shop than a high-security prison. I guess they just use strength of numbers. They're also all carrying Tasers and pepper spray so that would even things up with any violent buggers. It would be interesting to see what would happen if half a dozen of Paremoremo's meanest descended on here, though. That'd create some carnage!

I wander back to my room. Despite my piss in the shower, there's the urge for 'toilet-time' building in me, although this time its number two. I sit down and eye up the toilet nervously. Various guards and inmates mill around and peer in at me. It's quite intimidating and I keep putting the task off. After an hour I just decide to get it over with.

My diet for the last month has been rice at every meal and my turds have definitely become more solid. I meander, as casually as I can, over to my humble toilet and sit down.

'This is like giving birth,' I say to myself quietly. Making the situation worse are the guards and inmates who continue to glance at me.

'Just ignore them,' I keep thinking, as I try to just get the job finished. It's hard to look staunch when you're taking a dump. It doesn't matter how many tattoos you've got, how ugly you are, or the size of your muscles, pooing in public 'just ain't cool'.

There's a certain lack of dignity about prisons — or this one at least. Parting your cheeks and lifting your balls, bathing and toilet duties, strip searches, they're all on public display and it just sweeps your dignity aside. I remember Sharyn describing the maternity ward and how her dignity was left at the front door as she walked in. Prison is the same.

I struggle away with my business. I think I need a crowbar to lever the beast out. I'm wiping my bum as two guards come to the door. Apparently, I have visitors.

'*Chotto matte* [Just a moment],' I say quickly. A quick wipe and my pants are up. I can't help admiring my handiwork as I flush the toilet. It's a monster.

'You'll need to call "barge control" if that ever makes it into Tokyo Bay in one piece,' I think. A big grin erupts on my face at the joke. I'm still laughing as I walk out the door for my unexpected visitors.

Three staff from the New Zealand Embassy are waiting patiently for me as I enter the little partitioned interview room. Jenny, seated in the middle, starts talking with a somewhat intellectual Kiwi accent. (Some would consider that an oxymoron.)

'How are you being treated in here?' she says in a soft, compassionate voice.

'Yeah, fine. I've got no problems.'

'That's good. Just so you are clear, the New Zealand Government cannot intervene in the legal process here. All we can do is ensure you get the same treatment as a Japanese national.' I nod my head. 'If you feel you are not being treated fairly, or you would like to contact us, then send us a letter. They cannot stop you from having access to us.'

'Yep, no worries.'

'There is a delicate matter to discuss as well and it's a little bit personal.' She looks slightly embarrassed as she hesitates. 'Many of the Kiwis imprisoned in Japan get very . . . um . . . constipated.' I'm tempted to tell her about the python I've just released, but think better of it.

'Oh, I'm fine in that regard, thanks,' I reply.

We move on to the relationship between New Zealand and Japan. Jenny explains that the two countries are gradually moving closer together, and long term, New Zealand is hoping for a free-trade agreement (FTA) to be signed off.

I used to be strongly in favour of these. Keynesian economics tells us that countries will have particular things that they are good at. By entering into free trade, countries can specialise a bit more in those areas of strength and the sum total of goods and services produced between the two countries will increase, so the average wealth of the two countries also increases. There are a few issues surrounding this, though.

Firstly, as wealth increases, so does consumption. I'm not saying I want us all to be poor, but I'd rather see increased wealth directed into positive areas for the benefit of humankind, rather than just the purchase of shite.

Secondly, FTAs have a tendency to increase income disparity. People at the top of the food chain get more, while those at the bottom get less. An agreement between New Zealand and Japan, for example, would certainly push a few more Kiwis onto minimum wages, while in Japan a number of farmers would be forced out of business. Of course, we'd both get access to some cheaper goods, but I'm questioning that we really need this.

Thirdly, small countries often get screwed in signing deals with dominant economies. Hardened negotiators from countries such as China and the United States will exact a heavy price from other countries signing up for FTAs with them. Small nations become prostitutes and they sell their soul in the process. Consider Australia — they went galloping into Iraq with the United States, despite overwhelming public outrage at home, and all on the promise of a trade deal that has still not eventuated.

So as I sit here with the Embassy officials, I'm not really sure New Zealand needs a free-trade deal with Japan, even though we might get cheaper laptops in the process.

The meeting finishes and I'm led back to my room for dinner. It's a quiet evening tucked in my cell listening to the radio. At 9pm I sling on my green pyjamas, then it's into a hurriedly made bed. The room remains cold and damp and, despite the blankets, a cold chill once again envelops me. I curl up into a foetal position, hoping enough of my head is poking out to satisfy the guards.

I lie there pondering how to keep warm. Maybe the guards will let me keep an extra layer on under my pyjamas. Whenever you change, the clothes get swapped through the hatch, so to wear something extra requires the supervisor's permission. I think I'll pose the question to him in the morning.

The other issue is dampness. This morning there was a thick layer of condensation on my window. It's probably not helped by having a toilet and basin in the room. Although putting the toilet lid down may help a bit. That'd be a first; a male voluntarily putting the lid down on a toilet. What's the world coming to? Thinking about it, most of the condensation will be from my breathing, and there's not much I can do to stop that.

I try to sleep but my mind is way too active. It meanders around on various topics. Prison isn't quite what I'd expected. While there are some evil-looking inmates, none is the big scary monster I was worried about. They all seem pretty wary of me, in fact. Maybe I've fooled them with the 'What you lookin' at?' snarl I've been dishing out. Whatever, people are keeping well clear of me and I'm most relieved.

The bath was amazing. It's probably the highlight since I boarded the *Shonan Maru*. I can get used to two of them per week, that's for sure. The exercise yard — well, it was disappointing, but at least you get out for half an hour each day. Finally, the food is average, but as Vincent said, 'Prison is no "hi-de-hi" camp for the elderly,' so I reckon a month in here will be fine, really.

The worst thing is it's another month away from my girls. Unfortunately, it's become the norm in recent years. Now the poor things have news of their old man being locked up in prison plastered all over the TV and newspapers. Regardless of the cause I'm sure it's embarrassing for them. I'll write them a letter in the morning.

There's a bang down the far end of the hall that drags me out of my slumber. A guard with a bad limp hobbles past. Another bang, then an inmate starts yelling. He gets more and more agitated about something. It sounds like he's trying to smash a window with the little desk. It takes about two minutes for the stormtroopers to arrive — 25 of them running in unison down the hall. I hear one of them bark instructions to the inmate, but that just seems to wind him up even more. It's now a torrent of screams and shouts from the inmate. There's a quick scuffle and then silence. A short time later they drag him past my room. He looks unconscious, with his legs dragging listlessly behind. Note to self — do not yell and scream in the night.

Thankfully, I do finally get to sleep, and it's not until about six o'clock the following morning that I start to stir. I roll onto my back and look up at the ceiling. There's a black dot in between the two fluorescent tubes that I'd never noticed before. 'What is that?' I wonder. I lie there looking at it. Why would they put something there? Then it occurs to me that it's probably a camera. I shove my mini desk under it and climb up for a look, and sure enough there's a little wee camera lens pointing at me. The sneaky buggers.

It's back to bed, but now there's another bit of dark nudging at me. It's up in the corner of my room by the window. Is that what I'm thinking? I jump out of bed, this time climbing up on the toilet and there's a little spider looking back at me from a partially built web. You little beauty! I'm busy admiring him when there's a sharp tap on my door from one of the guards. 'You stay in bed till roll call,' he says sternly. I scramble back into my scratcher and lie there admiring my new pet. It's funny how such a little thing could have any significance for me and yet I'm really happy to have his company.

When I was a kid I had a pet spider. I called him Hercules. Well, I thought of him as my pet, but in reality he was just a spider that lived out the front of our home. I'd feed him flies every night and he grew into quite a remarkable specimen with a big bulbous bottom on him. I used to joke that he had a bum like that because he was an African spider.

Then one day he just disappeared. I'm not sure what happened to him. Most probably a bird finally got him. His bum alone would make a tasty little hors d'oeuvre for a discerning starling. At that time, though, losing the little guy just broke my heart. I bawled my eyes out for hours.

I look back at my new pet. 'I'll call you Hercules,' I say to him. It's amazing he even made it in here. The only gaps are a few millimetres by the air vent outside, and a few millimetres by the door. It then dawns on me that young Hercules has not found the most productive rainforest to inhabit. He's the first bit of life I've seen in my room. Not even a fly have I spotted in the sterile confines of my cell. He's going to find slim pickings in here.

The chimes come through the radio announcing 7am wakeup. I jump out of bed and climb up to check out Hercules. 'Good morning,' I say cheerily. He doesn't say anything. When he starts talking, I'll know it's time to escape.

I get started on a letter to Sharyn and the girls, interrupted briefly by roll call and breakfast. I can't even remember the last time I actually hand-wrote a letter, as opposed to tapping it out on a keyboard — perhaps when I was trying to woo Sharyn with my wily charms, many years ago. It's a slow and ponderous process despite the limit of only five pages.

As soon as it's finished I press my buzzer and Probus comes over to my hatch.

'I'd like to send this letter to my family please,' and I pass the brown envelope out to him. His eyebrows slope into each other as a frown forms slowly on his face.

'But you are on communication ban. No letters.'

'What do you mean "No letters"?'

He shrugs his shoulders. 'No letter!' and he holds his hands in a cross.

'Not even to family?' I ask, bewildered by this.

'*Sou desu ne* [That's right].'

'Well, how come everyone else can send letters?'

'Hmm. They got no communication ban. Only you and Yakuza have it.' With that he slams my hatch and wanders off.

I remember Jenny from the New Zealand Embassy talking about letters. I fossick through all the papers on my shelf. It seems crazy I'm not even allowed to communicate with my family. Apparently, the ban is imposed where inmates might continue in their illegal activities which for Yakuza I can understand. For me — it's not like I'm a career criminal.

I finally locate the paper from the New Zealand Embassy. It explicitly states that I have access to them via either letter or prison visits, so they can just forward it on for me.

I press my buzzer and Probus comes back with an agitated look on his face.

'It says here, I can send letters to my Embassy,' and I hand the paper out to him. I don't think he reads English, but he looks at the paper nonetheless. 'So I'd like to send this letter to my Embassy please,' and I cross out our home address and scribble on the Embassy's. Probus looks at it dubiously as I pass the envelope over to him.

'But this the same letter!' he protests.

I give him a little smile. 'Yes. It was my mistake. I always meant it to go to the Embassy. Very sorry.'

He shakes his head, his big nose jiggling as he does so. I think he's about to refuse when there's a commotion on the other side of the hall. He looks over for a second, then hurries off to investigate, thankfully still clutching my letter.

There's an inmate outside the door to his cell, yelling abuse at one of the guards. Probus arrives and starts giving him instructions, but this just seems to agitate him even more. He turns towards me during one of his rants and it's my old mate 'Chicken-head' from the exercise yard. A minute later there's the unmistakable rumble of stormtroopers on their way. Chicken-head stops yelling and freezes for a few seconds. There's a horrified look on his face and his head starts jerking. Then for a second time he freezes, only this time he pisses his pants. There's cackling and laughter from the other inmates as the liquid spreads down his grey trackpants and onto the floor. I'm not even sure he knows what he's done. He looks terrified out of his mind, or what's left of it at least, as the sea of blue uniforms surrounds him.

There's a trail of urine past my door as he's dragged out, much to the amusement of the other inmates. Maybe I was a bit mean in snarling at him yesterday. He has no friends in here. In all fairness, he belongs in a rehab clinic rather than a prison. Life can indeed be cruel.

Speaking of cruel, a short time later, I spot my first Yakuza. I'm on my way to the exercise yard with the image of Chicken-head pissing his pants still floating around in my mind, when I spot an inmate about to climb into the bath. His back, arms and neck are all covered in garish tattoos, mostly dragons and serpents by the looks. He's mid-fifties, short, stocky and a bit overweight, but there's an arrogance about his stare. Cold, cruel eyes glare at me for a few seconds, then he turns and climbs into his bath. I'd later learn that this guy was one of the most feared gang leaders until his arrest last year.

As I continue up to the exercise yard, I realise what a diverse group of people are contained within these walls. It's interesting watching the other inmates, trying to figure out their stories. Some are obvious, like the druggies, some of the violent offenders and maybe old Yakuza back there. But some in here, you look at them and you wonder how on earth they ended up in this trap. There's a few 'wolves in sheep's clothing' of course — inmates who are sweet and fluffy on the outside, but underneath lies something more sinister.

Thankfully, today there's no rain, so skipping is allowed. My plan was to do half an hour, but after about 10 minutes I'm knackered. I switch over to press-ups again and then it's back to my room.

Another guard I haven't seen before is waiting for me. He sits down just outside my cell.

'My name is Takashi,' he says abruptly. 'I am warden here, and I must talk to you.' He's tall and wiry with a slightly gaunt face and unsmiling eyes.

'*Mondai nai* [No problem],' I reply nervously. He shifts around on the floor to get comfortable.

'It has been reported to me that you are intimidating other prisoners.' I'm about to say something but he holds his hands up to stop me.

'It is forbidden to communicate with other prisoners in any way. If you continue looking for trouble things will be very difficult for you here.

I think you have enough trouble in Japan already.' He motions that I can speak now.

He's referring, I guess, to my 'What you lookin at?' assassin snarl, which remains my only communication with any other inmate. This morning I added a 'bro' on the end and gave it a Maori accent, which sounded particularly vicious. My nephew would have been so proud of me. It has actually become a defence mechanism. I strut around like a puffed-up and angry peacock, but it's all a sham. Underneath I remain anxious and uneasy among all these violent people.

To be fair to the prison staff here, it's not quite the rampant WWF with weapons I was anticipating. 'Hulk Hogan' and 'The Rock' have yet to make an appearance in their 'budgie smugglers', so while I might be nervous, I'm not the terrified 'chicken in a pen of weasels' that I was originally expecting to be. And if I've fooled the guards with my snarl, hopefully I've fooled the inmates as well.

I look back at Takashi.

'Sir, I'm not looking for trouble. I just want to get out of here in one piece.' He forces a faint smile.

'Pete. My job is to keep you safe . . . and the other prisoners as well. This is a warning for you. You must do what you are told. And you must not cause any trouble with other prisoners.'

I nod, and he sits there for a few more seconds studying me, then gets up to leave.

'You have visitors by the way — *bengoshi* [lawyers].'

I'm led downstairs to the interview room where Miyake-san is waiting.

'*Ohayou gozaimasu* [Good morning],' he says politely, as I enter. He's wearing a dapper little tweed suit with a waistcoat — a bit like what the English gentry might wear, only missing the gold pocket watch. He waits patiently for me as I get seated.

'So how was the prosecutor?' he says smiling.

'Hmmm . . . I don't like him so much. He is very arrogant.'

Miyake nods his head.

'Yes, well prosecutors in Japan are mostly like that.'

'I know he's just doing his job . . . but he doesn't need to be such a wanker.' Miyake looks puzzled by my last word, but says nothing.

'While I think about it Miyake-san, they are doing lots of investigation of the boarding. How do we make sure they also investigate the ramming?'

He cocks his head for a few seconds while he contemplates this.

'Under Japanese law the coastguard must investigate all collisions involving Japanese vessels. If they will or not . . . I do not know . . .' He opens up his little diary.

'You are meeting the coastguard this morning. Maybe you can ask the Investigator.'

I nod in agreement.

We move on to the case, most of which I know already. We remain hopeful the court will settle for a summary offence, the decision of which will be made in a few weeks. Until then I just continue with the prosecutor, as well as the coastguard now it would seem. Miyake is about to leave when he remembers something. He pulls a big folder of papers out of his bag and smiles.

'Sea Shepherd has set up a "Supporters' Page" for you, so people can send you messages. Already, though, is too many.' He puts his hand on the folder. 'This is just a few. I think is over 500 now. What we will do at each meeting is hold up a selection to the glass for you to read.'

'Oh fantastic,' I reply. Miyake places an A4 sheet against the glass partition and I start reading.

'Hi. My name is Izabella. I am 11 years old. I am from Brazil. I think is very bad that Japanese keep you in prison. You are doing what is right. And the great whales and God thank you for your brave actions. I am studying English and as soon as I am 18 I will apply to join Sea Shepherd and I would like to be crew on your boat. You are my hero. God bless — Izabella.'

A lump forms in my throat as I read the last lines again. How cool is that! Miyake pulls up another email but I can't help but think about

Izabella's. The actions of Sea Shepherd have impacted on a young girl on the other side of the Pacific. She's been motivated enough to send us a message but, more importantly, to set some goals that one day just might make the world a fractionally better place.

I've always believed that we affect the planet in two ways: firstly, our actions have direct consequences. We save some whales, we stop nuclear testing, we tip oil down the drain, we chop down native trees; these all impact on the environment in positive or negative ways.

Secondly, through our actions we influence those around us. If we consume lots of shite, our kids probably will as well. If we use public transport, our friends are more likely to do so. We all have a spider web of relationships linking those around us. Being involved in things such as *Earthrace* and Sea Shepherd increases the size of our web. We're able to reach people as far away as Izabella, who we might never actually get to meet. The obligation then is to ensure this influence is used in a positive way.

I work my way through another dozen messages. They are from all over the world and many sectors of society — quite astonishing really. I was aware we had received strong media coverage in Japan, with, admittedly, the 'dangerous assassin' bit not reflecting on me so well. If the supporters' messages are anything to go on, it seems like the story has had almost global reach.

The final message is from Larry. He's decided to stay on the *Steve Irwin* for the Mediterranean tour. It finishes with a series of Japanese sayings that he feels will be useful to me. The English translations are as follows.

'Is that your soap? Let me pick it up for you.'

'No, that doesn't hurt at all.'

'Yes, I like that a lot.'

'Would anyone else like a go?'

'I would like to share a room with a sumo wrestler.'

There's the same thread wound through all his messages. I can just picture Larry's little yarpie head poking out from under his sheets as he dreamed these up. He'd be sniggering away to himself, admiring his masterful crude wit, then he'd hipitty-hop off to see the translator. She wouldn't quite understand him, of course, but she'd diligently do the translation all the same, given Larry's earnest expression as he sits there like a gnome in his 5XL hoodie.

I finish up with Miyake, then am escorted to another room where a coastguard interviewer by the name of Hajimoto is waiting for me. He's a short, stocky man with broad shoulders and powerful-looking arms. He'd make a good rugby prop or a weightlifter perhaps. Short, stocky people are a bit limited for options when it comes to elite sports.

He commences with a series of questions related to the net I cut in boarding the *Shonan Maru*. After an hour of this I start to grow impatient.

'You should get the prosecutor's notes,' I suggest to him. 'All these things you ask me now, those questions have been answered already.' Hajimoto frowns.

'There will be two investigations — one by coastguard and one by the prosecutor. And some cross-over is expected.' He goes back to his notes. His body language suggests the matter is closed.

'Can I ask what you will actually be investigating?'

He looks back up at me. 'We do not know exactly what crimes have been committed yet. My job is to find that out.'

'That is good. I am assuming that you will also be investigating the ramming.' He breathes out with a heavy sigh.

'I am not sure a crime was actually committed with the collision.'

'Yes, well, surely that's why it needs to be investigated? To find out if a crime has taken place.'

'It is not part of my brief.'

'With all due respect sir, you're asking all these questions about a $300 net, implying I have caused significant property damage, but you're not prepared to ask questions about the destruction of a $US3 million super-boat. Perhaps the ramming should be your brief.'

He puts his pen down on the desk and looks at me.

'Perhaps it is another investigator who will cover this.' He then waves his hand dismissively and goes back to questioning about the net.

I remain surly with him for the rest of the morning, before being escorted back to my room for lunch. In the afternoon, it's another long session with the prosecutor, with yet more questions relating to the net and my boarding. As I'm escorted back to my room, I start thinking about Hercules, hoping that will cheer me up.

It's been a couple of days since he arrived in my life. He seems quite content to sit up in his corner, but I do fear his mortal coil might expire soon, if he continues on his fast. He's not fasting deliberately; it's just that he's selected a barren wasteland in which to start his new life.

'It's a pity you can't eat cabbage,' I sigh later while I'm having dinner, my spoon stirring up a lifeless fluid. There's suddenly a moment of divine inspiration, a flash of brilliance even. I'll just hang food outside and catch insects for him. Brandishing a pale shard of waterlogged cabbage, I poke the bait out the narrow gap that Hercules probably came in through. I check it every half hour and, sadly, even by lights out at 7pm, nothing has been fooled onto it. Similarly, all the following day, nothing is tempted.

'The life has been sucked from it already,' I say to Hercules. 'It's got no smell left.' I'm pondering this over dinner, which serendipitously tonight includes an orange. Another great flash of brilliance; orange peel has lots of smell. A right insect magnet I reckon. I squeeze a bit of juice on a peel and poke it where the cabbage has been. I'm again disappointed as the evening draws to a close.

The following morning I slip out of bed at 'sparrow's fart' and again nothing. Then just before lunch, a bonanza. Not just one, but five little insects, all gnawing away on the inside of the skin. I eye them up anxiously as I peer through the glass. I gently tug the skin back through the slot and three fly off. One gets squished on the way in and is dead on arrival, while the last one is merely injured. He looks a bit like a big sandfly. I'm not sure what he is, but I'm sure Hercules will love him. I climb up on the toilet and poke him into the web. I end up damaging a few strands but, thankfully, the little insect is stuck fast to the silken trap. Hercules is a bit wary at first. He sits there sizing up the situation.

'Come on Hercules,' I urge him. 'Get stuck in!' He takes a couple of tentative steps, decides his dinner has arrived and springs into action. There's a mad dash as he careers down and grabs his helpless prey.

A thought enters my mind. Maybe I'll get in trouble with Sea Shepherd for interfering with nature. Today, I've killed two little insects. It's easy to frown on such escapades sitting in your hemp-covered lounge suite eating a tofu burger, though. Not so easy when you're going mad in a max-security prison and you're not allowed to speak to anyone. Hopefully, my sanity can take precedence over insects. Just this once.

11
Shocks to the system

Over the following days and weeks my life starts to fall into a solid routine.

7.00	Wake-up call. Clean room.
7.20	Roll call.
7.30–8.00	Breakfast
8.30–9.00	Exercise (Mon–Fri)
9.00–9.15	Bath (Mon, Thurs)
9.30–11.30	Coastguard interrogation
11.30	Lunch
1.00–4.00	Prosecutor interrogation
4.30	Dinner
5.00	Evening roll call
6.00–9.00	Prosecutor interrogation
9.00	Lights out.

I'm spending eight hours each day in interviews and the time seems to just blitz by. Sadly, neither the coastguard nor the prosecutor show any interest whatsoever in the collision. I have an astounding five days of questioning simply verifying the gear I wore when I boarded the *Shonan Maru*.

Towards the end of the investigation period, there's an increasing number of questions regarding 'Whale Wars I' and 'Whale Wars II', campaigns with which I wasn't involved. Despite my continued protests that I have no comment to make, they remain intent on showing me episode after episode in search of my elusive opinions.

The prosecutor has gradually mellowed and I almost like the guy now. I wouldn't go to a pub for a beer with him, but he's still decent enough. He'll be very formidable in court; his voice has such strength about it and he's very adept at how he uses it. He also knows my case so well now, having spent over 100 hours interviewing me.

Hercules and I manage to get a good little routine going as well. Any fruit that arrives — which sadly isn't often — I cut some up and use it as bait. I've found that just some juice around the window crack is enough to coax the odd insect inside, and once in, it struggles finding its way back out again — a bit like an eel trap.

Already I think Hercules has grown a bit. He seems to know now that me standing on the toilet is often mealtime because he races to the corner and gets all excited. He's a fussy little fellow, too. He doesn't eat everything. He must just suck the juices out of each one then he drags them over to a long thread on the side of his web and hangs them there like trophies. By the time I leave, it'll be a full cabinet, I believe. Or perhaps he realises my stay here will be brief and he's saving up some 'ready-to-serve' meals for when I'm gone. Either way he's got an impressive row of insect carcasses nicely lined up — a very Japanese spider perhaps.

Using the Embassy as an intermediary has been a godsend for letters. Each weekday between 5 and 6pm I churn out a letter, normally back to Sharyn and the girls. They're probably bored to death — five pages with content dribbled through them sparingly. I'm not allowed to write about any other prisoners or the events thereof, so I suspect the content has as much life as prison soup does. Nevertheless, it makes me feel good to be in touch with the whanau (family) back home.

It's a wet and windy day that heralds the end of the investigation period. As soon as I walk in the room I know the news is bad. Miyake and Fukuyama have long, forlorn faces as we exchange greetings.

'I am sorry to say that the indictment is not good,' Miyake says. 'They have charged you with the lot.'

He holds a piece of paper against the glass and I read the charges:

Boarding a vessel without just cause;
Destruction of property ($1300 net);
Disruption of commerce;
Possession of a deadly weapon (knife);
Assault causing injury.

I read the charges several times. 'Do we still have the trial in 10 days?' I ask.

Miyake shakes his head. 'No Pete-san. That was only if the court went for a summary offence. It would have meant you plead guilty and they let you go. All these charges are too much. It will have to go to a full trial now.'

I put my head in my hands, collecting my thoughts. I had an inkling they would charge me with more than one offence . . . but five! A couple of them are so petty as well.

'Can we defend against the charges?'

Miyake goes on to explain the difficult situation we face.

'The destruction of net — $1300. We should just accept it and pay compensation.'

It irks me to pay $1300 to those bastards when they sank a three million dollar boat, but $1300 in the scheme of things is negligible. That's three hours' work for one of the lawyers.

'For the knife,' Miyake continues. 'We just accept that. It is a minor charge . . . and the unlawful entry on a vessel, we are suggesting we accept this charge as well.'

'Even though they sank my boat? It seems so unfair. I have all these charges levelled against me by that *Shonan Maru* crew . . . .'

Miyake shrugs his shoulders. 'I know it seems unfair. But they are not on trial. You are.'

'Yeah, but they should be on trial. The system here is just corrupt.'

There's a long silence between us and my frustration is starting to show. Miyake turns to Fukuyama and they whisper in Japanese. Finally, he comes back to me.

'We are suggesting we contest the assault charge and the disruption of commerce charge, but only in a small way. To defend the charges fully may take years.'

'So what you're saying basically is we just plead guilty,' I spit at him.

'In a way, yes. If you want to get home as quickly as possible that is the best way.'

'And what about the IWC Resolutions, CITES and International Law that all say the whaling is illegal, does that have no bearing on the case?'

Miyake looks down at the floor again. 'I am sorry, but these things do not matter. In Japan, whaling is legal and to argue aspects of International Law would just drag the trial out, maybe even for years. You would be in prison for all that time. And in the end you will still be found guilty. Over 99 per cent of cases brought to trial in Japan result in convictions.'

'Ninety-nine per cent!' I reply incredulously. 'You're not serious?'

'Yes. A not guilty verdict in Japan is very rare.'

'Well, why am I bothering with lawyers then? Maybe I should just sack you lot and plead guilty.'

Fukuyama starts to speak. It's almost the first time she's said anything other than a greeting. Her voice sounds soft compared to my increasingly belligerent tones.

'Pete-san. Our job is to get you out of Japan as soon as possible. That is what we are trying to do. Despite all the charges we still think a suspended sentence is possible.'

I take a deep breath, trying to calm myself down.

'So when can you get me out of here?' I say finally. She pulls out a diary and the two of them consult it.

'We think mid-July is the earliest,' she replies. I flop my head back in my arms. July is another three months away. I've already done two — one on the *Shonan Maru* and one in Japan. Another three seems like an eternity. We sit there in silence.

I lift my head back up.

'What's the good news then?' I try to smile. They look at each other. Then Miyake explains he has a letter from Sharyn. He grabs his briefcase and starts rummaging through the pages, then places one against the glass.

I start to read. It's mostly about my girls. Danielle has just turned 15 and passed her learner's car licence. I cast my mind back a year to when I was teaching her to drive and she ran over a flax bush in an industrial estate. I smile at the memory.

The words in the last paragraph then leap out and slap me in the face.

'I am now seeing someone else.' I read them again and a sudden sadness comes over me. It shouldn't really. We split up over six months ago, and that she has a new partner is a good thing. But for some reason it touches a really raw nerve in me.

'I'd like to finish now please.' I can hardly get the words out between sobs. I press the buzzer and a couple of guards arrive to escort me back to my room. I'm a blubbering mess as the cell door is locked behind me a few minutes later. I collapse on the floor, my throat sore and tears cascading over my cheeks.

I crawl over to my mat and slouch on it. What the hell am I doing here? I look around my sterile room. Hercules sits up in his corner waiting for dinner. It's a sad life when two months have passed and he remains the highlight. All those people who advised me against joining Sea Shepherd will be saying, 'We told you so.'

Sharyn and I got together almost from school. I was studying engineering at Auckland University while she worked in Hamilton. She'd drive up to see me each weekend with bags of mussels and bottles of rum. We'd eat during the day, drink in the evening and have more fun at night.

After I left uni, she was always happy to follow along and support me in the various locations that employment and adventure took us.

It wasn't until *Earthrace* that we had our first ever fight, and regrettably since then they became increasingly regular. The weird thing about *Earthrace* was I only ever envisaged a one-year project, but it just kept growing and growing. It took a full year just to get clear in my mind what we were going to do, then another year to raise some sponsorship. Sadly, though, the sponsorship was nowhere near enough, so Sharyn steadfastly stood beside me as I sold off our company, our forestry block and our shares. In the end we sold everything and racked up debts of nearly $1.5 million. In 2007 we made the first record attempt, but it was a total disaster. Funding it nearly sent us bankrupt and we failed miserably.

I looked at selling the boat, but no one was interested; it was just an odd-looking vessel that had failed a record attempt. The mountain of debt hung over us like an ominous dark cloud, and staring financial ruin in the face, I'd gone back on the sponsorship trail. I felt like I had a tiger by the tail, and if I let go it would devour us. This became a very difficult time. Financial pressure, incessant absence from family and disappointment at the initial failure bit deeply into me, and I was probably the most miserable I'd ever been.

Cracks started to appear in our marriage. We fought, and sometimes about the most minor thing. I was struggling keeping the wolves at bay, while Sharyn battled raising two girls while working full-time. From there we started to drift apart.

In 2008 we made the second record attempt, circumnavigating the globe in 61 days, smashing the old record by over two weeks. We completed the tour and sponsor obligations, arriving back in New Zealand in early 2009.

Arriving home, though, things were tense. It was a bit like we didn't know each other any more. Sharyn had changed a bit and little things she'd say or do would piss me off. At the same time, I don't think she really liked what I'd become. *Earthrace* was this monster and fighting it had changed both of us.

Part of the problem had been Sharyn was an outsider. She had bravely put her house and mortgage on the line to allow me to follow something I believed in, but others, me included, were running the project. Sharyn and the girls did join us on some great voyages — a tour around UK and up the Seine to Paris, the east coast of Australia and some great little stops around New Zealand. But Sharyn by now hated the boat. She was an outsider on it, despite her mortgage and assets having created it. The boat was a wedge that continued to cleave us apart. .

Where previously we'd shared news of everything, when I returned home there were always little secrets. Instead of Sharyn being my soul mate that I'd tell everything to, she'd only get the good news, or the edited 'highlights' package at 10pm. The more this pissed her off, the more the news was edited. Secrets and marriage, they don't work.

We talked about splitting up, but each time it was like looking into a black hole. You want to jump, but you don't know how far the bottom is. So you back away from the abyss and patch things up again. When you've been together since school, splitting up isn't so easy, and especially when the time together has been so rich. Sharyn was also the only love I'd ever had, and the thought of abandoning that was dreadful.

Finally, we made the decision to separate shortly before I left for Antarctica. In the back of my mind I'd harboured thoughts of coming home after the campaign and I'd have my old Sharyn back — we'd be soul mates again and start afresh. In reality it was probably never going to happen, so I've joined the long list of losers with failed marriages and I've split from the most awesome lady I've ever met.

That Sharyn has a new partner is a good thing, but for some reason, her words, 'I am seeing someone else', continue to reverberate around in my head as I wallow in self-pity. Dinner being passed through the hatch brings me back to reality briefly, but I quickly revert back to numbness. My stomach is all balled up in a knot. Maybe Larry was right about me.

Maybe I am destined to be a 'bull elephant' and just roam the world with no ties. The thought of not seeing Sharyn, my girls and my family, though, that'd be a stark and bleak future.

I lean back against the wall and look up at Hercules' web in the corner of my room.

'Maybe Sharyn and I can be great friends,' I say to him. 'For half my life she was like my best mate anyway.' Various friends of ours who've gone through broken marriages have all ended up in bitter acrimony, though. The kids, the house, the money, the guinea pigs; it all ends up in a matrimonial brawl, while lawyers suck the couples dry. Well, at least we won't end up fighting over the money, because there isn't any. Ha ha.

And Sharyn is an amazing lady; probably the most generous and giving person I've ever met. If anyone were going to forgive my ample flaws and weaknesses and accept me as a friend, it's her. She accepted me for untold years anyway.

I get a pen and paper out. 'Dear Sharyn, It's good that you now have a boyfriend,' I write. 'What's his name and what's he like?' Then I start wondering if maybe he's someone I know. Maybe I don't want to know just yet. Hmm . . . better to wait till I get home perhaps. I then scrub out the last sentence.

What about my girls? Will they want anything to do with their criminal dad? I've seen so little of them these last few years. In many respects I've betrayed them as much as I have Sharyn.

I cast my mind back a few years. I came home from work one day and Danni had scrounged up a Barbie pedal car from someone's rubbish. She had the older kids from our neighbourhood sweating away pushing her around in it. Half an hour later, I looked out and there they were still heaving and grunting at Danni's bidding. I was upset that she wasn't sharing, but at the same time I was really proud of her. I remember thinking, 'What potential she has: very clever, always scheming, a born leader.' Better just hope she hasn't inherited too many of her dad's flaws.

A guard appears and I hand my uneaten dinner out to him. I get back to my letter. Writing it starts to lighten my mood fractionally.

By the following day, I'm mostly over it — and thinking about the future. My job is to get out of here, and to use my incarceration and trial in a positive way. To do that, I need to get on top of the whaling issue. 'Why is whaling illegal?' the lawyers had actually asked me that the other day. My reply at the time was far from eloquent. I decide to make some notes on the subject. If it will be used by the lawyers or not I don't know — probably not. They seem inclined to just enter guilty pleas and accept the judgement. I start writing:

Whaling is illegal because . . . it just bloody well is, OK!!!

'Yes, Pete, that's going to go down well in a Japanese court, isn't it?' I sit there tapping the paper with my pen; it is almost like 'Where do I start?' Hmmm . . . how about at the beginning?

Whales have been hunted for thousands of years, mostly in the form of coastal whaling. In the eighteenth century, ocean whaling began in earnest, and heading into the 1930s, consensus for a body to oversee the industry grew among various countries.

In 1937, a Norwegian by the name of Birger Bergensen put together the text that became the foundation document of the International Whaling Commission (IWC). Part of the text included a section titled Clause VIII. It said that nations who are part of the IWC may issue special permits to enable the killing of whales for scientific purposes. This was in addition to any commercial whaling activities. At the time Bergensen was quoted as saying he thought a maximum of 10 whales per year would be ample, but the number was never included in the text.

In 1946 the documents were signed and the IWC became a reality. At that time, war-ravaged Japan was in ruins and malnutrition was evident throughout the country. America decided to assist and part of the package included converting many of Japan's naval vessels into whalers. Guns were replaced with harpoons, the fleet was back at sea, mostly in the North Pacific, and whale meat became a cheap source of protein for the masses.

Over the following 40 years hundreds of thousands of whales were killed in legal commercial whaling activity, and many species were on the brink of extinction. In 1986 the IWC introduced a moratorium on all commercial whaling. Several nations including Norway, Japan and Iceland protested bitterly about the ban, arguing they had traditional and cultural reasons to continue whaling. The following year (1987), Norway and Iceland decided to leave the IWC. Since then their respective governments have issued their own permits for whaling and ignored pleas from the IWC to cease. As they are no longer signatories to the IWC, they are restricted to whaling in their own waters and there is little the IWC can do about it.

Japan, however, took a different approach. In 1987 they issued a special scientific permit for 150 minke whales from Antarctica. Then the following year it became 300, then 400 and it has gradually increased with the 2010 quota being set at 1000.

The IWC passed a series of resolutions classifying the permits as invalid because they lacked scientific merit, but Japan has largely ignored these. Next the IWC, led by New Zealand and Australian contingents, had the entire Antarctic area classified as a whale sanctuary, banning all scientific and commercial whaling. This was enacted by majority resolution.

Since then Japan has argued that the Clause VIII regulation takes precedence over the resolution, so their scientific programme may continue. That the original intention of the scientific programme was a maximum of 10 per year doesn't matter since it wasn't specified in the 1946 document. Japan's view is considered very narrow and most legal opinions suggest the resolution enacting the whale sanctuary, prohibiting all whaling activity within its Antarctic boundaries, is valid. With no enforcement mechanism, however, Japan has simply continued to submit their research results each year and ignore resolutions, claiming they are merely political statements with only a simple majority. Note, the resolutions require a 50 per cent vote to be enacted, while regulations require 75 per cent.

In recent times the IWC has descended into what resembles a dysfunctional family split down the middle. Japan has become the abusive father that comes home drunk and smacks around the kids but the family can do little to control him. If Japan is kicked out, the fear is it will just go back to wholesale slaughter of whales. So the family tolerates the abuse.

Even taking Japan's view that Clause VIII takes precedence, it still requires the research to be valid. Between 1946 and 1986 Japan took 700 whales in research. In the last 23 years it has taken over 10,000. That's an awful lot of research. It can easily be demonstrated that commercial aspects dominate the science. The number of supposed researchers in the programme is minimal compared to actual whalers. A few lab technicians in white coats fossicking about with faecal samples under a microscope do not make this a valid research programme. There was begrudging acceptance by the IWC scientific committee in the early 1990s that the results were of some value, but in recent times the Japanese papers tend to be similar to previous years, but with a new set of data cut and pasted in. It is research in name only.

If you consider revenues from the so-called scientific programme, it has made over $US1 billion, which is a massive research project. For that amount you might expect a new form of renewable energy or a cure for heart disease. Instead we are given bogus papers confirming that 'Yes! Minke do eat krill.' Of course, the research component is but a fraction of that. Some estimates put it at about $US100 million, or around 10 per cent of revenues. Even that, I believe, is overly generous.

To sum up, under IWC resolutions, Japan's whaling in Antarctica is illegal because it breaches the whale sanctuary resolution, and this is backed up by the Scientific Committee of the IWC. Furthermore, this body has repeatedly passed resolutions requesting Japan to cease its lethal research programme because it is lacking in scientific merit. As mentioned already, though, there is no mechanism in place to enforce the resolutions.

In recent times there have been significant advances in non-lethal research techniques, and the data gathered is in many ways superior to that for lethal methods. Biopsy simply involves firing a small dart into the animal's back as it surfaces, retrieving it with a two-gram sample of skin tissue. I know it doesn't sound that nice, removing a chunk of flesh, but if the whale is given the choice — biopsy sample, or explosive harpoon followed by nimble Asian fingers on the sushi tables of Tokyo restaurants, I know which option they'd go for.

This small sample enables a whole raft of analytical options. DNA analysis reveals population dynamics. Stable isotope analysis of tissue gives dietary details covering the last one to six months; compare this with a stomach analysis which only gives you a single snapshot of what each whale ate in the previous 24 hours. Hormone analysis provides pregnancy details. Some toxins can be measured from small biopsy samples. It is true that liver and kidney analysis can reveal more information of toxin build-up, but this hardly has relevance in Antarctic populations where, thankfully, toxin levels remain low. Additional advantages of the non-lethal methods are the much larger number of samples possible. Thousands of biopsies can be taken cheaply with no deaths. There is also the possibility of repeated sampling of the same animals over time, allowing trends to be established.

There are other legal avenues to explore. Both New Zealand and Australia have staked claims in Antarctica, and marine charts, for example, recognise the areas as belonging to New Zealand and Australia. Japan has said that it does not accept the claims, but it has never attempted to dispute this in an international court.

So we have the interesting situation where under New Zealand law, for example, the Ross Sea is classed as New Zealand territory. Whaling, scientifically or otherwise, is banned in all New Zealand territory, so Japanese whaling in the Ross Sea is illegal. Under Japanese law, however, they classify the Ross Sea as international waters, so under Japanese law it is legal (ignoring IWC). That brings us back to enforcement. Unless New Zealand or Australian governments are prepared to send down a patrol boat to enforce their laws (and territorial claims), Japan can continue to hunt down whales with impunity.

There is one further legal body to consider: the Convention on International Trade in Endangered Species (CITES), to which Japan, Iceland and Norway are signatories. Japan's programme qualifies as manifest and persistent infractions of CITES, specifically.

- Extraction from the sea of strictly protected whale species, for primarily commercial purposes.
- Non-compliance of reporting duties for marine species.
- Failure to designate a 'scientific authority' independent from the management authority for marine species.

Unlike the IWC, CITES does have enforcement options. Member nations can cease trade with Japan of all species covered by CITES (over 30,000 plants and animals), which would effectively halt all food imports and exports. In recent times, such measures have been threatened in dozens of cases, and the threat is normally sufficient to bring recalcitrant countries into line. It is the last resort, with diplomacy having failed already. Surely we are near that stage now with whaling. Japan's 'scientific programme' has been running for 23 years and it has just issued the new JARPA II plan, extending research for another 18 years.

The programme breaks a couple of other conventions. Japan is signatory to the Antarctic Treaty. Among other things this bans refuelling in Antarctica (water below 60 degrees south). Japan refuels all its vessels in Antarctic waters. In 2010 they were photographed refuelling near the French base, for example. Secondly, all waste products must be removed. When the whales are butchered, about 40 per cent of each whale is pumped back into the sea. Once again, enforcement becomes the issue.

Antarctica is the Wild West with no marshals, and as long as countries such as New Zealand and Australia continue to watch on the sidelines, it is likely that Japan will just continue illegal operations.

It takes me a couple of days to finalise the notes. What I've come to realise is that, legally, whaling presents a real quagmire, with different treaties, governing bodies and jurisdictions, all conflicting against each other; which is perhaps why Japan has been able to continue with its programme for so long. For someone to take them on and argue the case fully would be a mammoth undertaking. It would potentially tie the courts up for years, with the only guaranteed outcome being fat lawyers milking the plaintiffs. We must do something, however. Future generations will look back at us in horror, wondering why we sat on the sidelines for so long when we all knew what was happening.

The days begin to tick by. With interrogation over, my life descends into bored monotony. Where before I had eight hours each day of debate and discussion, now it's almost zero. The days just drag out. I find the evenings the worst. Dinner is all wrapped up by 5pm and the four hours to lights out seem like an eternity. As I climb under my blankets each night, I'm just so grateful to have crossed out another long and uneventful day.

I remain on a visitors' ban, which I find oddly absurd. The prosecutor's reasoning for this is that I may try to subvert my witnesses if they visited me; as if anyone from Sea Shepherd is going to come to Japan and risk similar imprisonment. My lawyers continue to visit me twice per week, normally on Tuesday and Thursday, and I treasure the conversations and company.

I came here fearing violence, and while I see the odd bit of nasty stuff, it is the mental side that starts to weigh on me. I'm not allowed to speak to any other inmates, and I'm only allowed to speak to the guards if spoken to. Some days my total number of words you could count on one hand, and it merely involves '*Arigatou* [Thank you]'. To sit by yourself all day and to not speak to anyone must start to screw your mind.

I remember many years ago my twin brother and I went 'bush' down near Fiordland and we met this really weird guy who was there hunting possums. He'd been in there for five years and he had a month out of the bush each summer to blow his money. The way he treated us you'd think we were the first visitors he'd ever seen. There was definitely something odd about him, too; he had these made-up words he would sling in the middle of his sentences, almost like a tic. He'd be an interesting case study for budding psychologists, I reckon — how isolation affects the human body and mind. I'm hopeful then that by the end of this book you won't start spotting liberal sprinklings of words not found in the *Concise Oxford Dictionary*.

The baths, two per week, remain the biggest buzz for me. I jump in and close my eyes, while my butt crack is still screaming from the scalding heat. It's pure unadulterated bliss until Probus starts barking at me that my time is up.

I love the exercise time as well. Or, not the exercise, but the fact it gives me a brief respite from the loneliness in my cell. I have always found exercise a chore; about the only bit I enjoy is the relief when it's over and done with. My fitness has improved a bit. In my half hour in the yard, I now skip continuously, cranking out about 4000 jumps, then in the afternoon in my cell I'll do 500 press-ups and 500 sit-ups. That takes care of another hour or so.

The great thing about the exercise yard, the bath and visits, is it gets you out of your cell and in contact with others. That a bloke stands there and watches you clean under your gonads while you're taking a bath, I don't mind really.

The most exciting day was a visit to the courthouse when I was indicted. They didn't bother with the hood this time, just handcuffing me and strapping me to one of the guards. I still felt like a muzzled dog, and I still kid myself that I'm a really bad arse. The other prisoners all mill around freely, while I have my own personal entourage of 10 guards and a luxury coach. If it weren't for the guards and the handcuffs I'd rip you guys all to shreds . . . ha ha.

Anyway, since I am such a vicious criminal the bus was all curtained up, so you couldn't see in or out. But the curtain beside me wasn't closed properly, and pushing with my knee, I managed to open it just a smidgen. I felt like a little schoolboy who's snuck into his first peepshow, as the river, cherry blossoms and high-rise apartments zipped by my window. The scene wasn't amazing in any way compared with many places I've been, but it still seemed incredible to me. My excitement lasted about three minutes before one of the guards realised that a serious security breach was taking place and he pulled the Velcro tight on my curtain.

It was early evening when I was finally dropped back to the prison. I felt like a dribbling old biddy who lives in a rest home but who got a visit to the local zoo. An exciting day it was, too. In addition to seeing cherry blossoms and buildings, I spent some time in a courthouse cell, I got to meet a judge, my lawyers and the various court officials. It highlights, perhaps, how the deprivation of senses in prison makes one more perceptive, and the mundane takes on a whole new appeal.

The courthouse cell, for example — normally, I wouldn't give a toss about what a cell is like. It was a bit different to my current cell, but not by much, and yet I spent half an hour going through it: the different screws, the welding, the camera, the toilet and basin. It all just represented something new and different.

I've noticed, too, how most of us in prison resemble meerkats. At the slightest noise in the hallway, we all immediately poke our heads up for a quick look out. It may be the only exciting thing we see in the day, even if it is just a bowl of soup tipping over. Also, for many, it's a defence mechanism. You are looking for the new inmate and judging where on the food chain they sit. I remember when I first walked down the hallway, and every single cell had an inmate peering out at me. They were wary like caged animals looking for the next threat. Most inmates in here are violent in some way or other and you can sense this simmering away under the surface. The cell, however, is your safe haven. It's your burrow and no one messes with you in there. But as soon as you step out, you're exposed.

12
The long wait continues

I'm increasingly noticing the sadness in here. When I first arrived I was apprehensive about many things, but there was also a sense of excitement and adventure. That is now long gone. There's a pervasive depression and gloom about this place, and the longer I'm here, the more I feel it.

Prisoners, on my floor at least, are in for serious and violent offences and very few will be out any time soon. With a conviction rate of 99 per cent it's not like anyone on my floor will be found 'not guilty'. They're all just slowly watching their lives pass them by, surrounded by fellow rapists, murderers and mafia, in similarly unfortunate circumstances. I am probably the only one with any chance of a suspended sentence and while that will still see me incarcerated for four to five months, that's but a walk in the park compared with most of them here.

One of the guys across from me is a case in point. He's on his second offence and he's up for murder after a drunken fight. The other day he returned just before lights out and was balling his eyes out. Apparently, he had just signed a document confessing to manslaughter in the hope they will drop the murder charge. At the very least he'll still be here when he is 40. For someone in their early twenties that must be a horrific concept to get your head around. The best years of your life and you'll just sit it out in a blank cell, with cabbage soup to look forward to. The tragic part

The long wait continues

is so many inmates here are in the same boat. I've lost count now of the number of grown men I have seen or heard crying.

The prison experience is a bit like a cauldron; the interrogation, court appearances, loss of dignity, violence, isolation — it's like you get boiled, and a little bit of your spirit evaporates away every day. You see this in many inmates. They sit in their cells staring despondently off into space. The highlight this week will be a bath and the lowlight will be getting smacked up, but you have little control over any of it.

The theme song for *Whale Wars* is the Smashing Pumpkins track 'Bullet with Butterfly Wings'. There's a great line in it: 'Despite all my rage, I'm still just a rat in a cage' and it sums up what prison is like. You lose control of your situation. It doesn't matter how angry you are, you have no ability to influence your situation. You just have to sit it out while others determine your fate.

It engenders despondency and a loss of self-respect. Most inmates do not care how they look, aside from not wanting to appear weak. Very few of them exercise. Some do go upstairs for their half hour in the yard, but they just stand in the sun and when their time is up they just amble listlessly back to their cell. I haven't seen any other inmate skip for longer than two minutes. They just don't care any more. Why keep fit when you're faced with 10 or 20 more years of this crap?

There was a period of five consecutive days of Japanese holidays and we remained in our cells for its entirety. Prison resembled a ghost town, with but a single guard patrolling our floor and the stormtroopers hidden in the basement, eating doughnuts no doubt. The only human contact was food being passed through the hatch. They were the longest days of my life; it just drove me mad sitting all day and with nothing to do. So I started pacing around my cell. It was about an eight-metre circuit. Once I started I couldn't stop.

I remind myself of a polar bear that used to be caged at the Auckland Zoo. I was about six when I first saw him. He would pace backwards and forwards in a pathetically small enclosure, his steps always in exactly the same spot. At the time I thought he was so cool. Then our family returned about five years later and this time I wasn't so enamoured with his condition. He still just paced backwards and forwards. We returned a third time and I felt so sorry for the poor guy. What a horrendous existence for such a noble creature. His life was spent pacing to the amusement of kids and an occasional treat at meal times. We are so cruel to inflict such misery on animals.

Part of our problem has been we refuse to question such things — or at least until recently. Capture animals from exotic locations and cage them so we can admire their beauty, strength, cuteness or ferociousness — that was what zoos did. Little thought was really given to the animals themselves, aside from keeping them alive and on display.

Thankfully, attitudes are now changing, and zoos are under increased scrutiny to improve things. There has been a definite promotional shift towards the wildlife rescue or endangered species breeding programmes, as an excuse for the continued existence of zoos. I remain dubious. If we are serious about these issues, we should put in funding and create a dedicated breeding or rehabilitation programme rather than squeezing the animals into what is often little more than an animal circus.

Here's a thought. An equivalent zoo for humans is this prison. Allow tourists to pay 20 bucks, and they can walk through here and watch us fossicking around in our cells. For an extra five dollars you can come at meal time, and if you're really lucky you may see one of us taking a dump. The SAS assassin from New Zealand would be the star attraction right now, but be quick because this ferocious beast may only be here for another month before he heads back to the wild in New Zealand.

As the days pass, I start to think more and more about food. I'm obsessed with it. An hour or so before each meal and I can think of little else. Then when dinner is announced by the guards, I immediately start licking my lips and salivating. I've become a hominid version of Pavlov's dog.

Part of it is the repetitive nature of existence in here. The sights never

The long wait continues

change, the sounds never change, the room remains cold and damp, and the smell is the same except when the old grogan gets wedged in the toilet bowl. The one thing that does change is the glorious food. Each meal, despite being bland, is eagerly awaited, and every so often a treat is served up. On Saturday lunchtime we get a single roll with a little sachet of jam. Luxury! Every third Sunday, we get a bowl of sugary sweet coffee. Pure indulgence! The most amazing bit of grub was over the long weekend. They gave us each a single chocolate biscuit with puffy cream in the middle. It was like a symphony of tastes. I'll be a cheap date when I do finally get out of here. A couple of toasties and a rum 'n coke and I'll be ecstatic.

A few weeks ago Probus brought me a box of biscuits and a note. I couldn't read the text, so I have no idea how or why I was the recipient of such generosity. Not that I cared. All I cared about was the box of savoury treats sitting patiently on my desk.

'I'll save them,' I said to Hercules at the time. 'Maybe have a few with dinner.'

'Good idea,' he replied. I sat there trying to write my book, but I couldn't help but look at the biscuits. So I shifted the box out of sight behind my basin. Still they kept entering my consciousness — little wee tugs at the back of my brain. Half an hour later, and all I'd written a sentence about food. Finally, I succumbed.

'Just one, eh Hercules.' I sounded like Jake the Muss outside the pub — 'Just one, eh Beth.'

I jump up and grab the box. Inside are three smaller packs, each with about 30 Snax biscuits. I tear open the first and sling one of the round morsels into my moist gob. What hits me is the delicious three-punch sequence — first the salt, then the sugar, and finished off with a lingering scent of fat. I close my eyes and savour it. Savoury biscuits like this used to have very little sugar. Then food companies discovered the addition of sugar gave them wider appeal. McDonald's perfected this with their burgers, each loaded with the trifecta of tastes the human palate responds to.

Well, that little Snax biscuit hit the spot, but it's nowhere near enough. So I gobble a second biscuit. Then a third . . . Next I try two at once. Before long the first pack is finished so I'm into the second. Then the third. Half an hour later and the entire box is gone. My jaw aches from so much chewing.

I sit there almost satisfied. Amazingly, though, I could still do with more. I look down at my desk. The box lies there like a disembowelled carcass. On the floor are the three foil packs carelessly discarded during my frenzied attack. A few crumbs are scattered around, so I lick my finger, and scrape up every last crumb of goodness. I'm like a fat Labrador determined to devour every last molecule of food.

I know a few ladies who regularly eat a whole packet of Tim Tams in one sitting. It would seem like I've now joined their illustrious ranks, but I don't even need Tim Tams. Any old biscuit pack will do.

I lean back against the wall with a smug look on my face. There's a slight tension in my stomach. To release it I relax my throat, and roll out the most bountiful burp. Even my daughter Alycia, the best burper I've ever known, would have been proud. The rasping sound echoes around the prison, and a little of my stomach contents, consisting mostly of biscuit, regurgitates up through my gullet with a sudden rush of air. I savour the rich taste a second time and swallow.

Interestingly, the burp elicits not a simple comment from my illustrious company. Such a fine demonstration of masculinity, you would expect at least some acknowledgment from my fellow villains, yet the block remains eerily silent.

'Well, I thought it was a good burp,' I yell out. Still all quiet, accept for Probus at my door with a sharp rebuke.

Then it hits me. A small epiphany. The Japanese don't burp. I've been in the company of Japanese for four months, and the only burps I have heard have been my own. Or maybe they do burp, but they sneak them out. Thinking about it, I haven't heard them fart either.

I cast my mind back to those two weeks on the *Bob Barker*, where our diet consisted largely of lentils. There was a nuclear physicist on board who explained that the lentils ferment inside our gut, which leads to, in her word, 'excess flatulence'. At times, sitting in the TV room was like experiencing a symphony of wind, with trombones, trumpets and the occasional squeak of a clarinet, all competing for space. Those notes of special opulence were usually followed by the crack of a high five somewhere within the confines of the room,

Well, I've been farting away like 'Little Toot' doing circles in my cell, and yet I've heard not a single peep from anyone else. I'm in the company of men who rape, pillage and steal, and yet they politely slide out their farts in silence so as not to offend anyone. Or maybe the Japanese have a gene that inhibits their ability to expel large volumes of air. Or maybe they are taught from an early age the ancient technique of expelling air through one's skin. Or better still, they are born with noise cancellation.

We once took *Earthrace* along one of Germany's northern rivers, and there was this strange sensation that came over me. I couldn't put my finger on it, but something seemed out of place. Strange gusts of wind, and faint low-frequency sounds. It was like a spirit surrounded us. I ignored it for several minutes before finally extricating myself from the driver's seat to investigate. I didn't expect to find anything, but as I opened the rear hatch, a massive rush of air slammed into me. The sound had grown slightly to a faint Whop! Whop! Whop! I emerged outside and looked up, and there, just 20-odd metres above me, was a massive black attack helicopter. It was like a giant insect eyeing up its prey. The most extraordinary thing, though, was its silence — the only real noise being the gusts of air that each blade sent hurtling down.

It turns out that this menacing-looking beast was a joint European development and it deploys active noise cancellation. The noises emanating from the chopper are complex and loud — high frequency from the gas turbines and low frequency from the blades. A series of sensors mounted around the chopper detect these sound waves then the corresponding opposite wave is transmitted from a series of speakers.

The result was astonishing. You'd normally hear one of these from several miles away, and yet here it was just above me and I could hardly hear it at all.

The chopper was packed with all sorts of weapons, and secret squirrel hardware, but as soon as one of the *Earthrace* crew emerged with a camera it disappeared indignantly over the horizon.

Here's something else interesting about choppers. When they are travelling fast, the blades on the forward stroke can just surpass the speed of sound — that is, they become supersonic for a fraction of a second, creating the distinctive thuds which are mini sonic booms. So, if you're in the ocean waiting to be rescued, and you hear the 'thud, thud, thud' of the chopper, it is travelling towards you. If the thuds stop, it is either stationary or travelling away from you. Hopefully, of course, you'll never need to know that piece of information.

Anyway, I've digressed somewhat. Back to my speculation that Japanese use active noise cancellation to mask their burps and farts. So when they fart, they emit at the same time the corresponding but opposite fart sound from their mouth. That would mean of course that they can make burp noises from their bum to cancel out burp noises from their mouth, which is even less plausible.

I look up at Hercules. He's unimpressed with my musings. Maybe I am going mad? Not only am I talking to a spider, but now I'm also pontificating active noise cancellation of flatulence that is genetically inherited by certain races. The truth is I was already mad, demonstrated ably by my boarding of the *Shonan Maru*, and the Japanese are just an incredibly polite race that don't let their farts be heard or smelt by anyone else.

There's something else curious about the Japanese — their penchant for bowing. As a rule they don't shake hands at all, rather they bow deferentially when saying 'hello' or 'goodbye'. The lower they get the more respect they are showing. I remember watching the crew on the *Shonan Maru* as they said their goodbyes on the dock. There was so much bowing that it looked like a bunch of cuckoo clocks in action, and each subsequent bow seemed to be deeper than the last until their noses were almost touching the ground. It was quite charming really.

You also see the politeness in their language. There are over 10 ways, for example, to apologise. Commonly used words will often have different levels of respectfulness. Some would be used among friends, some among equals, then very respectful words when speaking with people older than you or superiors. It's almost like three languages wrapped in one. In English, respectful language usually just has the swear words removed.

There's a definite reverence held for older people here. In prison, for example, young guards are incredibly polite to the older ones regardless of rank. There's a deep respect afforded the elderly. They value the contributions they've made and the wisdom they hold. In many Western cultures, we associate old age with senility, trundling our grandparents off to rest homes, rather than really valuing what they have to offer us. The power in this country is also contained mostly within the ranks of retirement-aged people. The Japanese parliament, for example, would keep a proctologist fully employed as there are so many wizened old men within its confines. Interestingly, and unfortunately, this age group also remain the strongest advocates for continued whaling.

Something else I've noticed with the Japanese is their love for rules and regulations. Life for the crew on the *Shonan Maru*, for example, was dictated by a plethora of formal procedures that had to be followed. Any deviation required the captain's consent, which crew were reluctant to ever request. The Japanese Prison Service is proud of the fact that prisoner lives here are among the most controlled of any corrections facility in the world. Even the way a business runs here is a demonstration of rigid adherence to formal procedures enumerated in countless manuals. A journalist explained to me that Japanese people prefer life like this. They would rather life be organised and exact than spontaneous and imprecise.

I remember wondering many years ago how 120 million people could live in such a small country. Japan has a similar land-mass to New Zealand, and yet 30 times the population. If you put 120 million Kiwis in this country, it'd be total carnage and chaos, and especially in Tokyo, which ranks as one of the most densely populated cities in the world.

Well, one of the reasons is they just lead organised lives where everyone obediently follows rules. Also, they are such a polite and respectful race. I don't think they form friendships easily, but in many respects they don't need to because they are all so courteous to each other.

It contrasts so markedly with India, which has a similar population density, i.e. way too many, and yet a total lack of rules, or certainly a lack of tolerance for any that do exist. We were lucky enough to visit India twice on *Earthrace*, and on both occasions the locals were incredibly warm, generous and supportive of us. Within minutes of meeting people we were their best friend and not, as you'd expect, because they thought we had money. We made it plain to all of them that we were nearly bankrupt. Indians are just naturally fast in forming deep friendships. We spent some time in one of the slums and the amount of love and support within that teeming mass of humanity was overwhelming.

Anyone reading this who wants to have their faith in humanity confirmed or restored should go and live in India for a while. Don't hang out in the tourist areas. Pick a poor area or a little village in the country somewhere, and you will be astonished. You'll also walk away with some true friends for life.

In some respects Japanese and Indians are opposites — one manages survival through politeness and order, while the other survives by love and chaos. A nightmare holiday for a pair of Japanese newlyweds would be getting dumped almost anywhere in India. They'd be as mad as cut snakes after a week of such filth and chaos.

It's interesting to watch some of the older Japanese tourists who visit New Zealand. They huddle in their group at Auckland airport before being ushered into their own air-conditioned coach. They all stay in the same luxury hotel. Japanese guides corral them through our wonderful country, and their only interaction with locals is watching Maori do a haka at Whakarewarewa.

The long wait continues

While on the *Shonan Maru* I'd asked Hajimoto about this. He explained that most Japanese speak English, but they don't want to use it with us, for fear they'll embarrass themselves, or offend us. He said they also wanted their holidays totally organised where they can tick off the little boxes in their itinerary as they go.

I have my suspicions that the Japanese all have obsessive compulsive disorder (OCD). I'm not sure if the OCD gene has been discovered yet, but I'll bet my bottom dollar that it's prevalent through much of the population here.

From their prisons, boats and cooking to their books, buildings and toilets — in fact their entire lifestyle, they are all just so totally obsessively organised. Little is ever left to chance or spontaneity. It's a life of cleanliness and sterility. I hate to imagine what sex between them would be like. Certainly, I doubt there would ever be action on the kitchen sink or dining-room table, let alone sneaking a sly one in the boss's chair after he's left work for the day. I expect showers would be mandatory both before and after coupling, but alas never during.

I am but speculating of course, and no doubt after this is published I'll be inundated with angry emails citing multiple orgasms from hot, steamy nights of dirty sex with carefree Japanese men and women. And to be fair, my view of Japan is presently slightly jaundiced towards seamen, the judiciary and hardened criminals.

Of course if you wanted someone to build you a good car or reliable electronics, those same OCD qualities suddenly emerge as quite desirable. Also, at times, living in an OCD nation can be rewarding. I have yet to have a single person be late for a meeting with me here. Punctuality seems compulsory rather than just virtuous. The public transport system is apparently the epitome of timeliness, although at peak hours a little bit of *frottage* with those in front and behind you is inevitable, as the last hundred passengers are crammed into each carriage.

The streets are incredibly clean. So when you're crawling home after a heavy night on the piss, you can fall asleep anywhere, safe in the knowledge that when you wake in the morning, you won't be lying in a pile of rubbish — although you might just find yourself being nudged by a street cleaner.

So I guess being an OCD nation has its pluses and minuses. When you're stuck within the jaws of their justice system, though, I feel it's all bad.

Along with their OCD, there is also a total obsession with safety. In our humble travels we'd previously found Australia to be the most safety-conscious country in the world. On the *Earthrace* tour, for example, we never had a single city refuse us to allow public entry onto our vessel — until we reached Australia. Four cities there cited safety concerns as their reason for refusing public access, and in every other city, without fail, getting permission was an ordeal.

As another example, our public liability insurance was US$750,000 in New Zealand, US$1 million nearly everywhere else, and in Britain it was US$1.6 million. Australia: US$16 million. It cost us more for premiums for a six-week tour of Australia than the previous 12 months of circling the globe. I suspect we might find similarly high premiums in Japan.

It's not that I'm opposed to seat belts or crash helmets, but if you wrap your population up in cotton wool they gradually become physically dysfunctional. This especially applies to kids. If they're not allowed to climb trees, swim in rivers, fossick around in the bush, they tend to be inept when suddenly thrust into a new environment.

I've seen this many times with prospective crew. They arrive on board thinking they are the equal of others, and yet they can't even scale the boarding plank without wetting their pants. Parents have protected them so much that they're a liability outside the shopping malls and video arcades.

This trend applies not just to Japan or Australia, but to most Western countries, I believe. Kids no longer explore for themselves or just play with their mates unsupervised. As soon as school finishes, they're picked up in a four-wheel-drive and dropped off to ballet practice, then soccer practice, then driven home for dinner and homework. Whatever

The long wait continues

happened to kids running amok after school: building a hut in the gulley, exploring the cave at the beach, and letting off a few fire-crackers in the neighbour's vegetable patch? Their lives today are so organised that they lack initiative to entertain themselves. We're also indoctrinating kids with the concept that to try something new, they must first be taught by paid professionals. The result is mediocrity. No wonder they find alcohol and drugs so appealing when the highlight of their week has been a trip to the shopping mall.

It's also little wonder that with such lifestyles we're turning into fat bastards. The other day, I was up in the exercise yard doing my little skipping routine and all the other inmates just stood around. A couple wandered listlessly in circles, while the others stared blankly off into space. Exercise just isn't on their radars here. I suspect most people play organised sport at school, but upon graduation their decline into flabbiness commences. Of the hundreds and hundreds of people I've seen in Japan, I don't remember a single fit-looking person with decent muscle tone — not one! This prison alone has so many man-boobs jiggling away it could sustain a medium-sized bra factory.

I've found the Japanese in general to be soft. In prison, for example, the slightest hint of a little rain and all the inmates scurry down to the comfort of their cells. They're allowed on average two hours per week in the exercise yard and yet, for many of them, a wet ground is sufficient to keep them indoors for half of this. When they've been raised indoors I guess this is understandable; their priorities don't lie in getting outdoors.

One of the things they do make a priority, however, is shopping. A journalist seemed quite proud of the fact the Japanese were in his words 'outstanding shoppers'. It sounded like it should be an Olympic sport — and if it were, I suspect Japanese 'shopping-athletes' would regularly grace the podium, as their red and white flag is raised to the tune of their national anthem.

Enjoyment and satisfaction is from buying and owning things. Part of their pleasure is the buying process itself — the trip to the mall, comparing alternatives, making the decisions, handing over the 'readies' and then heading home to unwrap their latest acquisition. I call this 'purchasefaction' — pleasure gained from the purchase process, and in Japanese people the urge to satisfy this craving is strong indeed.

Hajimoto gave me a magazine to read and it was about holidays in Okinawa. From the bits I managed to decipher, however, it was just another avenue allowing Japanese consumers to buy stuff. Each holiday package was crowded with recommended purchases to enhance the holiday experience. A shopping holiday, if you will.

There were several sections on dive gear and one of them enabled the purchase of customised wetsuits. There was a table where you entered a series of body measurements, like chest, waist and height. Incredibly, there were 34 different values required in placing the order. The only thing missing was penis length and the gap between your legs! Most people just buy S, M, L, XL or XXL. If there's a pie cart parked permanently outside your house then perhaps you might get an XXXL. But to detail 34 different measurements is insane. Wetsuits are stretchy, for goodness sake. The point is not that you need all this customisation in your wetsuit, rather it's another contribution to purchasefaction. Shoppers gain satisfaction in the process itself. They go to bed that night with a contented smile in their eyes and a warm little glow in their stomach.

Then there's another nice little shopping 'hit' a few days later when the package arrives. Shopping has become a drug, and the little 'fix' from each purchase is addictive.

It would be fair to say that certain populations around the world find alcohol incredibly addictive. The Aboriginals in Australia and Inuits in Alaska come to mind. Both have been ravaged with the effects of alcohol abuse. Well, the Japanese don't seem to have the same propensity for alcoholism, but they would rate among the most addicted to shopping. Unfortunately, the effects are not felt by the Japanese themselves, but rather the planet's limited resources that are increasingly depleted to satisfy the addiction.

The long wait continues

It's not that the Japanese are alone in this. Most Western economies these days have a certain fixation on consumption. However, the Japanese, I believe, are among the most hooked.

In summary then, and bear in mind this is merely based on my scant observations here, the Japanese are the most polite and courteous race in the world. They are also meticulous, thorough and extremely organised. This extends to cleanliness, and compared to my own debauched habits, they would seem obsessive. Their people place little value on fitness or the outdoors, preferring to spend their time indoors and shopping. They have a strong sense of duty, strong loyalty and reverence for the elderly. Power is held mostly by older men, which is similar to most countries of course, only here it is more pronounced. They are slow to form friendships. Oh, and also, they consume 10 per cent of the world's total seafood. Japanese companies, however, catch 40 per cent of the world's total fish take.

Going back to my own obsessions, I am becoming increasingly engrossed in my calendar. Perhaps it's the Japanese starting to influence my behaviour. Anyway, it's just a simple A4 sheet with the months January to July printed on it. I've been diligently adding on any significant events, like the day I boarded the *Shonan Maru*, when I was arrested in Tokyo, my birthday, court appearances, and all the way to 7 July, which is when I will be sentenced.

As soon as I hop out of bed in the morning, I eagerly cross out another number, and there's a sense of satisfaction that goes with the task. On some days I might take the calendar out 20 times, just counting forwards, backwards, and soaking up the data. Then at night I take one last look at it before I climb into bed. 'Just 36 more days till sentencing,' I'll say to Hercules, as I lie back on the hard floor. There's a nice feeling at the end of each day — an understanding that I'm one day closer to going home.

The time between crossing a date off in the morning and hitting the sack in the evening feels like an eternity. The days now pass so slowly, especially on the weekends when we're on 'lockdown'. On these days, the only human interaction is via a surly guard passing your meals through a hatch.

Saturday night is the worst. Off in the distance I hear the odd party, and 'hoons' blasting around the streets in their modified cars. It contrasts so starkly with our Spartan and monotonous existence in here.

Monday has now become my favourite day of the week. Guards arrive back on the floor and it changes from a ghost town into a bustling little community again. We get a bath and a half hour in the exercise yard. There's also a good chance of a visitor or a letter, now that my communication ban has been lifted. Monday is also shave day. The electric shavers are passed in, you do your thing, and then it is handed out and onto the next inmate. It's odd that a shave should hold any attraction for me really, but it's something to keep me busy for a short time.

I have a growing awareness that this is going to alter me a bit. One change I suspect is my temper is shorter. The other day in the exercise yard, the skipping rope was fractionally short — every 100 skips or so I'd trip on it. So I handed it to one of the guards and asked for a longer one. Actually, I didn't know the Japanese word for 'longer' so I asked for a bigger one. Five minutes later and he returned with one the same length. Or he'd just handed the same one back to me. Either way, it really pissed me off.

Next I'm off for my bath, but I discover on climbing in that it's only lukewarm. It takes about five minutes running the hot tap to get it up to temperature, and by now I'm ready to punch someone. We usually get about 10 minutes of soaking — in the end I got about five before the guards are yelling at me because my time is up.

I take about 30 seconds longer than normal in climbing out, and one of the guard starts telling me off . . . and I just lose it. I am totally livid. I stand there for 30 seconds hurling abuse at him, before I bristle off back to my cell itching for a fight. I was lucky the stormtroopers weren't called to sort me out. I've seen them called for much less. I suspect if the guards understood the words I slung at them I'd certainly be hauled off to a punishment room in the basement.

The long wait continues

If the worst thing to happen to you in a day is a short skipping rope and a lukewarm bath, life is probably OK. In here, though, events like a bath or exercise take on such significance that any disruption to them can tip you over the edge.

I've seen many prisoners in here just completely lose the plot, and for no apparent reason. They all have their reasons, of course, but to outsiders, you'd wonder why someone would get upset over it. Perhaps a crap letter from home, a guard winding them up, an inmate getting in their face . . . people seem to snap so easily and before they know it the stormtroopers come thundering along and drag them off downstairs.

The people who struggle the most are drug addicts. There has been a number of them arriving here over the last few months, and the tough challenge they face is 'cold turkey'.

The first week is the worst for them. You can hear them moaning and groaning down the hall until the guards eventually go and deal to them. If they keep making noises, however, they're pounced on and hauled off, reappearing a day later, with fresh bruises and looking even more broken. Once they're past a week of cold turkey, they normally manage to settle in OK. I've noticed the period 10pm until about midnight is the worst for them.

I remember old Chicken-head who I'd snarled at on my first day in prison. He was dragged off several times, and then one day he just never returned. The guards wouldn't tell me where he ended up, but hopefully it was a hospital or rehab clinic somewhere.

The longer I've been in here, the more that I try to avoid the present. Watching men like Chicken-head get dealt to, after a while you get numb to it. I spend much of the day, and night for that matter, just dreaming — sometimes while I'm awake and sometimes while I just doze. There's plenty of time for it. We're forced to lie on the floor for 11 hours each day yet my body only seems to need seven hours of sleep. It's like I'm not living in the present any more — I live in the past, remembering all the great adventures I've had, and I live in the future, contemplating what

I'm going to do upon my release, but little thought is given to the present.

Perhaps it's because the present is so unappealing. Anything exciting in my life right now is normally an ugly event at someone else's expense that I'd rather block out. I've seen enough unfortunate people in here with destroyed and shattered lives. The occasional letter from home is like a little star of light that illuminates for a short time, but it's not enough to brighten an otherwise black sky. The present is just dark and ugly. The past certainly isn't, nor is the future — in my mind at least. Dreaming has become a form of Tardis that transports me out of here, temporarily, at least. This is possibly the first time in my life that I've just wanted to send myself into the future — throw me in that Tardis and send me to my release date.

In some ways I'm the lucky inmate in this block. I'm probably the only one with a chance of getting a suspended sentence. With a conviction rate of over 99 per cent, it's not like any of us here will be found not guilty. The other inmates, though, are in for serious stuff — rape, murder, extortion, supply of narcotics — and none of these guys will be released anytime soon.

The result is palpable. As you walk the white line between cells, people's stories are written on their faces and, sadly, the story is nearly always just one of two. The first, and I see this on the bulk of inmates, is a loss of hope. They sit in their cells staring off into space, their minds just listlessly ambling around. I imagine the poor blokes facing 20 or more years of this. I can't even comprehend what that must be like, coming to grips with such a horrendous fate. Many I think just withdraw into themselves as the life is gradually sucked out of them.

The second group, and this is much smaller, are just angry — angry at getting caught, the police, the judges, the system. A rage simmers under the surface waiting to boil over. These are the ones who seem to snap for little or no reason, but after a while many of them get broken into submission and end up in deflated despair like the rest of the inmates.

There are also, however, a couple of exceptions. An old man down in

The long wait continues

cell number 30; he is always smiling and happy no matter what. I see him each morning as I wander out for exercises and he bows his head at me and opens his mouth revealing a toothless grin. He's a wizened old thing — bowed legs and an extreme hunch give him an animal-like quality as he hobbles around the floor. He's probably the closest to death on our floor and yet he's also the happiest guy here. A few recent arrivals, still basking in the warmth of freedom, remain smiling, but it's just a matter of time before they get squashed into anger or despair.

I remember the first convict I ever met. Just after I left school, my twin brother Bazza and I went hunting up the Haparapara River on the East Cape. We parked near the mouth, then hiked about 10 clicks upstream into the most amazing valley of native bush. We'd hunted there many times, and even today it remains one of my top places in the world.

On this trip, we built a bivouac under a giant rimu tree that towered above us. The river was just starting to flood on this evening. Heavy rain the previous night had seen the river rise progressively through the day, and the sound of small boulders moving along the river-bed rose above the constant rush of rapids.

It was an hour after dark and Bazza and I sat around the fire cooking dinner and drinking rum and coke. The bush was just starting to come alive. Morepork (native owls), weka and kiwi all started their various night calls. A possum that lived in the rimu came climbing down, his claws scratching their way down the smooth bark.

'This is the life, eh?' Bazza says to me. He's busy stirring a billy of venison stew, and the aromas drift around us as the wood on our fire crackles and burns underneath.

'Yeah, indeed. I wonder what the poor people are doing.'

Bazza smiles. 'Well, two of them are living like kings up the Haparapara River.'

He raises his metal mug and looks at me.

'Cheers to that, brother.' Our mugs clink together and we both take a deep swig of the syrupy sweet drink.

The urge to go bush like this has always been strong in us. We share a primeval satisfaction from a combination of fire, food, river and shelter — and two brothers who love each other as only twins can. Bazza suddenly cocks his head to one side. A startled kiwi squawks off in the distance, but this is followed by two more.

'Something moving this way, bro,' he says peering nervously upriver. There comes the sound of heavy hooves on rocks and dirt, as something large moves steadily towards us. Out of the darkness looms a massive Maori man with a horse limping behind him. We sit there watching him anxiously, as he ties the reins of his horse onto a log.

'Um . . . hi there,' I say slowly. He looks over at us and remains silent. Despite the cold, all he's wearing is a pair of boots, black shorts and a black freezing worker's singlet. He'd be about 195 centimetres tall and 120 kilos, I reckon — a fearsome sight for two little white kids. He wanders over to where we are sitting and looks down at us with calculating eyes.

'Do ya want a seat?' Bazza says hopefully, shifting along his log. The silence is deafening. A sneer crosses his face. An ugly scar runs down his cheek, across his mouth and down his chin. It's hard to tell what he's thinking.

'Nah, I'll just sit here,' he says finally and he squats down onto a rock across the fire from me. His voice is deep and resonating, and his words come out in a careful procession.

Bazza goes back to stirring the stew.

'Hey, you want some kai [dinner]?' he asks, looking at our guest.

'Nah, she's right.'

'You sure, bro. We got heaps. It's venison.'

He looks at Bazza again, then down at the stew bubbling away. A big smile slowly emerges across his scarred face.

'Oh, you sure?'

'Yeah. Bloody oath. And we got a rum and coke here with your name on it as well'. Bazza grabs the small pot and pours a 50:50 rum and coke into it.

The long wait continues

'Sorry, we got no spare cup. But it'll taste just the same in a pot,' and he hands it over to the smiling warrior.

Through dinner he gradually opens up to us. His name is Maka, and he's been hunting pigs further upriver. A few days ago his horse went lame so he's heading back out. I sit there watching him as light from our fire flickers across his face. His hair is long and unkempt, and starting to form 'dreads'. In addition to the scar on his cheek, there's another on his forehead and one on his neck. His Adam's apple has a spider web tattooed around it. His arms, shoulders and back are all heavily tattooed, and he's got 'HATE' inscribed on the knuckles of both hands. Not the sort of bloke you'd want to see your daughter coming home with.

The thing that really gets me, though, are his eyes. They look cold and hard, even when a big smile is spread across his face.

'What you fullahs up to?' he says finally. He's on his second helping of stew by now and slowing down.

'Oh, just a few more days' hunting and then back to work,' Bazza replies casually.

Maka nods his head. 'You know you two are the first Pakeha [whites] I've seen up here,' and he gestures with his hand out over the valley. 'I hunted this area heaps when I was a kid. Then like many I went to the city and forgot about it. Just recently I got a bit of time on my hands so I thought I'd come back to my roots'. He pauses for a few seconds to take a swig of rum. 'Ya know, I always thought of this as my valley. And it's wicked to come back and find its still here . . .' his voice trailed off.

Funnily enough, Bazza and I had always thought of this as our valley, too. We've been up here many times and Maka is the first person we'd ever come across. Maka puts his plate on the rocks. There's a contented look on his face.

'We're lucky in this country you know,' he says seriously. 'People in other countries would die for a valley like this. But if they owned it, it would be choked with people, houses, sewage, pollution, the animals would all be killed off. . . . We're the luckiest people in the world right here, but most of us have no idea.'

Bazza and I nod in agreement. We know all too well. A small weka comes creeping around the campfire. They're a flightless bird, a bit like a kiwi, only much cheekier. He steps gingerly up to the lid of our rum bottle, which is sitting on a rock. He eyes it suspiciously, then grabs it with his long beak and scurries off into the darkness with his stolen treasure.

'Best we finish the rum tonight, eh,' says Bazza with a chuckle.

'The trouble we got,' Maka continues, 'is our government is obsessed with population. "We have too few people," they keep telling us. When I was a kid I remember our Prime Minister telling us our two million population was too small. We needed three million. Well we're at three million and they're telling us we need four. We'll get to four and then they'll want five. And this amazing country will eventually be turned into another seething mass of humanity like Europe or Asia. We'll come back to this river in 50 years' time and it'll be choked with Asians all shitting in the river and killing the last few eels that remain.'

'In 50 years we'll be coming up in Zimmer frames,' I reply.

Maka laughs. 'In 50 years you'll be pushing me in a coffin I suspect.' He prods the fire with a stick. 'A country only has so much natural resource. There is finite land, rivers, lakes, trees, kina, crayfish, pigs — each time our population doubles, we halve the amount of natural resource per person. And in the end the government will decide that this valley needs to be converted into farmland to support the needs of all these new people and it'll be stolen from us. Or they'll decide to mine it or sell it off to foreigners.'

'So what's your point?' says Bazza. 'We stop all immigration?'

'Bloody oath we stop it! Maybe we still take a few refugees, but that's it. Otherwise our mokopuna [grandkids] will end up inheriting a bloody cesspit like all the other crowded countries.'

The weka is back. He skirts around Bazza, fossicking among some cutlery lying around. He finally picks up a teaspoon and scurries off like a little criminal with his booty.

The long wait continues

'Hey, what do you do for a living?' says Bazza, changing the subject.

Maka's face scowls a little as he considers us through hard eyes.

'Actually, I'm just out of prison. Been in Parry for the last few years and I haven't sorted a job yet. Not so easy getting a job when your CV has all these blank periods in it.'

Bazza and I try to remain nonchalant, like we meet convicts every day, but he's the first we've ever come across. And Parry (Paremoremo) is New Zealand's toughest prison where they send the real bad bastards. It strikes me as odd that a convicted felon should have a well thought out argument against immigration. Although I guess prison gives you lots of time to ponder such things.

'What'd you get done for?' I ask him. In the back of my mind I'm praying he doesn't say murder.

'Oh nuffin much. I was in the Mongrel Mob and did a few jobs,' he replies casually.

'What's prison like?'

He sighs and pokes the fire again.

'Ya know prison is hell. It changes you, but not in a good way. There's so much violence, hatred and anger. People always trying to shaft ya. The screws trying to shaft ya. And boredom makes ya mind fester. You end up with scars,' and he touches the ugly scar covering his cheek. 'But these ones heal. It's the ones up here that don't,' and he touches his temple. 'Prison screws with ya mind and ya never the same again.' Maka's voice is controlled, but there's anger beneath it. He passes his pot to Bazza for another rum and we sit there in silence.

'You know I can tell someone who's done time. You can see it in the way they move and in their eyes. Especially in their eyes. They're always looking around, but they don't move their head. They try and pretend they're not on the lookout for trouble, but they always are. They can't help it.'

I look over at Bazza, there's a big cheeky grin on his face.

'Actually I've always been able to tell the people who've done time as well,' he says seriously.

'How's that?'

'Well, firstly, they're big Maori fullahs like you,' and Bazza starts to chuckle. 'And, secondly, they're all walking funny 'cause they've been shagged by other big Maori fullahs like you.' Bazza bursts out laughing and rolls off the back of his log in a heap.

A smile crosses Maka's face.

'See I can tell you never done time. If you said that in prison and one of the bros heard ya, it's fifty fifty if they'll laugh at ya or knife ya. People doing time are unpredictable. Ya never quite know what they're gonna do.'

There's a clanking noise behind Bazza. The weka is trying to steal the billy lid now, but it's too awkward for him to run with.

'Piss off ya bastard,' Bazza curses and chases him into the bush.

The fire has died down and it's now just a glow reflecting on Maka's face. Without the scars and tattoos, he'd actually be quite a handsome man in a warrior kind of way. He looks up at me. 'You two don't need to worry about prison anyway. Guys like you don't do time. You go to university, get married, have two kids, and live happily ever after. And if you do anything a bit suss, you'll employ a white lawyer who will get you off.' I just smile and nod my head.

Well, it was many years ago now that we met Maka. Bazza and I went up the Haparapara River many more times, but we never saw him again. Funnily enough, he was right about many things. New Zealand's population is now approaching four and a half million and the government is telling us we'll be economic when we reach 10 million. They're also trying to open conservation areas to mining. And I went to university, got married and had two kids. He was wrong about me not going to prison, though. He'd be so proud if he could see me now, locked up in the notorious Tokyo Detention Centre.

Looking back on those years of hunting, I have mixed feelings about them now. There's no doubt that Bazza and I have the 'hunter-gatherer' instinct. It is buried somewhere in our genes. That desire to go to the bush, river or beach and gather food for our family is a primal urge that I know many people don't experience or understand, and yet I cannot deny it exists within me. Sharyn's smile as I wander up the drive with fresh venison, a few snapper or a fat crayfish gives me a sense of worth, and I'm not alone in experiencing this. Of course, this is nothing new. Humans were experiencing this back when we were swinging in trees.

I sometimes wonder whether I just failed to evolve. Most of you represent the new and improved humans, while I'm stuck with an old and increasingly irrelevant set of traits. I missed out on the new 'money-making' genes; instead I inherited the hunter DNA sequence that is gradually disappearing from humanity's gene pool.

Or perhaps we all have the hunter sequence, but in most people it just lies dormant. It never kicks into play because of the environment or upbringing. In Tokyo, it's hard to imagine a hunter lifestyle ever flourishing, unless you wanted to join me in prison. Or maybe the urge is there in all of us, but it's satisfied in other ways — going to the shopping mall and buying food or presents for your family could be the modern equivalent of bringing home a tapir carcass.

Whatever the answer, I knew from the first time Dad took Bazza and me rabbit shooting with his little .22 single-shot rifle that hunting would be part of my life. The rabbits and hares were plentiful and on most trips we'd bring home at least a couple for the pot. We also started eeling and fishing, and then years later we progressed (or regressed, depending on your point of view) into pig hunting and deer stalking. In many respects it provided the ultimate in free-range food. The animals roam the bush, far from fertilisers, chemical feed lots and barns. The meat is superior — rich in taste, low in fat and free from hormones and genetic engineering. Many people these days go paying extra for 'free range' farmed meat and yet, in New Zealand, genuine free-range animals are in the bush all around us.

There was a time when I never cared where my meat came from. Sharyn and I lived in Australia for a few years while I was doing automation jobs in various meat plants scattered around the country. One of these jobs was at a large beef plant in Queensland, and on the first day our engineer, Regan, offered to show me around. We started off in the boning room where meat is cut into smaller chunks and packaged into bags and boxes. Regan grabbed a big hunk of flesh off the white conveyor and handed it to me.

'This is what it's all about,' he said proudly. I rolled the meat over in my hand but it didn't look anything special, or not in my mind at least.

'Is this a good piece?' I enquired. Regan's face lit up.

'It's not a good piece, mate. It's a bloody great piece.' He pointed at little tears of yellow fat interspersed among the red flesh.

'This here is marbling,' he explained, 'and the more marbling ya get in ya meat, the more money ya get for it. The Japs and the Yanks go ape-shit over this stuff. Can't get enough of it.' He slung the meat back onto the conveyor, which shot it along to a woman who picked it up and stuffed it into a plastic bag.

'And how do you get marbling, exactly?'

'I'll show ya later. But first we'll go through the slaughter floor.' He led me out through a passageway and into a giant hall full of shouting men and clanking machines. It looked like an assembly line of discrete stations all performing different tasks; some had men, some machines and some had both — although 'disassembly line' is probably a better description. At one end were entire animals with everything still attached; they worked their way along snaking chains of moving meat workers, and then they finally exited as a dressed carcass ready for freezing.

'It's impressive, isn't it?' says Regan. As an engineer, a lot of his time would be spent in this room keeping the machines and robots ticking over. I've worked in many meatworks, however, and there was nothing impressive about this one. The bit that was amazing was the size of the animals. As we worked our way along the chain, I couldn't help but stare in wonder at the enormously fat beasts hanging beneath each meat hook. They were simply massive.

The long wait continues

We came to the end of the floor then passed through a passageway to the killing room.

'We employ Malaysians in here,' Regan explained to me as we entered. 'This is a *halal* plant, which means our meat can be exported to Muslim countries. But that means the killing has gotta be done by Muslims.'

I watched a huge beast lumbering along between rails. It was so big that I wondered how its legs could carry its weight. Snot and saliva hung off its nose and mouth, as it swung its head from side to side. Gates closed behind the beast, locking him in place and his big brown eyes were filled with terror. He raised his head up and bellowed and the noise reverberated around the concrete room and through our bodies. His breathing came in short rasping gasps. Two little Malays stood on either side of the anguished animal.

One of them reached over and deftly placed some kind of gun gadget against the animal's skull and pulled the trigger. There was a click and hiss from the device, barely audible over the din of other animals outside waiting their turn, and the stricken beast just collapsed with a solid thump onto the floor. It lay there motionless, aside from a rear leg that twitched in the air, like when a dog is being scratched. A second Malay darted forward, thrusting a long narrow blade into the neck of the animal. It sent a bright gush of blood out over the concrete floor.

'It's not a real gun of course,' said Regan, as we leaned against the wall watching.

'It has a needle that fires into the skull of the animal and it then shoots a blast of air into the brain to mash it . . . bloody clever, eh?'

I glanced at Regan who was smiling at me.

'The guy slits its throat to keep the Muslims happy . . . and the animal, when it dies, is pointing at Mecca.'

I nodded my head slowly but said nothing. Eventually, Regan led me through another passageway and outside into the sweltering Australian heat. We're greeted by the chorus of a lone kookaburra. I've heard their little ditties many times. For me, it's the sound of Australia — or one of them at least. He sat proudly atop a power pole looking out over an endless array of yards full of bloated cattle. Another Australian sound is that of the ever-present blowfly. It's a few seconds before a couple started pestering me and they followed us as we descended the stairs and crossed an area of dirt.

'These represent the very best beef in the world,' said Regan as we reached a pen full of animals. 'To get that marbling in the meat like I showed you before, the cattle gotta be real fat. But ya can't get that by just leavin em to run around in a paddock to eat grass. What we do is we chuck em in pens an feed em an feed em. And not just hay. Man, these guys get the very best grains an stuff designed to pump em up real big. Some of em here even get fed beer. The Japs like that, apparently. Beer-fed beef.'

I looked out over the sea of sad brown eyes, many of them looking back at us. Some had their heads buried in the feed bins, but most of them just stood there, their ears and flesh twitching at the incessant flies that hovered around them. Urine and faeces covered the ground and a rank smell permeated the air.

'Does making them this fat cause problems?' I asked Regan finally.

'Hell, yeah,' he replied excitedly. 'They get so big they can no longer regulate their heat. So on the hot days they used to just roll over and die. That's why we got em sprinklers.' He pointed to a labyrinth of overhead pipes shooting a fine mist of water out over the pen.

'During the day we turn em on and the cattle just hang out in the shower to keep cool.' He swatted at a fly that kept trying to land on his face.

'The other problem is the animals get so big in the last month or so that if they lie down, they're unable to get back up. But, mostly, in the end they just stay standing.'

Now for someone who has hunted animals almost all my life, I found the killing room and pens quite unnerving. In the end I watched six animals get slaughtered and it definitely affected me — the joviality of Regan and the Malays, despite the brutality of what they were doing, and

The long wait continues

the terror that blazed in the eyes of the cattle. I bet your average person would stop eating meat were they forced to pull the trigger and kill the cattle on which they were to dine.

There was also a growing doubt that started to creep into my mind about the feeding pens. To fatten those poor animals up so much that they can hardly walk cannot be right. I'd never had a problem with cattle running around in a paddock, but to imprison them in small pens and force feed them chemicals is pushing the moral boundaries too far. No doubt it's an addictive concoction of grains and hormones. The faster the animal grows the more money the farmer makes presumably.

The problem, I realised, was not limited to Australia, nor is it limited to beef. Both the chicken and pork industries have appalling and ongoing records of abusive and inhumane practices. The sad part is that these practices are what make the most money — consumers demand cheap meat and that requires squishing the animals into smaller areas and feeding them chemicals. The solution, in part at least, lies in government regulations, but alas most are too busy selling assets and coaxing in foreign investment to be bothered with the welfare of animals.

The solution also lies in the pockets of consumers. Take an interest in what you eat. Don't just buy on price. See if any products are free range or local. Or maybe consider going vegan or vegetarian.

I remember my daughter Alycia coming up to me a while go.

'Dad, I'm going to be vegetarian from now on,' she'd said confidently. I was so proud of her, although at the time I figured she'd stick it out for a month or two then give up. Well, I got a letter from her a week ago and she's just celebrated two years as a vegetarian. Good for her!

I ran *Earthrace* for about a year as vegetarian. Some of the crew were initially sceptical about it, but once we got into the swing of things it was great. Then I was vegan during the campaign in Antarctica and, much to my surprise, the food was outstanding.

It's been many years now since I last went hunting. Will I go again? Probably not, but I respect people like Maka, and their right to catch eels, kina, crayfish, pigs and deer to feed their whanau. I have little respect, however, for the food industry that continues with its horrendous treatment of animals with seeming impunity, and I have even less respect for the Japanese while they insist on harpooning whales and watch them slowly bleed to death.

I know that some of you will see this as hypocrisy, supporting some people's right to kill animals and not others. It's an argument the whaling industry has propagated for many years. In my mind, however, there's a big difference between a Maori fullah catching an eel in his local creek, as he has done for hundreds of years, and a factory ship poaching endangered animals in a whale sanctuary.

Going back to a subject I touched on earlier, I've just realised something really curious. You'll remember that *halal* killing requires animals to be facing Mecca when they are slaughtered. Well, consider this. Wherever we are in the world, there are two directions in which we can head in a straight line to reach Mecca. The first is the direct route and the distance will always be less than half the globe's circumference. If we go in the exact opposite direction, we will also eventually arrive at Mecca, only the distance travelled will be greater than half the globe's circumference. What it means is that when the animal's head is facing towards Mecca, so is its bottom.

There's something else curious as well. If you go to the location on the globe that is the exact opposite to Mecca, any direction you face will automatically be towards Mecca. So, if you built a meat plant here, for example, the animal can be facing any direction and will always be facing towards Mecca, although the location for this imaginary meat plant will be somewhere east of New Zealand in the Southern Ocean, so I doubt they'll be building a factory there any time soon.

13
The most hated man in Japan

Dinner is passed through the hatch and, tonight, it includes a big, fat, juicy orange.

'Look at this Hercules; they've given us fresh bait.'

I grab the orange and start spinning it like a cricket ball. It rolls out the back of my right hand, gives the ceiling a little nudge then tumbles back down. I switch to my left hand, and on the third throw it comes out at a funny angle. I can't quite catch it — the fruit bobbles on the tips of my fingers . . . then plunges into my toilet. It sits there bobbing up and down like an apple at a county fair. Thinking about it, I doubt they'd do apples any more. Any self-respecting kid these days would surely turn their nose up in disgust at a humble apple. You'd need a Kit Kat or Mars bar to get them interested.

Either way, it's a sad sight — my luscious orange bathing in a bog. There's a gross skid mark down the side as well, evil germs within it no doubt hearing about a rave in the big orange marquee that just arrived in their midst.

I reach down and gingerly pull out my fruit. I give it a quick clean under the tap, wondering if I should still eat it. The diet in here is so bereft of fruit that I can hardly throw it away. I clean my hands, dry the fruit, and place it on my little table. I look up at Hercules. It's been a few days since he's eaten. At least he'll be happy, with the peel guaranteeing us a few insects in the following days.

I pick the orange up again, convincing myself it should be eaten, despite the E coli busy replicating on its skin. Thinking about it, the skin is a decent barrier in any case. God, nature or evolution has already blessed fruit with a perfectly adequate layer of packaging.

Which reminds me. Have you noticed this idiotic trend in supermarkets to package up all fruit and veggies into Styrofoam and plastic? Instead of just grabbing a capsicum, you're now forced to buy three, pre-packaged into wasteful amounts of hydrocarbon and energy.

It's not just the produce department doing this, though — the entire food industry has become obsessed with packaging, and none more so than here in Japan. Food manufacturers here must run competitions to see who can pack the least amount of food into the largest amount of packaging. I first noticed this on the *Shonan Maru*. I recall a large box of biscuits. Inside the box was a large plastic bag. Inside this were foil packets . . . and inside each foil pack were three lonely biscuits. Nine measly biscuits with enough packaging to wrap up Vincent's lycra-clad body in its entirety.

I put the nine biscuits in the original box and they barely occupied a third of the volume. Packaging is obviously cheaper than food. I guess in a way they are packaging air and tricking us into thinking it's food.

I finish peeling my orange, putting a little piece aside for insect bait. 'We'll get you some dinner yet,' I say to Hercules, who as always, sits motionless in his corner. Next I poke a wedge of orange in my mouth, the sweet taste of my first fruit in over a week is delicious, despite the memory of it bobbing up and down in my toilet.

I sit there devouring the rest of the fruit, when something, generally inauspicious, catches my eye. 'I do declare,' I say to Hercules proudly. 'Check out my calf.' My humble little calf muscle now looks decidedly big. Well, bigger than he was before prison anyway. Or am I imagining it?

I remember overhearing a conversation between two crew members several years ago, in which they were comparing calf muscles.

'Oh, your calves are so toned. What do you do to get that?' one of them had said in admiration.

'Um . . . Well I . . .' In fact the conversation lost me at this point. I never really figured a calf muscle would ever be thought about, let alone admired. Well, those two crew members certainly spent a bit of time dwelling on theirs. And now perhaps I can see something in what they were saying.

Herein lies the secret to muscly calves. Get locked up in prison for four months, and spend half an hour per day skipping. The prison bit is optional, though, but it does at least guarantee you have the time available. It's an investment of just 50 hours, and you too can have those beautiful sculpted calves you've always dreamed about. Insert here a picture of some goddess who's had enhancement surgery, tanning sessions and works out six hours a day . . . and has muscly calves, of course. Oh, you'll need to buy a five-dollar piece of rope as well.

As we get closer to trial date, I start to grow a little uneasy with my lawyers. They visit me regularly, and are super-polite and courteous, but there's reluctance on their part to present much in the way of defence. Including any material on the illegality of whaling, for example, raised considerable debate. They did finally agree to the submission of written evidence, but their reticence was all too evident.

They also don't understand that our goals are wider than purely getting me released from prison. Japanese in general believe their whaling programme is entirely legal, and to have a counter-argument presented professionally in court and reported widely through media here would be good progress.

It's the assault charge, however, and my defence thereof, that really starts to vex me. It comes to a head just a few days before the trial. Miyake-san and Fukuyama-san come to see me, loaded up with boxes of papers and a laptop. 'We have here the prosecution evidence for review,'

Miyake says jovially once we've dispensed with the usual pleasantries. As we sift through, I realise the case against me is rather compelling. Written testimony, images and video all linked together and suggesting I injured three crew. The testimony reads a little like a contrived story, which it is, but it's still a well-constructed argument.

Alarm bells start going off when I ask to see our defence evidence.

'But we are relying mostly on your testimony,' Miyake-san replies confidently. He pulls out the questions I'd been rehearsing the previous week, but which are mostly related to my character, rather than the assault itself.

'What about the videos of them shooting themselves?' I ask.

Miyake shakes his head. 'We don't think it really adds to your case.'

'What do you mean?' I spit back at him. 'It shows them shooting themselves with their own impulse guns. Of course, it adds to my case. My defence should be based on that damned video.' Miyake's smile is wiped from his face, and he looks forlornly at the floor. 'I want that video included. We did agree on this ages ago.'

There's a long awkward silence which Fukuyama-san finally breaks. 'Pete-san. It is too late to include that video. The evidence is already finalised...'

'And the video of those bastards running me over. Is that included?'

'Pete-san. We have not submitted any photo or video evidence.' I put my head in my hands and close my eyes. I cannot believe they left out all that good video.

'You need to understand this is Japanese court. It is not like New Zealand or America. The prosecution still needs to prove their case against you.' Her voice is soft, but it does nothing to reassure me.

'Just so I understand this, my defence rests on those questions,' and I point at the list in front of Miyake, 'and the written evidence we've already submitted.'

'Um... Mostly... Yes.'

Again I shake my head. It doesn't seem like a defence, but rather a faint hope that the prosecution won't sufficiently prove its case.

'Perhaps Pete-san we can practise your questions again?'

I look back at these two lawyers costing Sea Shepherd $500 an hour each. They were supposedly the best money could buy here. They seem such a waste of money. As if the patsy questions about taking a boat around the globe will have any bearing on an assault charge. We sit there for a minute just looking at each other. In frustration, I decide to just leave. It's not like we're achieving anything constructive anyway, so I press the buzzer, and a guard arrives to escort me back to my room.

Through the afternoon and evening, I sit in my cell and fester. Paul will be livid when he finds out we've failed to include any video. It feels like no defence at all. It's like these lawyers just want to ask forgiveness and collect their cheque. Miyake claims I just don't understand the Japanese system, and yet I'm sure it is still based in some way on logic. When I look at the prosecution case, it is just a nicely laid out and well-constructed argument, supported by evidence. Why can't my team do the same?

The prosecution case is essentially circumstantial. There is agreement on some things. I fired a bottle of butyric acid and, around the same time, two crew on the *Shonan Maru* fired their impulse guns. Three crew, including the two with guns, received pain in their eyes a couple of seconds later.

So the question becomes is it conclusive, based on presented evidence, the injuries were caused by the butyric acid? If so, I'll certainly be found guilty. If not, hopefully, they'll find me not guilty.

One thing I've found perplexing is how the injuries occurred in the first place. All crew were wearing helmets with visors pulled down over their faces. How can the chemical go up under the visor and into the eyes? It takes half an hour before the answer suddenly illuminates my dull mind. It can only be caused by a mist! Tiny liquid droplets suspended in air. As crew breath in through the nose, the mist is sucked up, and some remains in the cavity under the visor. Once there, it is free to settle on the eyes and the skin.

The question then is can an impulse gun generate a fine mist? In fact that is exactly what they are designed to do. They use high-pressure air to force a low-viscosity fluid out a divergent nozzle, producing a spray or mist.

Could my bottle of butyric acid hitting a wall also form a mist? Again it takes me a while to figure this out. Glass is inflexible — as soon as it starts to bend, it breaks. So, inside the bottle, there is little pressure build-up. The bottle shatters, but little pressure is released because it has no chance to build up. The liquid will then just flow in whatever direction offers least resistance. The faster the bottle was fired, the faster the flow will be, but there is little in the way of pressure, and there are no tiny holes through which the liquid is forced. The result of this is the liquid will splash, but it will not produce any mist.

The other thing curious is prosecution claims of how far the liquid was spread. If you throw a bottle of liquid at a wall, it will normally radiate outwards on the surface, forming a circle. Some of the liquid will also sit a little out from the wall, then basically drop onto the deck. This in fact is what the prosecution photos show — most of the liquid is in a circle on the wall, then some has splattered on the deck directly beneath this. Any remaining liquid will be little splashes that can be in any direction, but their volume will be small.

Now the crew with the impulse guns, some 18 metres from where the bottle landed, claim they were covered in butyric acid. This defies logic, when you consider most of the fluid will be back close to where the bottle landed. It is possible, by some small miracle I suppose, that a splash could make it that far, carried by the wind and momentum, but this cannot then suddenly go up under the visor, let alone also drench all three crew. It is just impossible.

Our defence was so easily proven with the video — you see the crew fire their guns, the spray sweeps back and envelops them, then all three show considerable distress. Unfortunately, thanks to my legal team, the footage was unavailable to us in court. However, there is still evidence and logic that can perhaps help prove my innocence. Whether my lawyers will be inclined to use it remains to be seen. All I can do is present it to them and hope they can be convinced of its merit. I pull out my notebook and start a list to hand to the lawyers.

- Distance to crew. The bottle landed by the bridge. This is 18 metres from where crew were injured. It is highly unlikely that the small amount of fluid (375 ml) can cover such a large area.
- Evidence of butyric acid. There are marks on the door and deck where butyric acid landed, but none on the deck where injuries occurred.
- Helmets protecting face. All three crew were wearing helmets with visors down protecting their faces. For them to receive eye injuries requires the liquid to be a fine mist. This can be produced by an impulse gun, but not by a bottle smashing.
- Burning of jackets. Crew claim their waterproof jackets were covered in butyric acid so they burned them in the vessel incinerator. Generally, you do not burn plastics in boat incinerators because they give off toxic gases. They also leave behind a sticky mess that clogs up the base and eventually must be chiselled out.
- Impulse guns loaded just before encounter. Crew claim the impulse guns were filled with water just before the encounter. The impulse gun is an anti-boarding measure, so it will always be stored ready to go. They never know when Sea Shepherd will try to board, so they will remain prepared.
- Filling of impulse guns with water. Crew claimed the impulse guns were filled with water. When used in law enforcement or crowd control, impulse guns are loaded with pepper spray. To fill them with water is illogical. The fine spray would be effective in watering plants or putting out a fire, but little else. Also, the *Shonan Maru* has water cannons that shoot 100,000 litres per

hour, and fire hoses that shoot 40,000 litres per hour. Why then bother with a third water device with only 10 litres total. Unless of course the liquid is not water . . . in which case it may be a reasonable anti-boarding measure.

- Access to pepper spray. Crew claim they would not have access to pepper spray. The whalers use LRADs and stun grenades, both of which require military clearance. This same clearance would likely also give them access to pepper spray.
- Testing of impulse gun contents. Prosecution tested the impulse guns contents and found water. The guns were not seized until a week after the *Shonan Maru* arrived in Tokyo, however, so there was ample opportunity for crew to clean the guns and replace the contents.

As soon as the 7am chimes go off for wake-up, I'm out of bed. My big day in court has finally arrived. Or the first of them, at least. I eye up the suit that sags dejectedly from a hook on my wall. It's been six years since I wore it last — a meeting with South Canterbury Finance where they loaned me the final half million to get *Earthrace* launched. Since then I've always managed to avoid the burden of such attire. When you skipper such a cool boat, I just figured I didn't need the suit any more.

I put on the pants and crisp white shirt but they feel foreign to me, like they belong on someone else's frame. The shirt collar chafes on an area of neck that has long since forgotten the feel of smart clothing. I wriggle into the jacket and peek at my reflection in the polarised glass. It looks wrong on me somehow, as though I'm a farmer on his wedding day, grizzled hands and weather-beaten face incongruous with the hired tuxedo. I cast the thought aside and get ready for roll call.

An hour later I'm fed, watered, searched, handcuffed and seated in the back of a prison bus. Inmates are assembled into rows of 10 outside, and handcuffed to long lengths of rope. A series of elephant chains composed of angry and broken men with disappointment etched into their faces, and, like me, all on their way to court for a seemingly inevitable guilty verdict.

Two buses in front suck up inmates then the last two rows come shuffling into mine. I sit insolently at the back with my entourage of guards. The inmates all eye us up suspiciously as they work their way along, anxious eyes dancing around looking for trouble. They are ordered into seats, the curtains are pulled, and we start rumbling our way onto the bustling Tokyo streets. It's a stop-start affair — the short journey to court taking over an hour, with much of it spent inching along in a long snake of vehicles.

There's another strip search in the court basement, then I'm escorted through a maze of concrete tunnels into a small meeting room where Miyake and Fukuyama are waiting patiently. 'Did you see all the protesters outside?' Fukuyama says with a smirk on her pretty face.

'I heard them from the bus,' I reply. 'But I never saw them. Our curtains were pulled.'

'Mostly they are right-wing nationalists. They are not so nice. But in Japan most people are afraid of them. They can be very violent . . . and they are calling you racist. They are also demanding you get a 15-year sentence.'

I give a little chuckle. Hopefully, they'll be disappointed. If people are out protesting, at least it will generate media around the trial.

'They are all applying for seats in the courtroom. There are maybe 500 of them. So you will get to see a few of them soon.' Fukuyama pauses for a few seconds. 'Court officials are very worried about security, but you will be safe.' She looks so earnest and concerned for me, but safety is the last thing on my mind.

We move onto the day's proceedings, then I pull out my list of points concerning the assault charge. 'I'd like you to include this in my defence please,' I say as politely as I can. I hold the list against the glass and Miyake starts reading. A frown gradually furrows his brow and he lets out a long sigh. 'Pete-san. This talk of pepper spray will not help you. The impulse guns were tested and found to contain only water. It is not wise to raise this issue.'

'Yeah, but they had a week in Tokyo before they were seized. Of course the prosecutor only found water in them.'

There's an exasperated look on Miyake's face, and he manages just the faintest hint of a forced smile. 'Pete-san. Three of the crew testified they filled the guns with water. If we proceed with this, we are calling them liars.'

'Bloody oath we're calling them liars. Their whole industry is based on a lie. What makes you think the whalers aren't capable of lying?'

He goes back to the page and continues reading. 'This point about splashing and spray,' he says slowly. 'That is speculation only. It needs an expert witness and it is too late for that.'

I shake my head. They just always seem to have an excuse. No wonder the conviction rate here is so high — their defence attorneys don't defend. 'Look Miyake. I'm an engineer. I have a degree in fluid mechanics. I'll be more of an expert than anyone else in the court. I know those things. They are not idle speculation. When I testify, all you need to do is ask me those questions.'

He sits there spinning his pen on the tips of his fingers while he considers me. 'Miyake, I didn't injure those three crew. They injured themselves. My crew saw it. Hell, you've seen it on the video . . . and I'm damned if I want to get a conviction for their incompetence. That charge will follow me for the rest of my life. Now we need to put up a defence. This is the best we have,' and I hold the list back up against the glass. 'What you have planned is not a defence. It is a combination of doing nothing and asking forgiveness. For the other four charges I'm OK with that. But this assault charge is nonsense. They have concocted their story. I can't just roll over and accept it.'

'Pete-san. At this late stage . . .' His voice trails off.

'Look Miyake. Let's do this. After court today, you take these notes and work on it.'

He bows his head and he goes into the Japanese sulking mode, which I've become familiar with. He exchanges a knowing glance with Fukuyama, who is equally morose. 'Very well. We will look at it for you,' he says finally. Resignation lines his face, and the two of them excuse themselves and leave for the courtroom. Two guards arrive to escort me to a small holding cell.

Half an hour later and I'm again searched and handcuffed, then escorted by six guards through another series of corridors to an elevator. We then go up and emerge outside a back entrance to the courtroom. A wispy little woman holds the door slightly ajar and peers in. We wait there in silence, waiting for a cue to enter.

I stand there nervously, with the guards keeping a wary eye on me. My heart pounds away and my breathing quickens. A few minutes pass, and the lot of us look at nothing in particular. Finally, we get the signal, and I'm sandwiched between the six guards and we shuffle into the court. It is deathly quiet, and I can feel everyone's eyes on me as I follow diligently over to a row of seats. My handcuffs are removed and I'm motioned to sit, with a burly guard on either side.

Three judges are seated behind a large bench. The one in the middle, a man around 60, with thick grey hair and a generous face, smiles faintly at me. To his left is a rather plain lady, except for dark and penetrating eyes. The final judge is about 40, with a neatly trimmed beard and hair brushed back over his head. They all wear big black gowns and there's a certain regal presence about them, perched up on their imposing bench and peering down at us.

The main judge starts talking, then, at the end of a few sentences, he pauses, while an interpreter translates for me. Her pronunciation is outstanding — probably the best I've come across in Japan. She could get a job on the BBC, I muse, as her words shuffle around in my head. The judge rabbits on about various things — cell phones, weapons, electronics, leaving, protesters and security.

I scan around the gallery looking for a familiar face. Jenny from the

New Zealand Embassy is seated in the corner, and there's also a lady from TV3. Aside from that, it's a sea of angry Asian faces glaring back at me. Few women are present. Among the 90-odd people, just five are female. Half a dozen journalists in the front row are busy sketching me. Or I assume that's what they're doing. With no photos allowed it's the best they can get. A dozen guards are strategically placed around the gallery, standing stoically at attention and looking for trouble.

The trial starts in an orderly fashion, with the prosecution submitting enormous amounts of written evidence and written testimony, mostly from the *Shonan Maru* crew. The bulk of it is just handed over, with the head prosecutor drawing attention to anything he feels particularly relevant. After an hour of this, they call their first witness. His name is Kurisu, and he was a young deckhand on the *Shonan Maru*.

He looks awkward in his suit and tie. His shoes are way too big. They look like flippers. Probably borrowed from his big brother. He takes a seat and looks at his hands nervously. Beads of perspiration roll down his forehead and his hands are shaking.

Prosecution ask him a series of rehearsed questions, mostly related to the eye injury. His voice wavers as he tries his best to answer. A wee pang of guilt seeps into me for putting the guy through this. He's just one of the crew doing his job. I chatted to him on the *Shonan Maru* and he wasn't even pro-whaling. He just works 12-hour days and hopes to get married later this year. Whaling for him is basically a non-issue.

I then remember he was one of the crew who fired an impulse gun at us. He readily admits his injury occurred a couple seconds after he fired, and he also concedes the spray from his gun came back over him due to the wind. Interestingly, he claims his visor was not pulled all the way down, although from the video you can see it clearly was. I rue again our inability to get the video included as evidence.

The prosecutor then asks what he thinks should happen to me. Kurisu-san looks over at me for a few seconds before answering. 'I think he should be severely punished. He should spend a long time in prison. He shows no remorse for his crimes.' I feel like jumping up and smacking the little bugger. This prick was one of the crew that rammed and sank my boat, and yet he's suggesting I should have remorse! He also injured himself through his own incompetence and is trying to sling the blame at me. I glare back at him but he now has his head bowed in that humble Japanese manner.

My lawyers then ask a series of questions, but they don't get stuck in as I had hoped. I anticipated a bit of rough and tumble, but it all seems so polite and courteous. Much to my chagrin, there are no questions related to the impulse gun, the filling of them, the pepper spray, the visors, the burning of jackets. The only interesting bit that does emerge is the crew cleaned off butyric acid near the bridge (where the bottle landed), but not in the area where injury occurred, presumably, of course, because there was no butyric acid there — just pepper spray. Also, no glass was found where the injuries occurred. No surprise there either.

In the afternoon, a doctor is called to testify. He was on board the *Nisshin Maru* and advised the *Shonan Maru* crew on treatment. I'm not sure he adds any value — there is no dispute on the injury, merely how it occurred.

Before I know it, the day is over and I'm on the bus back to prison for the night. The following day follows much the same pattern. Komini-san, another injured crew member, gives his evidence, but nothing new is revealed.

Day three sees me in the stand. I've just sworn an oath to tell the truth, when there's a sudden commotion by the main door. I turn to see a big fat man charging towards me and bellowing. His face is contorted in an ugly, belligerent snarl, and for a second it looks like he's going to reach me. He lunges a few steps then trips, collapsing into a jiggling heap of flesh on the floor. Half a dozen guards, now all awake from their standing slumber, pounce on him and wrestle him out the door. His booming voice continues to reach us for a good minute as the guards struggle with him down the hallway. I feel like turning to the gallery and asking if anyone else wants to have a crack at me.

The rest of the morning is spent answering questions from Fukuyama. We've rehearsed these many times, and the answers just roll off. It sounds fake and choreographed, until we reach the ramming. 'Can you tell us what happened during the collision?' Fukuyama says to me slowly.

I start to answer and my voice wavers. I can feel a lump welling up in my throat. I stop for a few seconds to compose myself, and a solitary tear rolls down my cheek. Three judges look impassively at me in the hushed court. I continue talking, and the anguish hangs there in my voice as I recount one of the most heart-breaking events of my life. The many times I'd rehearsed this I thought I'd breeze through it, but the emotions continue to come bubbling up. The bit that really upsets me is the injustice in all this: the fact that I am on trial for minor crimes, while the destruction of my boat has been ignored. The thought weighs heavily upon me, and I'm somewhat relieved when the final question is answered and I'm escorted back to my holding cell for lunch.

After a short break, it's the prosecutor's turn to have a crack at me. He hones in on the bottle of rotten butter initially. I have always admitted the firing of the bottle, yet his questions suggest in some way I've denied it. He prattles on and on, while I diligently sit there answering through the interpreter. Next it is the knife. I'd always considered this the most minor offence, given that most crew on boats carry knives anyway, that I needed it to cut the net to get aboard, and that I never had it on me when I confronted the crew. Nevertheless it seems to warrant another hour of pointed questions. Finally, he moves onto a series of photos and videos concerning Paul Watson. Under advice from my lawyers, I just make no comment about them.

Before I know it, three days of the trial are over. The time has passed so quickly — perhaps because a normal day in prison goes so slowly. It's hard to believe also that my defence is basically complete. All that remains is summing up by both sides, and my final words, which I'm going to attempt in Japanese.

If I was a judge, based on the evidence thus far, I'd certainly find me guilty of all charges. I can't help but feel we have just rolled over. In some ways I've been judicially raped, and I can see why their conviction rate here is so incredibly high. Given that I'll almost certainly end up with a false conviction for assault, I can see how easily justice can go wrong. How many prisoners in my ward are falsely accused I wonder? Perhaps heaps. In my case, it is possible the assault charge won't affect the verdict too much. I've pleaded guilty to four charges anyway, so hopefully having an assault charge tacked on the end will still leave me with a suspended sentence and a flight home in a few weeks.

Over the following days I get started on my final speech. I'd written what I wanted to say then my lawyers have converted it into good, seamless Japanese. At least I think they have. As I go through the translation, though, I can see how they have toned the language down, and it is a very humble statement. It is loaded with regret, apologies and asking forgiveness.

Over the following 10 days I gradually get a handle on the speech. Many of the words I don't know, so it is more like memorising full strings of syllables, which I find quite difficult. Each new paragraph takes hours to master and, try as I might, I don't seem capable of reciting the document in its entirety without something written to prompt me.

A day before summing up and my practising is interrupted by a visitor. I'm escorted to an interview room where Melissa from TV3 is waiting for me. Her big smile and lovely Kiwi accent is so welcoming. Despite only meeting her once before, she seems like an old friend coming to see me. As I sit, though, I see a worried look in her eyes.

'How are ya, Pete?' she asks with concern.

'I'm bloody marvellous mate,' I reply quickly. 'Summing up tomorrow. I'm on the home stretch.'

She looks at me for several seconds. 'Do you have any comments about your expulsion from Sea Shepherd?'

I stare at her blankly wondering what she is on about. 'What expulsion? I know nothing about anyone getting expelled.'

There's a long silence as she considers me carefully — a journalist figuring out if she's hearing the truth or not. 'You really haven't heard, have you?'

Another blank stare from me, but my veneer of optimism is starting to delaminate. 'I haven't heard what?'

Melissa holds an A4 sheet of paper against the glass partition, and I start reading. It's a press release from Chuck on behalf of Sea Shepherd. As I read, a sense of betrayal invades me. It seems I have indeed been expelled from Sea Shepherd because, according to the press release, I took a bow and arrow, a banned weapon, aboard the *Ady Gil*. I read the document several times trying to make sense of it all. I put my head in my hands.

'How do you feel?' Melissa says finally. This is journalistic gold, I guess. She'd be wishing she could get a camera in here to record it.

'How the hell do you think I feel?' I reply caustically. 'I've been bloody betrayed.' I shake my head.

'Well, do you admit you took a bow and arrow?'

'Yeah, I had a bow and arrow. So what? Paul gave me permission to take it. If the whalers are running around with explosive harpoons and 12-gauge shotguns, what is so wrong with me having a bow and arrow? It's not like it was intended for shooting people.'

A guard pokes his head into the cubicle. He holds up two fingers, indicating we have two minutes of interview time left.

Melissa rattles off her last questions, but my responses are distant. My mind is awash in theories, and I spiral down in self-pity.

By the time I'm locked back into my cell on D Block five minutes later, I am a mess. Incarceration has taken its toll on me emotionally. Little things like a skipping rope too short or a promised visitor not arriving can upset me now, let alone something major like this. Certainly, betrayal is the dominant thought. I languish in prison, in part, on behalf of Sea Shepherd. How can they ever justify booting me out? Also, Paul knew damn well I had the bow and arrow — he had approved it. Why do they leave it until now to kick me out?

Whale Wars III has just started screening in the US. Maybe it's related to that? My crew all had some practice with the bow and arrow that was filmed. I wonder if it was included in the first episode. Maybe Bob Barker or a key sponsor saw it and took exception?

The other thought that starts to form is the damage this will do to Sea Shepherd. I am sure some people will be really pissed off about this. Great organisations show loyalty to their team. This represents total disloyalty. Or am I missing something? Doubts creep in.

My afternoon is miserable. I try and practise my Japanese speech but my mind seems incapable of any concentration. I get a sentence or two out then it wanders back to my expulsion. After many attempts, I give up and sit there listlessly looking at the wall.

After dinner and roll call I start doing laps of my cell. For the first time in ages, I lose count. After several restarts I give up on the counting, and I just keep going for a couple of hours, which is about 10 kilometres.

Finally, it is 9pm and I'm ordered onto the floor. My blankets are rolled out and I climb under one of them, but I know sleep is unlikely. My mind races like I've overdosed on caffeine, and it keeps rummaging around my expulsion and what it means for me. The press release said Sea Shepherd would continue to fund my defence, but what about my flight home? What about the money I'm still owed? What about all my gear on the *Steve Irwin* and *Bob Barker*? Am I no longer welcome at any Sea Shepherd functions? It feels like I am suddenly a leper — from hero to zero in the space of one press release. Sleep does finally come, but it's short and disjointed.

The following day I have a brief meeting with my lawyers before the trial commences, but they shed no light on the expulsion, other than debating the merits of mentioning it in court. Miyake starts to explain. 'The prosecutor is arguing for a long prison sentence with no suspension, to ensure you do not reoffend. If you go to Antarctica next summer, for example, it will look very bad for our justice system. Now, if you are expelled from Sea Shepherd, it will mean you can no longer reoffend, so the prosecutor's argument is weakened. On the negative side, it portrays you as dishonest. It implies you took the bow and arrow without the knowledge of your superiors in Sea Shepherd.' In the end, the lawyers decide to mention it in court, in part because it has been widely reported by media in Japan anyway, so the judges will already have knowledge of it.

The protesters outside are noisier today. Even in the courtroom, buried deep in the giant building, we can hear them ranting and raving with their loud-hailers. Miyake says it's the biggest crowd yet, although when you consider Tokyo has over 10 million people, it's maybe not such a large number. The few that won the ballots and made it into the trial, an assortment of angry old men, maintain their vigil of giving me the evil eye.

Court begins with a simple one-hour summing up by the prosecution. There's nothing new — just the low-down on all the evidence they already submitted. Their final request is that I be sentenced to two years' imprisonment with hard labour, and the confiscation of my knife.

Next my defence team has their say, and it, too, is a finely choreographed rendition of earlier testimony, with the only notable exception being my expulsion from Sea Shepherd, which has been tacked on the end. In terms of sentence, they suggest it be suspended, given I've already been locked up for four months, plus the month on the *Shonan Maru*.

Finally, it is my turn to speak, and I am escorted to the chair. 'I'd like to ask the court if it is OK to stand please,' I say to the interpreter. The lead judge gives has assent, I stand back up, and I take a deep breath. I stand there for about five seconds saying nothing. My breathing remains fast and my nervousness is all too evident. When I do finally start speaking, the first few paragraphs are a little fast and uncontrolled. I skip bits where I should be pausing, and I fail to accentuate key words. Gradually, I get into the swing, and after about three minutes, the words start gelling nicely, and I get some movement in my arms. I can see the judges listening attentively, all perhaps struggling occasionally with the accent, but for the most part understanding my words. The final few paragraphs, some 10 minutes later, I slow right down, and I finish with a gracious apology, that is full of emotion.

I have been humble. I have shown regret and remorse for my actions. I have apologised for injuring the crew, despite the knowledge they injured themselves. I haven't bitched about the *Shonan Maru* crew sinking my vessel . . . and I spoke 15 minutes of Japanese that was learned despite not being allowed to talk to any other prisoners or guards. In short, I've been very Japanese, and I have done my best.

It is funny how I put all that work into learning the speech, and it was all over in less than a quarter hour. There's a sense of relief that at least that is now finished. My defence rests, now it is up to the judges. In the back of my mind, though, I just know I'll be found guilty on all counts — all that remains is the sentence. Suspended or not.

The final act is the judge announcing the date of sentencing. My lawyers had suggested it could be as soon as just one week hence; however, much to my disappointment, it is a full month away — just another setback in this slow and cumbersome justice system that grinds you down.

The four weeks to sentencing drag by incredibly slowly. The visitors have all dried up. Where previously I might get two or three journalists a week visiting, with the trial all but over, now there are none. Over the one-month period, my total amount of human interaction is just an hour — a solitary visit from the Embassy, and one journalist. For someone who has always loved company, it is a difficult experience.

14
The day of reckoning

Sentencing day finally arrives, on 7 July 2010. It's exactly a year ago that I met Paul Watson in Friday Harbor where we hatched a plan to take the *Ady Gil* to Antarctica. What a crazy year it's been. After sentencing today, I'll either be going home or to another prison. I stand there in my cell for the last time. I look up at Hercules in the corner. 'Thanks heaps for all ya company mate,' I say, while a guard looks at me quizzically from the doorway. 'Good luck with ya next prisoner.' I wander out and stand in position, ready to be searched and handcuffed.

I look in at the inmate in the cell next to mine. He's been my neighbour since I arrived here, but all we've ever done is swap a few signs and words in hurried exchanges in the hallways and exercise yard. My jaw drops when I see what he's doing. He's shaving his balls with an electric razor — the same razor that is normally passed in to me next. Nice one. I've been rubbing his balls over my cheeks every Monday and Thursday. I shake my head. I am not going to miss this place, that's for sure.

A few hours later I'm back in front of the same judges, a packed gallery behind me, and the noisy protesters again agitating outside. The previous day, a journalist had taken great delight in informing me I was now, in her words 'the most hated man in Japan'. While I knew there were people who didn't like me, it surprises me there is that much feeling, especially given how contrite I have been in court. What concerned me more, however, was her prediction I'd get the full two years with labour, but with no option of it being suspended. Her words weigh upon me as the head judge starts to deliver the verdict.

He speaks slowly and deliberately, and I pick up enough of his words to understand it before the translation is made — guilty of all five charges. The sentence is two years with hard labour. My heart just sinks. Is that the end of it? I stand there while the judge looks at me. He then continues. 'The sentence is suspended for a period of five years.'

The words hang there in my head. The judge keeps talking for another hour, but I comprehend little of it. Not for the first time in this court, the tears well up inside me. I've been locked up for five months, and it has taken its toll. I don't feel elation, but just immense relief that it is nearly over. Thoughts of getting home with my family start to take over, and a smile creeps onto my face.

The judge finally finishes, giving me a stern warning not to reoffend, and I am free. I shake the hands of my legal team, the prosecution and the interpreter. I contemplate going up to the judges, but they are beating a hasty retreat through a rear exit. I take one last look at the gallery. Angry men are filing out, a few no doubt disappointed I'm not going down for a long lag.

My freedom lasts about 10 minutes, before Immigration officials arrive and arrest me for illegal entry into Japan. I'm again handcuffed then escorted to the Immigration Detention Centre, a half-hour drive from the court. My stay here will hopefully be brief — just long enough for a deportation to be sorted. Compared to the prison I've just come from, this is a holiday camp. My shared cell is massive, and there's a Coke machine outside. The food is also great. I'm allowed one phone call a day, although in the end I only manage to leave messages.

In the evening, I convince some guards to have a game of soccer on the roof. The yard is enormous — at least half a football field in size. The roof is covered in a massive steel structure that is probably there to prevent any chopper escapes, although today its job is to keep our ball from spiralling into downtown Tokyo.

It's three against four, and with no goalies the goals come thick and fast, and no one bothers keeping count. The exhilaration at just being able to run around, to yell, to jump is quite extraordinary. Having been cooped up for so long, the freedom here is intoxicating, and a smile is permanently etched on my face. I give the ball a big smack and it shoots off the side of my foot, smashing a light. Glass fragments tumble down onto the concrete floor, and for the first time since arriving in Japan, I laugh. It's a big, fat hearty laugh of someone who has missed out on a lot, and is happy to see it all coming back. The guards are not so pleased, but I just can't help myself. The laugh goes on and on, and I can see the guards eying me up nervously. 'You need keep ball down,' one of them says to me in halting English, as another starts picking up the little pieces.

'Yeah, no worries,' I say cheerfully. The game restarts.

The following day I'm escorted onto an Air New Zealand flight. The Immigration Security bus drops me right beside the plane. Thirty or so journalists behind a barrier film and click their little cameras as I emerge and walk over to the ramp. I give them a cheery wave and walk up and into the hushed confines of the latest Boeing 777 Dreamliner. I'm escorted by the Head of Security, who has decided to guard me all the way back to Auckland, which is disappointing really. I'd expected as soon as I got on the plane I'd be back to normal, my convictions a thing of the past.

One of the stewardesses comes forward with a big friendly smile. 'Mr Bethune,' she says with relish, 'we are so happy to have you on our flight. We all really respect what you've done.' I go to shake her hand, but she just reaches around me and gives me a massive hug. It's the first I've had in many months, and it feels amazing. I can feel her breasts against my chest, and her arms wrapped around my back. My skin feels like it is on fire. She announces my presence over the intercom, and the rest of the aircrew all hustle up with beaming smiles and shake my hand or give me a hug. It is so good to be among my own kind again.

Another one of the stewards steps forward and introduces himself. 'Hello Pete,' he says with accentuated gayness. 'I'm Richard, and I will be looking after you.' He leads me into the business class area. 'We've decided to upgrade you,' he says with a flourish, and ushers me into a window seat, with my security guard seated next to me. 'Now would you like something to drink?'

'You're speaking my language, Richard. Bring me a glass of your finest champagne.' I wave my hand in the air like I'm royalty. My guard turns to me with an apologetic look on his face. 'I am sorry Mr Bethune, but as a deportee, you are forbidden from drinking alcohol on this flight.' I raise an eyebrow but say nothing.

Richard opens his hands. 'What about an orange juice, Pete?'

'Yeah, that'd be great Richard. Thanks heaps.' The disappointment obviously shows on my face, as the guard spends the next five minutes apologising that he is simply following orders.

Boarding passengers start hustling past us, and I sit there looking at them all. Many come up and shake my hand or wish me well. One lady hands a flower to me. Where it came from or what she's doing with a solitary flower I have no idea, but the gesture is so nice. A man hands over a box of scorched almonds. Yet another sits down next to the security guy and starts a conversation with me, but is told to keep moving. Several film crews and photographers try to sneak shots but are pushed on.

Amazingly, I can smell the perfumes most passengers are wearing. I've never really noticed perfume before, except perhaps on the occasional old lady with some overpowering concoction flooding my nostrils. I'd thought of perfume as binary — you have it on or you don't. Well, today, I can tell the differences in all of them. The smells are so pungent and refreshing. Something else that strikes me is how tuned my eyes are to colours. The shades of people's clothing just leap out at me. It's as if my senses have all got amplifiers on them.

What interests me the most, however, are the people. I take great pleasure in looking at everyone that walks past — the smiles, the frowns and facial gestures. I try to figure out their story — are they going home, on business, on holiday? Then an ordinary guy walks past, and I glance at his eyes. I've seen the look before, but it's a second or two before it hits me. He has done time in prison. I can just tell. He looks exactly like those wary caged animals I thought I'd left behind at the Tokyo Detention Centre. He glances down at me nonchalantly then saunters on — someone trying to look tough on the outside but, inside, they are on the lookout. He can't help himself, and he probably doesn't even know he's doing it.

I wonder, and not for the first time, how this experience has changed me. Maybe I carry that same wary look with me. At the very least, I am a different person, just as the guy who passed me was affected by his lag. Maybe some changes are good and some less so. I am sure my priorities have shifted. What I do truly value now are the many friends and family who supported me through this. I will never again take them for granted. Sharyn especially has been a tower of strength, and despite our separation she remains my best mate in so many ways. She is an amazing lady, and I feel blessed to have had her support and love. And my two girls who said so many times that they loved me and were proud of me. Those few words meant more than anything else — a kid simply saying she values what her dad does, despite the list of criminal convictions he's ended up with.

Another change would be my lack of interest in money or material possessions. Prison has a way of stripping you bare, and it makes you realise the few things that truly matter. Family and friends come out on top, and money, cars and houses on the bottom. After sleeping on the floor for so long, I couldn't care what my bed was like in the future. Perhaps I will be very tolerant of my conditions from here on.

The plane takes off, and I watch Tokyo disappear out my window. I'm on the way home, and it is marvellous. I feel like a little weka — shiny objects take my fancy but I bore with them quickly, and I look for the next one. I watch a bit of a movie. Then I study the menu but I can't decide. I listen to Tiki Taane for a few minutes. Then I get another orange juice. Dinner is served and I become engrossed in it, but I only half finish before I go back to the movie for a short time. I can smell the red wine as it is served to passengers around me, and I crave it. The thought of the forbidden liquid consumes me.

I climb out of my seat and wander up to Richard in the service area.

'Hello,' he says warmly. 'Is there anything I can do for you?'

'Well, perhaps you could sneak me a wine,' I say hopefully.

Richard steals a quick glance at my guard who is busy eating dessert. 'I guess I could slip ya one,' he says with a conspiratorial wink. He grabs a glass and pours in some cabernet merlot. He fills it right to the brim, and hands it to me.

'You have two minutes,' and he stands beside me keeping a watchful eye down the aisle. The wine smells so rich and full. I take a swig and it is amazing. I'm no connoisseur, and so I'm not exactly sure what berry and fruit flavours it exudes. All I know is it is the most amazing glass of wine I've had in my life. I skull the last mouthful — hardly the recommended imbibing technique, but it is glorious nonetheless. I put the glass down with a satiated look on my face.

Richard turns back to me. 'Truthfully Pete, what we said to you before, we really meant it. Our crew was talking about your talents before you boarded. We all really admire what you have done. You have achieved something very special, and few people would ever have the guts to put themselves through what you just have. You're a bloody hero mate.'

I can feel a lump in my throat, and I'm almost in tears. Despite having left Japan and prison, it seems my emotions are still hidden just under the surface, and a little breeze is all it takes to expose them — another change in me that will hopefully fade with time. I don't want to go around blubbering all the time. Richard suddenly gives me a hug. 'Here, let me slip you another one,' he says with another wink. 'A wine that is.' He laughs at his joke, and a second wine is poured and thrust into my hand. I finish the wine, the second best glass I've ever had, and I meander back to my seat, with a curious grin on my face. I feel quite pissed, despite only consuming two glasses.

My mind wanders back to the trial and what I have been through.

There is much injustice in my treatment, relative to the crew of the *Shonan Maru*, whose crimes have been totally ignored. Japan's coastguard still refuse to even investigate the collision, despite numerous requests from Maritime Safety in New Zealand. There is little hope of the *Shonan Maru* crew facing any charges, despite a plethora of evidence against them. A cursory viewing of the *Bob Barker* video and a basic maritime understanding is enough to convince most people of the illegality of the ramming. Not to mention the whaling, which involves an annual litany of crimes and treaty violations.

Despite the apparent hypocrisy in justice, however, I did get out of Japan basically unscathed. I never had a single fight, nor did any sumo wrestlers get to bend me over in the showers and slap my arse. I went to prison fearing violence, and while I saw lots of nasty stuff, none of it was directed at me. I lived among a bunch of broken and angry criminals who had little chance of getting out anytime soon, while I snuck through with a suspended sentence. My family has been without income for 10 months, but friends and family have supported them. All up, I have much to be thankful for. Things could have ended up way worse. It would be easy to get angry at the lack of justice regarding the whalers, and yet it wouldn't achieve anything positive. Life is too short to dwell on the past and what might have been.

The other thing to remember is the impact this will have on whaling. Certainly, the spotlight is on the industry like never before, and I've been a key part of a team that has achieved this. According to journalists in Japan, my boarding the *Shonan Maru* saved around 40 whales and cost them around US$2 million in lost revenues. The total Sea Shepherd campaign has cost the whalers around US$12 million in revenues. For the first time as well, the issue has been debated in Japan. While the majority there remain supportive of whaling, for the first time, there is at least some debate on both sides. Finally, the price of whale meat in the last six months has dropped 250 yen ($2.50), a sure sign that the industry is struggling to sell its even reduced catch. Whale meat is now the cheapest it's been since the embargo on commercial whaling was first introduced in 1986.

In many ways it has been a good trade. Sea Shepherd lost a $3 million boat, spent half a million dollars in legal fees, and had one of its crew locked up for five months. The whalers lost US$12 million in revenues and had their industry exposed to media scrutiny like never before. It will go down as a historic year for whaling — the one when the world finally woke up to what is going on in Antarctica. It hasn't been enough to stop the industry yet, but it is a nail in the coffin of a practice that in a few years will hopefully be abolished.

I have been so lucky to be in the middle of this. I was part of a great team that has delivered, not always in the way we expected, but we have definitely made an impact. I have been a member of the Sea Shepherd tribe. I may have been voted off in true *Survivor* fashion, but it doesn't take away the incredible adventure that I have been part of. The tribe has spoken, but I will always cherish my memories from when I was in it.

Richard said I was talented, but he's wrong in this. I only have a few skills. I am a good leader, and I am unafraid of failure. Those two attributes can be very powerful, but by themselves they are very limiting. I am poor at so many things that if left to my own devices, I make very little happen. It's only by being part of a team that I can achieve anything of significance . . . and in Antarctica, I have certainly been part of an amazing team. I think back to the many wonderful individuals I worked with — the Gillbillies, Mal, Peter, Fi and Potsy on the *Bob Barker*, Paul, Chris, Pedro and Locky on the *Steve Irwin*, and that's just a few of them — so many gifted people who all contributed enormously through the campaign.

When you have such a team with so many complementary skills and positive attitudes, the extraordinary becomes possible. We all have something extraordinary in us. In my case, I was lucky to get to work with such a great and talented bunch. But, in many, the extraordinary just lies latent — through inaction and lack of opportunity, people don't realise their potential. The key is to look for the opportunities, to be part of a team, and to get out there and make it all happen.

Remember, too, that there will always be setbacks. It could be argued that I was a failure in Antarctica. I went down and lost my boat — the biggest loss in Sea Shepherd history. We also went with so many possible tactics and failed to use almost all of them. We did, however, stop the whalers for over a month, we harassed the hell out of them at various times, and we boarded a whaling vessel, despite all the earlier losses and setbacks. We just did our best with what we had, and that's all we can do. The successes we had were because we backed ourselves, and we just accepted our failures as the price we pay for giving things a go. We should never be afraid of failure, but rather of doing nothing at all.

A kid of about 10 comes up and stands looking at me shyly. 'Wasup?' I ask him, keen for someone to talk to.

'Oh . . . Um . . . I was wondering if you could autograph something for me . . . please?' His voice is soft and unsure, and I can see it's taken a bit of nerve from him to approach me. I reach over and shake his hand.

'Sure bro. Hey ya wanna sit next to me for a bit?'

My minder looks dubious, but the kid jumps into the spare seat before any complaints can be raised. A big smile lights up on his face. 'Hey what was prison like?'

We sit there and talk for half an hour, before his mum finally comes to drag him away.

'Do you have any advice for me?' he says as he climbs up from his seat. I look at this little kid full of promise, and so receptive to input. 'Yeah bro. Be strong and stand up for what ya believe in.' He heads off with 'Kia Kaha, Kia Toa [Be strong, Be a Warrior], Pete Bethune' signed on his boarding pass. It may well end up in a bin at the airport, of course. But maybe a small seed has also been sown in the kid's mind — one that will germinate, grow, and play a tiny role in turning him into someone special. That a little kid wants a piece of my time is a gift and I'm grateful for it. But it also comes with obligations that hopefully don't get ignored.

On the 12-hour flight home I don't even bother trying to sleep. After dinner I down two coffees, and my mind then races off at light speed in random directions. The voyage is a whirlwind of movie clips, music, food, drink and chatting to various aircrew and fellow passengers. Before I know it we are taxied into a terminal and I am hurried off to Immigration.

'Where have you come from?' the immigration officer says to me as I pass my passport over. He's part Maori, and has a great working-class Kiwi accent that I have sorely missed.

'Japan,' I say politely.

He looks down at me with curious eyes. 'Were you there for business or pleasure?'

I hesitate for a few seconds. I stand there like a possum in a spotlight. 'I'm not really sure, sir . . . I guess it was pleasure,' I finally reply.

He studies me for a few seconds then looks carefully at my passport. Suddenly he recognises the name and a big white grin appears on his dark face. 'Oh you were that anti-whaling guy, eh?'

'Yeah that's me . . . and you have no idea how happy I am to be here.'

'I bet. Well, welcome home, bro. It's good to have you back.' He hands my passport over, and three airport police then escort me in to see my family.

As I walk into the Airport Police station, I can hear Danielle's bossy voice echoing around the halls. She has inherited a bit of her dad. I follow the voice into a kitchen area. Sharyn, my girls, other family members and volunteers — they are all there waiting patiently.

Sharyn comes over. She looks amazing. Her hair has been done, and her figure is trim and taut from all the hours of running and cross training. Despite our separation, I still love this lady to bits. She'll always have a big piece of my heart. I admire her for a second or two then I wrap her up in a big hug. 'Hey, I am sorry to put you through all this, eh.'

She smiles up at me, and I can see the relief in her eyes. 'Well, it's wonderful to have you back.'

Alycia steps forward. 'I love you Dad,' she says shyly. She reaches up and wraps her arms around me in a loving hug. The lump is back in my throat and a tear rolls down my cheek.

'Yeah, I love you, too.' I cling onto her for ages, not wanting to let her go.

Danielle is standing to the side. She has new glasses on and looks so grown up. There is a cheeky grin on her face. 'I just want you to know Dad,' she says with a confident voice, 'that I am really proud of all that you have done.' She pauses for a second or two. 'Even though I now have a criminal for a dad.' She starts to giggle. I shake my head at her. I have missed these girls so much. 'And you owe me some driving lessons as well.' I give her a hug. It is wonderful to be back where I belong.

I'm interrupted by a call on Sharyn's cell phone. 'It's Paul Watson, Pete. He wants a word.' She hands the phone over.

'Hi Paul,' I say as politely as I can muster. I still feel bruised at being expelled, and a call from Paul is the last thing I'm wanting right now.

'Hi Pete.' His voice is warm and familiar. 'I want you to know that your expulsion was only done to assist your trial. There was never any intention of really expelling you.'

'So you mean I have not been expelled from Sea Shepherd?'

'Correct . . . and you are welcome to come back to Antarctica on the next campaign if you like.'

I sit there digesting the information. It means they pretended to boot me out of Sea Shepherd. I am not really sure if it did assist my trial or not. Or why they never bothered to tell me about the strategy. It was a miserable act to leave me in there festering over it for the last month. However, I am relieved to think I am not the social outcast or Sea Shepherd reject I thought I was.

Funnily enough I don't really care either way. I am home with my friends and family, I am in one piece, and I have much to be grateful for. If it was a masterstroke of strategy by Paul and his management team then I'm cool with that. It could have been handled better I guess, but then so can most things with the benefit of hindsight. I cast the thought aside and move back to my family, who are waiting patiently.

'So what's the plan from here?' I ask.

Danielle gives me a shove in the back. 'It's time to go, Dad. We have a big party for you tonight. All the family is coming around. Even Bazza is flying up from Riverton.'

'Oh, primo.'

'Did you buy me any duty free on the way through?'

'What sort of duty free were you expecting?'

'Like vodka perhaps.' I look at Danielle. Her cheeky smile remains on her face.

'Since when do you drink vodka?'

'Since I started drinking Red Bull and going to nightclubs, of course.' She laughs.

How I missed my cheeky daughters taking the piss. It is indeed good to be back where I belong.

Epilogue

I gave a press conference a few days after arriving back in New Zealand. Following is the prepared speech, which pretty much summarises things for me.

Press Conference: 12 July 2010

Since 1986 when the moratorium on commercial whaling came into effect, Japan's so-called Scientific Research Programme has killed over 10,000 whales, and generated over a billion dollars in revenues. To call this anything other than commercial whaling is farcical.

Japan has also tried to call it traditional, and yet they have no history of ever whaling in Antarctica. The only aspect that remains traditional is the way the whales die — they are speared through the back with an explosive harpoon, then they spend the last 30 minutes of their lives thrashing in agony, as they slowly but surely bleed to death. And while this may be acceptable to Japan, to most civilised countries, it's a disgrace.

- It brings shame on Japan
- it brings shame on the Japanese government
- and it brings shame on the Japanese people.

What upsets me the most about this, however, is where it happens. It is in my backyard. And it's in the backyard of all Aussies and Kiwis. That Japanese vessels sneak covertly past us each summer, to then slaughter whales in our whale sanctuary, is deeply offensive.

Given the events of the last campaign, I'm left wondering just what it will take for the Japanese to finally realise that this is unacceptable to us.

- Must more conservationists be imprisoned in Japan
- must more boats be rammed and sunk
- or must someone actually die?

We came so close to being killed in Antarctica. If the Captain of the *Shonan Maru* had turned his vessel two seconds earlier, I'd be bringing my crew back to their families in body bags. Our lives were risked daily in what has descended into an ugly war.

On more than one occasion, I was asking myself why I am doing this. And like all my crew, I always came back to the same answer. I am standing up for what I believe in, and I'm standing up for what is right . . . and I'm not alone.

When I stepped aboard the *Shonan Maru*, I did so as the Captain of the *Ady Gil*, but I was also representing all New Zealanders, Australians, Americans and others, who have had enough. It's time the Japanese packed up their explosive harpoons and their 12-gauge shotguns, and went back to their own waters. In going to Antarctica, that was what I hoped for. Instead, I ended up in a Japanese prison.

My trial in Japan represents a miscarriage of justice. Not because I stood before their court, but because the Captain of the *Shonan Maru* did not. He rams and sinks my boat, and Japan's coastguard fail to even investigate it. I then step aboard his, and I spend the next five months imprisoned with a bunch of rapists, murderers and mafia. If five months' incarceration is truly what I deserved, then he should be facing five years Sadly, however, he'll never be brought to justice. Collusion, between the Japanese coastguard, Japanese government, and the whaling industry, which ensured I felt the full weight of Japanese law, is also ensuring that the captain and his crew do not. Japan insists on upholding the law, but only when it suits them.

This is especially so when you consider all the international laws and treaties they continue to break with impunity, and on an ongoing basis. Here are examples from the last 12 months.

- Japan continues to hunt whales, in breach of numerous IWC regulations demanding a cessation of all lethal research.
- Japan continues to hunt whales in Antarctica, in breach of the IWC Southern Ocean Whale Sanctuary regulations.
- Japan continues to hunt endangered sei whales in the North Pacific, in breach of CITES, the Convention on Endangered Species.
- The Japanese fleet continues to refuel below 60 degrees south, in breach of the Antarctic Treaty.
- The *Nisshin Maru* continues its annual discharge of over 1000 tons of whale offal into Antarctic waters, in breach of the Antarctic Treaty.

All these crimes and treaty violations, and not a single one investigated, let alone prosecuted, and yet they convict me for possession of a knife and damaging a net. It demonstrates the blatant judicial hypocrisy that exists within Japan.

Of the five convictions I received, I do, however, agree with four of them.

- I did board the *Shonan Maru* without permission.
- I did damage a net.
- I did possess a knife.
- I did disrupt their business. That was my job.

I disagree strongly, however, with the assault charge. At the time of the incident, one of my crew saw the *Shonan Maru* crew shoot themselves with their own impulse guns. This is confirmed in the Animal Planet video. That I still received a conviction is testament to the Japanese legal system, rather than my guilt. With a conviction rate of over 99 per cent, a 'not guilty' verdict was always highly improbable.

Nevertheless, I am accepting of my punishment for the other convictions. I believe in the rule of law, and where I have committed a crime, I have no problem in taking responsibility. I only wish the Japanese judiciary was equally as proficient in prosecuting the whaling industry.

As a result of my actions, I was locked up for a total of 146 days, which includes 24 on the *Shonan Maru*. During this time, I was treated with dignity and respect by everyone. This includes crew of the *Shonan Maru*, coastguard, police, prison guards, court officials and Immigration. In short, I have no complaints whatsoever regarding my treatment in Japan. I simply accept the incarceration as the price I pay in standing up for what I believe in. Whether it will make any difference to whaling in the long term, I don't know, but like everyone on campaign in Antarctica, I tried my best.

Finally, there are a number of people I'd like to thank.

- Sharyn, Danielle and Alycia, who have remained loving, loyal and supportive throughout this, and despite my long absence from home.
- Ady Gil, whose financial contribution to Sea Shepherd got the world's coolest boat down to Antarctica.
- My father, Matt, Ronnie, Gundi, Bill, Lisa, and all the other volunteers who got the boat to Hobart, and then lobbied for my return to New Zealand.
- The amazing crews of the *Ady Gil*, the *Bob Barker* and the *Steve Irwin*. We had an outstanding team in Antarctica, and any accolades people wish to direct at me should be shared by all those who risked their lives in defending the whales.
- The New Zealand Embassy, who supported me during the trial and incarceration.

- My legal team, who worked tirelessly to get me free.
- My sponsors, and especially Planet SeaDoo, Simrad and Mudhouse Wines.
- Senator Bob Brown and his team in Hobart.
- The two Kiwi construction workers who turned up in Tokyo to protest on my behalf, to then be attacked outside the court by right wing extremists.
- Tiki Taane, Rhombus and friends who played at the defence fundraiser in Wellington.
- The many people from all over the world who sent letters and messages to me in prison. They remained the highlight of any day.
- Those of you who protested, Facebooked, blogged and generally stirred things up on my behalf.
- The government of Australia, who are taking Japan to the International Court of Justice of whaling. It is nice to see a government finally show some backbone over this issue.

Following the press conference, John Key, the Prime Minister of New Zealand, accused me of being 'downright ungrateful' for all their support.

On the day of the ramming, Murray McCully, New Zealand's Foreign Minister, suggested that we got what we deserved. Also, shortly after my arrest in Tokyo, John Key seemed to liken my situation to that of a criminal being caught and arrested in a foreign country. I'd hardly call these statements supportive of my cause, and I certainly won't be offering the New Zealand government my thanks for them. The government also tried to claim I was ungrateful for the embassy support I received, despite me specifically thanking them in the press conference. The embassy did a great job. It was ill-considered statements by my government that let me down.

My real complaint with the New Zealand government, however, is their lack of backbone in dealing with Japan over whaling. New Zealand has a proud record of standing up to big nations. We gave the French heaps after the *Rainbow Warrior* bombing. We told the Americans to piss off when they wanted to bring their nuclear ships into our waters. I think today we have gone soft — we are so worried about trade, foreign investment and tourism that we no longer stand up for things.

Australia, thankfully, has committed to taking Japan to the International Court of Justice but, sadly, New Zealand is not joining them. We should not leave Australia out on a limb like that, but rather be standing there beside them. Good on the Aussies for giving it a go, and I hope they are successful in what could be a long and drawn-out court battle. Time will tell.

The Maritime Safety Report was finally released, some eight months after the ramming. Following are the conclusions.

- The *Ady Gil* vessel had right of way at the time of collision.
- The *Shonan Maru* crew had a legal obligation to keep clear of the *Ady Gil* and failed to do so.
- The *Shonan Maru* crew deliberately steered dangerously close to the *Ady Gil*, and turned to starboard at the last moment, and this is the major cause of the collision.
- The *Shonan Maru* crew, in deploying water cannons and LRADs on the *Ady Gil*, may have contributed to the collision.

No legal action has been taken by Maritime Safety New Zealand against the Japanese. There is a six-month time limit for legal action, and this had already expired when the report was released. Also, Maritime Safety New Zealand has no legal jurisdiction over Japanese vessels, and they claimed it was the responsibility of coastguard in Japan to initiate a prosecution. Japanese Coastguard, however, has made no investigation into the collision, nor have they made any comment over the findings in the New Zealand report.

Sea Shepherd and supporter Ady Gil have both looked at taking civil action in Japan, but the costs and complexities of their system suggest it would cost more in legal fees than could ever be recovered in damages. So there is little hope of the *Shonan Maru* captain or his crew ever being brought to justice over the ramming.

Shortly after the campaign, Laurens de Groot was promoted to head Sea Shepherd in Europe, but he is like a gypsy, working in various locations. Jimmy has applied to the New Zealand SAS. Larry is now working in Mozambique on a wildlife park. The other Gill-billies went back to their old jobs and studies.

The *Steve Irwin* went to Europe to battle bluefin tuna poachers in the Mediterranean. The *Bob Barker* went into refit in Hobart, in preparation for another campaign in Antarctica.

As for me, I'm enjoying being Dad again. I'm not sure what I'll do from here. Some speaking engagements, perhaps? I like the idea of getting paid to just blabber on. After so many months with no talking, I can hardly stop these days. Ady Gil and Sea Shepherd are both talking about a new boat — bigger, better and meaner. Maybe there's a job for me there somewhere. Marine conservation is where my heart is, and I hope that whatever happens I can continue working in this field.

Or maybe I'll get a haircut and a real job. I'm not sure what jobs let you take a spud gun and rotten butter to work, though.

Anyway, dear reader, thank you so much for getting to the end of this book. I hope of course you didn't just jump to the end to see what happens. Although thinking about it, that's just the sort of thing I'd do. Either way, I am grateful for the opportunity to talk to you about this most extraordinary adventure.

Kia kaha, kia mana — Be strong, stand up for what you believe in.

To see what we're up to these days, or to get in touch, contact me at:

www.Earthrace.net or www.seashepherd.org
email: pete.bethune@gmail.com
facebook: Pete Bethune

Acknowledgements

I was fortunate to be part of an amazing team of dedicated people, all of whom risked their lives in Antarctica in the defence of whales. Below are crew of the three Sea Shepherd vessels, and I am indebted to all of them.

Ady Gil Crew

James Burrowes, Laurens De Groot, Jeff Hansen, Simeon Houtman, Larry Routlege, Mike Smith, Jason Stewart

Bob Barker Crew

Christine Bindal, Phil Edmonson, Arne Feuerhahn, Darius Fullmer, Andrea Gordon, Marcus Graham, Peter Hammarstedt, Campbell Holland, Malcolm Holland, Benjamin Jahnel, Matt Kimura, Ralph Koo, Bradley Latimer, Glenn Lokitch, Jo-Anne McArthur, Fiona McCaig, Joseph Narthey, Amber Paarman, Benjamin Potts, Bonny Schumaker, Lincoln Shaw, Chuck Swift, Dave Thompson, Luke Van Horn

Steve Irwin Crew

Tor Alsen, Teed Arvidsson, Chris Aultman, Dan Babawi, Zoe Becket, Stephen Bennett, Craig Booth, James Brook, Vincent Burke, Sophie Cook, Leon Cossar, Laura Dakin, Julie Donehue, Chad Halstaad, Susan Hartland, Veronika Kristof, Paul Livsey, Shannon Mann, Locky McLean, Kevin McGinty, Pedro Monteiro, David Nickarz, Nicola Paris, Anastassia Parmson, Andrew Perry, Brian Race, Merryn Redenbach, Lila,

Gustav Upsal, Wieste Van Der Werf, Barbara Veiga, Erwin Vermeulen, Daniel Villa, Bevin Washer, Paul Watson, Michael Williams, Anna Wlock

On shore Volunteers

There were also countless volunteers who helped get us to Antarctica and back again. Here are a few below. To the many I've not mentioned, my apologies.

Donna Adams, Lisa Baines, Scott Behrnes, Don Bethune, Tim Bevan, Chellez Bradley, Senator Bob Brown, Jenny Camp, Chris Carter, Anna Cochrane, Jerry Crumley, Tony Denly, Gabe Giddens, Ady Gil, Sarah Grant, Paul Hickman, Gareth Hughes, Jakey Kuschlein, Michael Lawry, Hannah Ley, Denise Jamieson, Ronald and Gundi Janke, Megan Jolley, Bill and Mandy Leckie, Michael May, Russel Norman, Kerry Payne, Amber Pearson, Malcolm Pollard, Rhombus, Annie Robinson, Stan Scott, Isabel Sykes, Tiki Taane, Gemma Thornton, Bill Watson, Tim Watters, Persia White